ROUTLEDGE LIBRARY EDITIONS:
EDUCATION IN ASIA

Volume 7

EDUCATION AND SOCIAL CHANGE IN KOREA

EDUCATION AND SOCIAL CHANGE IN KOREA

DON ADAMS AND ESTHER E. GOTTLIEB

LONDON AND NEW YORK

First published in 1993 by Garland Publishing, Inc.

This edition first published in 2018
by Routledge
2 Park Square, Milton Park, Abingdon, Oxon OX14 4RN

and by Routledge
711 Third Avenue, New York, NY 10017

Routledge is an imprint of the Taylor & Francis Group, an informa business

© 1993 Don Adams and Esther E. Gottlieb

All rights reserved. No part of this book may be reprinted or reproduced or utilised in any form or by any electronic, mechanical, or other means, now known or hereafter invented, including photocopying and recording, or in any information storage or retrieval system, without permission in writing from the publishers.

Trademark notice: Product or corporate names may be trademarks or registered trademarks, and are used only for identification and explanation without intent to infringe.

British Library Cataloguing in Publication Data
A catalogue record for this book is available from the British Library

ISBN: 978-1-138-30826-8 (Set)
ISBN: 978-1-315-14674-4 (Set) (ebk)
ISBN: 978-1-138-31006-3 (Volume 7) (hbk)
ISBN: 978-1-138-50138-6 (Volume 7) (pbk)
ISBN: 978-1-315-14393-4 (Volume 7) (ebk)

Publisher's Note
The publisher has gone to great lengths to ensure the quality of this reprint but points out that some imperfections in the original copies may be apparent.

Disclaimer
The publisher has made every effort to trace copyright holders and would welcome correspondence from those they have been unable to trace.

EDUCATION AND SOCIAL CHANGE IN KOREA

Don Adams
Esther E. Gottlieb

GARLAND PUBLISHING, INC. • NEW YORK & LONDON
1993

© 1993 Don Adams and Esther E. Gottlieb
All rights reserved

Library of Congress Cataloging-in-Publication Data

Adams, Donald K., 1925-
    Education and social change in Korea / by Don Adams, Esther E. Gottlieb
        p.   cm. — (Garland reference library of social science ; vol. 513. Reference books in international education ; vol. 23)
    Includes bibliographical references.
    ISBN 0-8240-6635-9 (alk. paper)
    1. Education—Social aspects—Korea (South) 2. Education—Political aspects—Korea (South) 3. Education and state—Korea (South) I. Gottlieb, Esther E. II. Title. III. Series: Garland reference library of social science ; v. 513. IV. Series: Garland reference library of social science. Reference books in international education ; vol 23.
LC191.8.K6A33   1993
370.19'095195—dc20   92-36748
                                                                             CIP

Printed on acid-free, 250-year-life paper
Manufactured in the United States of America

SERIES EDITOR'S FOREWORD

This series of scholarly works in comparative and international education has grown well beyond the initial conception of a collection of reference books. Although retaining its original purpose of providing a resource to scholars, students, and a variety of other professionals who need to understand the role played by education in various societies or regions of the world, it also strives to provide up-to-date information on a wide variety of selected educational issues, problems and experiments within an international context.

Contributors to this series are well-known scholars who have devoted their professional lives to the study of their specialization. Without exception these men and women possess an intimate understanding of the subject of their research and writing. Without exception they have not only studied their subject in dusty archives, but they have also lived and travelled widely in their quest for knowledge. In short, they are "experts" in the best sense of that often overused word.

In our increasingly interdependent world, it is now widely understood that it is a matter of survival that we not only understand better what makes other societies tick, but that we also make a serious effort to understand how others, be they Japanese, German or Chilean, attempt to solve the same kinds of educational problems that we face in North America. As the late George Z.F. Bereday wrote: "[E]ducation is a mirror held against the face of a people. Nations may put on blustering shows of strength to conceal public weakness, erect grand facades to conceal shabby backyards, and profess peace while secretly arming for conquest, but how they take care of their children tells unerringly who they are" (*Comparative Method in Education,* New York: Holt, Rinehart & Winston, 1964, p. 5).

Perhaps equally important, however, is the valuable perspective that studying another education system (or its problems) provides us in understanding our own system (or its problems). To step outside of our own limited experience and our commonly held assumptions about schools and learning in order to look back at our system in contrast to

Series Editor's Foreword

another places it in a very different light. To learn, for example, how the Soviet Union or Belgium handles the education of a multilingual society; how the French provide for the funding of a public education; or how the Japanese control admissions into their universities enables us to understand that there are alternatives to our own familiar way of doing things. Not that we can often "borrow" directly from other societies; indeed, educational arrangements are inevitably a reflection of deeply rooted political, economic and cultural factors that are unique to a society. But a conscious recognition that there are other ways of doing things can serve to open our minds and provoke our imaginations in ways that can result in new approaches that we would not have otherwise considered.

Since this series is intended to be a useful research tool, the editor and contributors welcome suggestions for future volumes as well as ways in which this series can be improved.

Edward R. Beauchamp
University of Hawaii

CONTENTS

	Page
INTRODUCTION	xvii
CHAPTER I	3
Historical Roots of Modern Education	3
Traditional Educational Patterns	4
Introduction of Modern Education	10
Period of Japanese Annexation	11
Independence Movement	13
Implementation of New Policies	14
Summary of Japanese Influence	16

CONTENTS continued

Page

Education Under the U.S. Military Government 17
Korean Education Under the First and Second Republics, 1948-1961 ... 19
Educational Goals and Laws ... 19

War-Time Education and Reconstruction 23

The Development Decades 25
Bibliography 32

Articles and Books 32
Dissertations 40

CHAPTER II 43

The Educational System: Structure, Content and Administration 43

Formal Education 45

CONTENTS continued

	Page
Kindergarten (Yuchiwon)	45
Elementary School (Kuckmin Hakyo)	46
Middle School (Chung Hakyo)	49
High School (Kodung Hakyo)	52
Academic High School	56
Vocational High Schools	58
Special Education (T'uksu Hakyo)	60
Higher Education	61
Junior Colleges	63
Colleges and Universities	65
Graduate Schools	66

Teachers and Teacher Education	67
Teachers' Organizations	70
Nonformal Education	70
Administration of Education	72
The Ministry of Education	72
Finance	78
Bibliography	82

CONTENTS continued

Page

Articles and Books 82
Dissertations 92

CHAPTER III 97

Transnational Transfer Of Knowledge And Its Influences On Korean Education 97

    The Transnational Knowledge System 98
    United States Influences On Educational Theory and Practice 99
    The Case of United States Teaching Methods in Korea 101
    Koreans Studying in Western Countries 106
    Building An Indigenous Knowledge System 107
Bibliography 111

    Articles and Books 111
    Dissertations 116

CONTENTS continued

	Page
CHAPTER IV	121
Educational Policy Making and Planning	121
Organization of Planning and Policy Process	121
Planning	121
Policy Making	125
Sequential Middle-Range Plans	127
The 1954-1959 Planning Period	127
The 1962-1966 Planning Period	128
The 1967-1971 Planning Period	129
The 1972-1976 Planning Period	130
The 1977-1982 Planning Period	132
The 1982-1986 Planning Period	134

CONTENTS continued

Page

The 1987-1991 Planning Period 135

Policy/Planning/Practice: The Example of Vocational Education 137
Long-Term Educational Planning 138
Summary 140
Bibliography 142

Articles and Books 142
Dissertations 152

CHAPTER V 157

Education, Economic and Social Change 157

Educational Growth 157

Contextual Explanation of Educational Growth 163

CONTENTS continued

	Page
Financing Educational Growth	165
Distribution of Educational Opportunity	169
Education and Economic Growth	174
Education and Social Change	177
Education, Politics and Government	182
Summary	187
Bibliography	190
Articles and Books	190
Dissertations	203
CHAPTER VI	211
Epilogue	211
Explaining Educational and Economic Growth	211
Educational and Social Problems	213
Trends and Strategies	217

CONTENTS continued

	Page
Goals and Ideology	220
Effectiveness and Quality	221
Equalizing Educational Opportunity	223
Bibliography	225
Articles and Books	225
Dissertations	226
INDEX	229

TABLES

Page

I.1	Kuk Ja Gam in the 12th-Century Koryo	7
I.2	Effect of War on Number of Classrooms	24
II.1	Kindergarten Enrollment, 1980-1990	45
II.2	Expansion of Elementary Education, 1945-1990	47
II.3	Primary School Curriculum	48
II.4	Middle School Expansion, 1945-1990	50
II.5	Middle School Curriculum	51
II.6	High School Expansion, 1951-1990	53
II.7	General (Academic) High School Curriculum	57
II.8	Schools for Handicapped Students, 1990	61
II.9	Expansion of Higher Education, 1945-1990	62
II.10	Korean Higher Education by Category, 1980-1990	63
II.11	Teacher Education Institutes, 1989	68
II.12	The Institutions of Non-Formal Education, 1987-1990	72
II.13	MOE's Expenditure Classified by Items, 1989	81
III.1	Korean Students in the United States, 1988	107
IV.1	Chronology of Major Korean Education Policies and Reforms	133
V.1	Enrollment Ratios and Percentages of GNP Spent on Education	160
V.2	Composition of Revenue Sources of School Expenditures by Levels	168

TABLES continued

Page

V.3	Share of Private Costs in School Education by Levels	169
V.4	Advance Ratio in 1976	170
V.5	Students Entering IQ Distribution Before and After the Implementation of the HSEP (in Percentage)	174
V.6	Korea Health Index	177
V.7	Social Class Evaluation Factor by Occupation	179
V.8	Social Class Evaluation Factor by Perception of Self's Class	180
V.9	Degree of Political Participation by Educational Level	185
V.10	Educational Level of Congress	186
V.11	Educational and Social Changes in the Development of Korea	188
VI.1	Major Reform Proposals by PCER	218

FIGURES

Page

I.1	School System in the Koryo Era (12th Century)	6
I.2	The School Structure For Japanese and Koreans in Korea in 1937	15
II.1	The Current Education System	44
II.2	Changing Trends of Enrollment in High School, 1979-1989	55
II.3	Distribution of Students in Vocational High Schools by Major Field, 1989	59
II.4	Students in Junior Colleges, 1989	64
II.5	Teachers' Promotion System	69
II.6	The Education Administration System	73
II.7	Organization of the Ministry of Education (Munkyo-Bu)	75
II.8	Organization of a Board of Education	76
II.9	Organization Of A District Office of Education	77
IV.1	Organization of National Education Planning	123
V.1	Illiterates as Percent of Total Population (Age 15 and over)	159
V.2	Total Enrollment Ratios by Level	159
V.3	Total Enrollment Ratios by Levels and Stages Of Development	161
V.4	Total Educational Expenditures as Percent of GNP and Percent of Total Government Expenditures	167

FIGURES continued

Page

V.5	Percent of National Educational Expenditures by Level	167
V.6	Enrollment Ratios by Gender - 1st Level	172
V.7	Enrollment Ratios by Gender - 2nd Level	172
V.8	Enrollment Ratios by Gender - 3rd Level	173
VI.1	PCER Analysis of Educational Problems	216

INTRODUCTION

South Korea, along with Taiwan and other Pacific Rim countries, has captured the world's attention with its rapid economic growth and development of human resources. In the early 1950s Korea by some economic indicators appeared to be one of the poorest countries in the world. By the 1970s Korea had become one of the "newly industrialized countries" (NICs) and as the 21st century approaches Korean leaders and scholars envision the emergence of an "information society."

The growth and evolvement of Korean education paralleled and often led national economic and social changes. By the 1990s the quantitative dimensions of the educational effort, depicted in enrollment rates at the various educational levels, more resembled the educational structures of Western European countries than those of most of the third world.

Yet, mixed with accomplishments many severe political, social and educational problems may be found in contemporary Korea: full political democracy has not been achieved; inequities in incomes between different occupational groupings may be growing; opportunities for high-quality advanced education tend to be associated with income; gender bias is visible in the distribution of higher education and even more pronounced in the labor force where few women are found in professional and managerial positions. These conditions and others, together with certain persistent issues pertaining to the purposes, structure, and pedagogical characteristics of schooling make for serious contemporary debate.

Education and Social Change in Korea attempts to provide students and scholars with an introduction to Korean education and the dynamics of interchange between the educational system and the rapidly changing Korean society. Because of constraints of time and reference materials attention is given only to the Republic of Korea (South Korea). Although the authors made use of some sources written in the Korean language, primarily statistical and graphical materials, the references found at the end of each chapter include only English language works, many of which may be found in any good university library or acquired on interlibrary loan. Other references, primarily publications of agencies or affiliates of the Korean government, may be obtained by contacting the identified publisher. Copies of most of the fugitive materials will be made available upon request to the author.

The book is organized into six chapters. Chapter one sketches the main historical developments of Korean education. The second chapter describes the contemporary educational system, its organization, curriculum, personnel, administration and size. The third chapter critically examines the transfer from the U.S. to Korea of educational knowledge and models. The fourth chapter summarizes the major formal efforts at national educational planning and policy making. Chapter V takes a broad view of changes in the educational system and analyzes its interaction with the Korean society and state. The final chapter briefly reviews the current educational issues, directions and challenges.

The authors would particularly like to thank Emin Karip, Judy Sylvester, Boomyang Han, and Namki Park, for their research assistance. Special appreciation is extended to Ms. Yvonne Jones for her skillful and patient preparation of the manuscript.

Education and Social Change
in Korea

CHAPTER I

Historical Roots of Modern Education

For several millennia prior to the 20th century Korea was linked politically and culturally with China. Chinese art, literature, social philosophy and language dominated the tastes of the Korean court and upper classes. In education, the continuing impact of Chinese influence was visible in the content of studies and in the structure of educational advancement. Learning centered around Chinese language and literature. The writing of Chinese ideographs, in addition to being a basis for written communication, was an art form much admired.

Korean culture and education in the 20th century continue to be molded by international forces. In addition to the Chinese legacy, the Japanese, during their period of hegemony, introduced patterns of governmental organization and administration whose influence persists today. Further, since World War II and the division of the country along the 38th parallel, the special relationship between South Korea and the United States has left its mark in many of the modernizing trends and especially in educational policy and practice. Lastly, industrial Korea looks outward to the world and has been very conscious of the powerful globalization process of trade and technology shaping its future.

Contemporary Korea linguistically and ethnically is a remarkably homogeneous society. With a few natural resources it has had one of the highest economic growth rates in the world over the last 20 years and during the same period one of the highest rates of educational growth. Its institutions, often reflecting a lineage of foreign influence in form, are fully Korean in substance. Korea has evolved its own unique national identity. A nation of approximately 40 million people, Koreans in the last decade of the 20th century remember the turbulent past, but give most of their thought and energy to reshaping the present institutions in order to better meet the challenges of the 21st century.

This chapter offers a brief overview of Korean education from earliest times to the present. The history is important not only to complete the picture of educational change but also to understand fully contemporary educational problems and issues. Korea's educational past is part of the context of contemporary debates and decisions.

Traditional Educational Patterns

The religious, cultural, and ideological influences of ancient Korea are dominated by the cosmology of shamanism, present since ancient times, and the introduction through interactions with China of Buddhism and Confucianism. Shamanism, its mythology and rituals, appears to have given little attention to life hereafter or to previous life, but rather concentrated on the needs and interests of the ongoing life of the people. The gradual introduction of Confucianism and the later introduction of Buddhism in the 4th century brought two powerful and lasting influences on Korean culture. Buddhism and Confucianism have exerted profound impact on social, political and educational institutions throughout ancient and contemporary Korean history.

Confucius, a Chinese sage, is assumed to have lived during the 6th century BC. He and his followers left for posterity several books which came to be regarded as basic classics and over the years volumes of commentary have been added by scholars. Confucius "set up an ideal ethical-moral system intended to govern all the relationships within the family and the state in harmonious unity. It was basically a system of subordinations; of the son to the father, of the younger to the elder brother, of the wife to the husband, and of the subject to the throne. It inculcated filial piety, reverence for ancestors, and loyalty to friends. Strong emphasis was placed on decorum, rites, and ceremony. Scholarship and aesthetic cultivation were regarded as the prerequisites for those in governing other official positions" (COIS, *A Handbook on Korea* 1979:200) particularly allegiance to the sovereign.

Formal education in Korea is usually traced to the Three Kingdoms period when the geographical area roughly encompassing contemporary North and South Korea was controlled by Koguryo (37 BC-668 AD) in the north, Paekche (18 BC-661 AD) in the southwest, and Silla (57 BC-935 AD) in the southeast of the Korean peninsula. The first public educational institute, modelled after Chinese (Confucian) institutions, was created in 372 AD in the Koguryo period. Sometimes referred to as the National Confucian Academy (Taehak), this institution fostered certain core Confucian ethics.

Although little is known about educational undertakings in the Paekche period, several educational institutions developed and prospered under the Silla kingdom. A training system for young aristocrats was initiated early in Silla's history and eventually developed into *Hwarangdo* a "public semi-official social educational system" (Park, Sun-Young, 1991:13). The teachings of *Hwarangdo* were grounded in Shamanism, Buddhism, Confucianism, and Taoism, and at various times emphasized such virtues as patriotism, loyalty, filial piety, and martial arts. The elaboration of the bureaucracy and increased power of the sovereign led to the establishment of the National Confucian College (*Kukhak*) in 682, an institution modelled after Chinese institutes of higher education. Park describes the Confucian domination of the curriculum of the *Kukhak*:

> Its curriculum, which focused on subjects keyed to the inculcation of loyalty to the monarch and filial piety to parents, was divided into three different courses of study based on elective subjects which varied from philosophy to history and literature. Upon graduation from the college, students underwent a state examination in the Confucian classics and were appointed to public posts according to their grades. It was the first of a long tradition of state examinations for civil service recruits which later came to be known as (*Kwago*). (Park, Sun-Young, 1991:14)

The kingdom of Silla was eventually absorbed into *Koryo* which further developed many of its institutional structures. Although Confucianism continued to exert strong influence on education, *Koryo* (918-1392) accepted Buddhism as its official religion. The educational system slowly evolved with several *Hyanggyo* located in the countryside teaching Chinese classics and history, and private village schools, *Sudang*, which introduced the reading and writing of Chinese ideographs. The *Kuk Ja Gam*, somewhat similar in function to the earlier *Kukhak*, provided advanced education. (See Figure I.1) The *Kuk Ja Gam*, however, developed a curriculum which included in addition to Confucian classics such practical studies as calligraphy, accounting, law, and military tactics.

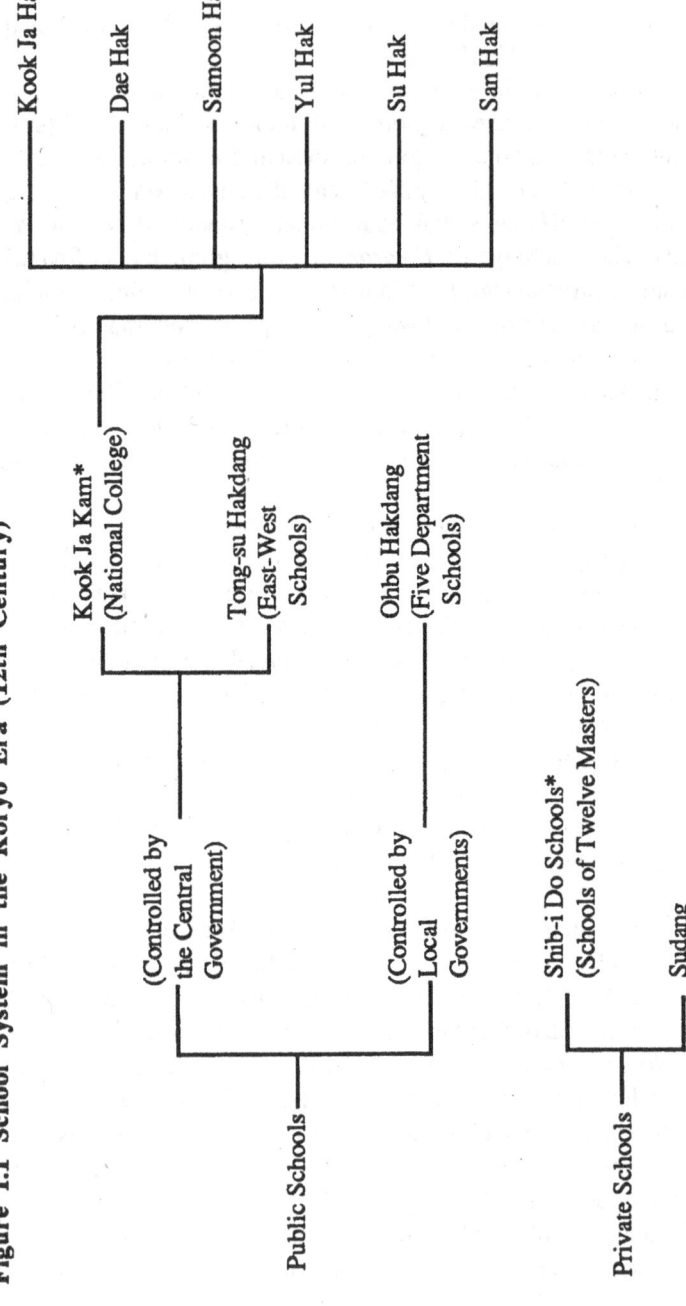

Figure I.1 School System in the Koryo Era (12th Century)

Source: Kim, Jong Chol. *Educational Development*, Seoul University Press, Seoul, 1985: 147.

Table I.1

Kuk Ja Gam in the 12th-Century Koryo

Name of Dept.	Student Qualification for Admissions	Student Quota	Faculty	Programs
Kuk Ja Hak	Descendants of Officials in Civil and Military Services Ranking 3rd or Higher Grades and Their Equivalents	300	Doctors & Assistants	Book of Changes, the Odes, Book of History, Book of Chou China, Life of Kung Yang, Life of Ku Liang, Book of Rites, the Spring and Autumn Annals, Life of Tuso, Book of Filial Piety, Confucian Analects, some books on medicine and fortune-telling (common for three depts.)
Dae Hak	Descendants of Officials in Civil and Military Services Ranking 5th or Higher Grades and Their Equivalents	300	Doctors & Assistants	Laws
Samoon Hak	Descendants of Officials in Civil and Military Services Ranking 7th or Higher Grades and Their Equivalents	300	Doctors & Assistants	Five Canons of Confucianism calligraphy, etc.
Yul Hak	Descendants of Officials in Civil and Military Services Ranking 8th or Higher Grades and Their Equivalents	Unknown	Doctors	Mathematics
Su Hak	Same as the above	Unknown	Doctors	
San Hak	Same as the above	Unknown	Doctors	

Source: Kim, Jong Chol. *Educational Development*, Seoul: Seoul University Press, 1985:148.

Choson in 1392 replaced *Koryo* as General Yi declared himself king initiating the Yi Dynasty (1392-1910). Perhaps the most important intellectual development under the latter stages of the *Koryo* had been the introduction of Neo-Confucianism. Historically, Buddhism and Confucianism had existed in relative harmony; however, corruption of some Buddhist monks and subsequent blame placed on Buddhists for their influence in weakening the *Koryo* court, which led to a military victory by the Mongols, had generated anti-Buddhist outcries among Confucian officials. Neo-Confucianism professed to have added to the philosophical depth of Confucianism by further explanation of the good (righteousness, wisdom, empathy) and the bad (material and ego-centered desires) sides of human nature.

The overall Confucian educational goal was to extend learning and self-cultivation. The ideal man was a "sage" (Gun Ja) whose wisdom contributed to the guidance of the state; the state itself had a responsibility to educate the people, that is, to lead them in the right direction. Good education was assumed to lead to good government and good government was assumed to guarantee a good society.

The selection of Confucian scholars was limited to the Yangbang or nobility class and the key to acceptance as a scholar was a set of national examinations which were created in the *Koryo* period and functioned until the latter part of the 19th century. Success in a number of examination hurdles could take a scholar to the final test in the presence of the king. The level of civil service appointment or social status depended on the ranking on the examinations.

The royal examination system played an important role in the life of Korea from the 10th century until the latter part of the 19th century. Achievement in these examinations became the highest individual educational goal for such achievement was not only practically a guarantee for a lifetime official position and a promise of coveted social prestige but also a devout expression of filial piety. The immediate purpose of these literary examinations was to select government officials on an unprejudiced basis of knowledge and scholastic ability. Another purpose for filling vacancies to official positions by means of free competition was to create a continued stimulus to cultural advancement. Neither purpose was fully achieved in Korea. First, this system had been originally developed to serve the peculiar needs of the Chinese power structure, where few nobility existed between the monarch and the people. In Korea, however, a numerically and politically strong landed gentry which jealously sought to maintain its privileges obstructed the usefulness of these examinations.

The educational system undergirding the examination system was a combination of public and private institutions of various quality and level of curriculum. At the top of this loose configuration was *Songgyun-gwan*, the national university. *Songgyun-gwan* could trace its origin to 1288 AD and from this date until Japanese annexation it was considered the highest educational institution in the nation. In 1398 this school settled at its present site in Seoul. More than merely an advanced school, the *Songgyun-gwan* was long the educational center of Korea. On its faculty were some of the most distinguished scholars of the nation and in its library was a priceless collection of the finest works of Chinese scholars. Its grounds served as the location for the royal examinations. The original purpose of the *Songgyun-gwan* was that of ". . . reorganizing the people's life demoralized by the preponderance of Buddhists in the former dynasty and of training able officials for the administration." To accomplish this goal ". . . it gathered here the best gifted youth of the Chinese classics so that they might acquaint themselves with Confucian moralism and philosophy as a guide for politics and economy" (Rim, 1952).

Thus from *Hyanggyo* or private *institute* to *Songgyun-gwan* the scholar traveled along an extremely narrow scholastic path. He studied to understand the ancient Confucian canon. The epitome of scholarship was the polished essay which typically reflected an attempt to produce a balanced mosaic of classic wisdoms. This process of emulation of a near sacred body of knowledge eventually was to prove inadequate preparation for the changes stirring in the late 19th century when Korea confronted western institutions and learning.

The 500-year history of Choson was a period in which Confucian roles and precepts were incorporated into the life and institutions of Korean society. Confucian principles became deeply infused into the structure of government, community, family and education. Each person, i.e., mother, father, daughter, son, teacher, student, official, ruler or subject, had a prescribed role defining in considerable detail appropriate behavior and responsibilities in social relationships. The purpose of education was to impart the rules, ceremonies, and moralistic principles associated with each status or rank. As Park Sum-Youn (1991) has noted, the influence of this period is visible today:

> It (education) was structured and the basis of rigid class distinction and male centered values. The social tendency of authoritarianism, sexual discrimination and aversion to menial labor is the Confucian legacy that is still very much felt in educational sectors today. . . .

But the Confucian educational tradition has provided Koreans with a reasonable way of thinking, a strong moral sense, and zeal for education by stressing that man can be a man only through education (22).

Introduction of Modern Education

The latter part of the 19th century was a period of turmoil and change in Korea with strong advocates emerging for the introduction of western culture and institutions and other Koreans committed to maintaining Korea's isolation and preserving traditional ways. The struggle between the traditionalists and the modernizers was reflected in the mix of "western" and "eastern" educational philosophies and institutions which competed for attention well into the 20th century. Confucianism interpreted education as a process of preparing privileged males through study of the approved classics in order to serve an aristocratic society. However, in contrast the impact of Western culture:

> . . . was manifested in the development of the *sirhak* or pragmatic school of learning. Literally *sirhak* means a pragmatic learning of politics, economics, history, and natural sciences, with greater concern for real problems than theoretical metaphysics. By advocating a realistic approach, *sirhak* provoked a fresh look at the world and facilitated the shaping of a new national outlook (KOIS, 1982:669).

The impact of *sirhak* was largely translated through *silhak* or Koreanized Western Studies developed and advocated by a small number of Korean scholars. A few *Yangbang*, often those out of favor with the king, were willing to explore Western studies and even embrace Western institutions.

With the opening of Korea to the West, Christian missionaries began to arrive and participate in education by holding classes and establishing schools. At first, the curriculum was often limited to the Bible and English-language instruction. As resources improved and suitable teachers were found, the curricula were sometimes extended to include Chinese classics, mathematics, geography, physics, chemistry, music, art, and gymnastics.

Modest in scope, early missionary efforts during this period often consisted of a few orphan children attending classes in a missionary's home. From these humble beginnings the influence of missionaries, largely Catholic and Protestant, grew to be a major force in educational development. At least four distinct contributions have been traced to the missionaries: 1) educational opportunity was provided to some Koreans who otherwise would have had none, 2) new methods of instruction were introduced, 3) practices reflecting enlightened views toward education of women were initiated, and 4) in general a small window to the West was opened. Some of the mission schools grew from humble beginnings to become distinguished institutions. Ewha Haktang, founded in 1886 by Methodists, became the first girls' school in Korea and evolved into Ewha University, the largest women's university in the world. Choson Christian College, founded in 1905 for males later became Yonsei University. These two institutions along with Korea University which evolved from Bosung professional school remain today among the more respected private Korean universities.

The end of the 19th century found a wide variety of educational institutions, private and public, indigenous and western, often in tenuous existence. One survey of the educational conditions in the mid 1890s in addition to the many private venture schools identified the following: a Government University (Songgyun gwan), Government vernacular schools, a Government English-language school, foreign language schools, and mission schools. The long-standing civil service examination system had been abolished but had not been replaced by a fully articulated educational system. Although a primary education system was officially in place it was financially ill-supported, and generally low in quality. Furthermore, arguments persisted over the pure use of Hangul as the written language of instruction versus some combination of the Chinese and Korean script. At the higher levels a variety of institutes and colleges had appeared, yet only sporadic attempts had been made to develop vocational, technical or engineering schools.

Period of Japanese Annexation

After testing its position during a five year Protectorate (1905-1910) and judging correctly that little outside interference would be forthcoming, Japan proceeded in 1910 with its full annexation of Korea. The Korean nation and Korean institutions thus became part of the Japanese Empire.

The general purpose and direction of education throughout the empire was given by the Japanese Imperial Rescript of Education and with much ceremony the privilege of obeying this honored document was extended to the Korean schools. The philosophy propounded in this Rescript was designed to weld together all elements of Japanese society by producing a common devotion to the Japanese Emperor. The schools, an official report indicated, should be used to ". . . give the younger generations of Koreans such moral character and general knowledge as will make them loyal subjects of Japan, at the same time enabling them to cope with the present conditions existing in the Peninsula" (*Annual Report* 1910-11:201). Initially, a dual system of education was created with separate Korean and Japanese schools. The Korean track included a 4-year common school followed by 4-year higher common school and a variety of 4-year "industrial" schools. Graduation from the higher common school permitted entrance to 3-year "special" schools for advanced study of the arts and sciences.

One Korean scholar described the Japanese policy as one of Denationalization, Vocationalization, Deliberalization, and Discrimination. As defined by Rim (1952) these terms mean:

1. *Denationalization*--forcing the Korean people to substitute loyalty to the Japanese Emperor for that formerly given to their own rulers.

2. *Vocationalization*--emphasizing schooling for Koreans only adequate for becoming low level tradesmen.

3. *Deliberalization*--ignoring both the humanities and the advanced scientific and technical courses in the Korean schools.

4. *Discrimination*--offering the Japanese better and more advanced educational opportunities than the Koreans.

Independence Movement

In 1919, Japan, as well as the rest of the world, was shocked by a sudden widespread independence movement in Korea. On March 1st of that year, 33 of the most prominent Koreans signed the Proclamation of Independence and sent a copy to the Japanese Governor-General. Special copies of the proclamation were read throughout the entire country and the independence movement was under way.

A number of educational changes followed the demand for independence. In the introduction to the Japanese *Annual Report of the [Colonial] Government (1918-1921)* a significant reference is made to the Independence Movement.

> Great as the improvement effected in the administration of Choson was, the change in spirit of the times following the Great European War demanded a readjustment of the administrative system, and though this could not be done at once owing to the outbreak of the Independence movement in March 1919, it was duly carried out in August 1919. The main points of the reform lay in the appointment of either a civil or military official as Governor-General, the change of the gendarmerie system into that of an ordinary police system, *the ensuing of non-discrimination between Japanese and Koreans, and the raising of the Korean people to the same standards as that of the Japanese, by means of a cultural policy.*

Specifically, with regard to education this document states:

> In the 10 years that have elapsed since the annexation, the yearning of Koreans in general for education has become far more intensified and this has necessitated the introduction of far-reaching reforms in the educational systems aiming on the one hand at the full provision of educational organs and on the other hand conducting the education of Koreans on the same level as Japanese, thus enabling them to enter schools of higher education on the same terms as Japanese students.

The Educational Ordinance of 1922 referred to both Japanese and Koreans. Under the new ordinance a continued emphasis was placed on proficiency in the national (Japanese) language. A second stipulation of this official policy provided for an expansion of educational facilities, and plans were formulated to start a building program at each educational level. Privileges to attend normal and university education were extended to more Koreans and the period of time needed to complete elementary and secondary schooling was increased to that found in Japan proper. However, the Japanese did not consider that existing conditions warranted compulsory education. Under the previous (1911) educational ordinance Korea's heritage was treated as being synonymous with that of Japan, however, schools under the new law were advised to be more cognizant of the needs of the Korean culture. For example, encouragement was given to the teaching of Korean history and geography to comply with the desires of the Korean people.

Korean authors generally pointed out that the depth of these modifications was not sufficient to bring about lasting improvement. Rim (1952:112) asserted that the greatest educational need of the Koreans was still ignored. The educational system in Korea, Rim argued, was still a foreign system with all ultimate power for the making of decisions resting in the hands of foreigners. There still were not adequate means for participation of Koreans in matters of important educational policy.

Implementation of New Policies

The Japanese authorities were cautious about expanding educational opportunities for Koreans. Higher education was considered especially dangerous because advanced schools could become centers for political activity. Nevertheless, during the early 1920s the Korean school enrollments expanded rapidly. Japanese statistics, generally considered reliable until military preparations obscured scholarship, show the number of public common schools more than doubling and the number of boys in higher common schools nearly doubling during the period between 1919 and 1922. Growth in higher education was also recorded with the establishment of the first separate institution for teacher training in Seoul in 1922. Soon, each province attempted to found its own normal school and although these schools were abandoned due to inadequate funds and small enrollments, their place was later taken by a few strategically located government-run teacher training institutions. Perhaps the culminating activity of the Japanese in respect to higher education was the launching of work, in 1922, on the long-awaited university. In 1826 Kyungsung Imperial University was established with two faculties: the Faculty of Laws and Literature and the Faculty of Medicine. A Faculty of Engineering was not added until 1938. Both Japanese and Koreans could attend the university, although the students and faculty were disproportionately Japanese (*Japanese Colonial Government* 1926-1927). Figure I.2 shows the integrated structure of schooling for both Japanese and Koreans in 1937.

A variety of other institutes of higher learning existed during the latter stages of the colonial period. Many of these were labelled professional schools (*Jeonmum Hakyo*) and included both governmental and public institutions, and private schools, most of which were originally mission. Professional schools (sometimes described as colleges in English sources) usually provided short-term courses in such areas as technology, agriculture, fishery and home economics. By 1943 there were 28 such institutions in Korea. Korean scholars often refer to them as advanced trade schools since their programs included little general education and no research activities. Some of the professional schools eventually became universities in the post-colonial period.

Figure I.2   The School Structure For Japanese and Koreans in Korea in 1937

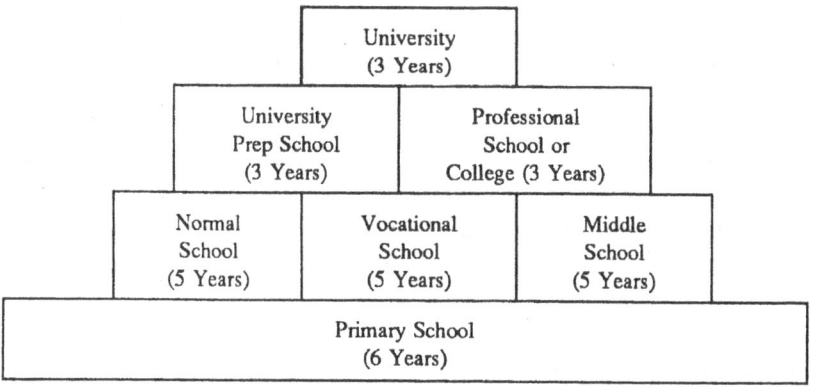

One Korean author refers to the latter years of the annexation as the "educational destruction period" (Lee M. K. 1949). This judgment was based largely on the manner in which the Educational Ordinance of 1938 was enforced. According to these new regulations all public elementary and secondary education now followed the Japanese system in name as well as in structure. The new guiding principles of the schools were twofold: "Clarification of the National Polity, Japan and Tyosen (Korea) as one Body; and endurance and training."

In this new law was the fulfillment of the non-discrimination promise of 17 years earlier. Koreans and Japanese were now to attend the same schools and study the same curriculum. The study of Korean language was completely discontinued and students outside as well as inside the school were rigidly forbidden to speak the native tongue. By 1940 the process of assimilation had gone so far that the Korean people were required to adopt Japanese names. Thus, Japan and Korea in official colonial documents came to be treated as "one Body."

Increasingly, as Japan's battle lines embraced two hemispheres, the schools of Korea became more narrow in purpose. To promote "endurance and training" secondary schools and colleges were required to send students to work on war production. To carry on its war effort Japan needed a large labor supply, additional soldiers, and more technicians. Before the end of the second World War the Korean schools were to have made contributions to all three needs involved in this guiding principle. Under a draft system all students were required to work where the Government dictated and school terms were shortened to give more time for production. As the need grew the Government multiplied its publicity to obtain Korean volunteers to swell the military ranks.

The colleges in particular were utilized to fulfill the need for specialists for the war effort. To meet technical requirements, courses in the liberal arts were reduced in number or dropped from the curricula of the colleges and private and public schools alike were required to educate for war. Choson Christian College, for example, one of the best known mission colleges, now became the Technical Administration College. And two of the most prominent women's colleges, Sukmyong and Ewha, became institutes for the training of leaders to work in rural communities in order that Korea's rural population might fully contribute to the war economy.

Summary of Japanese Influence

Japanese documents claim that their policies brought the first public education system to Korea. The Japanese interpretation of the Korean educational needs consistently emphasized vocational and technical training and a general deformalizing and modernizing of educational content. However, Japan in its haste to shower the educational and societal benefits of modernization and Japanization on Korea at first completely ignored Korea's ancient culture, later promoted insufficient reforms, and lastly reverted to assimilation by force.

Cole and Lyman (1971) as well as others point out that although annexation restricted Western influences and inhibited development of Korean institutions certain modernizing influences resulted from Japanese colonization. The imposition of a Japanese-style government structure had long-term impact on post-independence Korean bureaucracy and legal administrative institutions. Second, Christianity, increasingly oppressed by the Japanese, came to be highly regarded by Koreans. Although only a small percentage of Koreans converted to Christianity, the impact of Christians on education, politics and economic development has been significant.

Education Under the U.S. Military Government

With the Russians accepting the surrender of the Japanese troops above the 38th parallel and the Americans doing the same below this line, Korea in 1945 was freed from 35 years of Japanese colonialization. In subsequent agreements the U.S.S.R. and U.S.A. were charged by the United Nations with forming a trusteeship over Korea and the 38th parallel became a line of demarcation between Russian and American zones of responsibility and influence. Unfortunately international friction caused the two zones to become completely severed and the arbitrary line of demarcation took on the appearance of a national boundary. This boundary became a reality in the summer of 1948 after the United Nations sponsored an election in the American zone. Thus the end result of a trusteeship, created to establish a self-governing sovereign Korea, was to produce two Korean governments (the Republic of Korea and the People's Republic of Korea) each claiming jurisdiction over the entire peninsula.

The three years of Military Government in South Korea were fraught with political instability and economic hardship. Many of the U.S. military advisers lacked experience and adequate knowledge of the Korean culture. Meade (1951) was highly critical of the U.S. actions:

> [The] Military Government concluded its first year of occupation by foisting upon the Koreans a governmental structure in which one of the most certain

safeguards of democracy, local self-determination, was completely lacking. The resolve to instruct Koreans in the American democratic way appears to have become strangely distorted. It was not abandoned. The Interim Legislative Assembly was established in October 1946; universal suffrage was planned; and the popular election of provincial governors, mayors, and other local chief executives was introduced in November. The paradox was a strange one; for while the people could choose their officials, the latter were cogs in a machinery that made them responsible not to the electorate but to the authority of the United States Army Military Government in Korea (80-81).

In principle, one of the basic educational problems of the military government was to aid the Koreans in examining the educational needs and societal role which they wished their schools to play. Unfortunately, continual political conflict among the Korean students and teachers complicated and at times obscured the more technical educational issues. The multiplicity of political points of view led to conflicts between cliques of students, developed animosity among faculty members, and disrupted the administrative routines of the schools.

Such actions of the schools did not go unnoticed by the Military Government which at times took drastic measures. As early as March of 1946 directives reminiscent of those of the former Japanese colonial government were issued, ". . . forbidding school participation in political demonstrations and dissemination of political propaganda . . ." (United States Military In Korea [USMIK], 1946:19).

With regard to education some confusion persisted as to U.S. goals. Meade candidly states that the objectives of education under the Military Government were to ". . . eradicate the Japanese system and replace it by the American . . ." The official USMG reports describe their efforts as "democratizing" and "modernizing" Korean education. Perhaps in practice the difference in language was unimportant.

The Korean schools reflected the difficult and uncertain times. Teachers as civil servants were poorly paid and when caught in the periodic bursts of inflation, dissatisfaction and even resignations were the results. The students, and faculties as well, often became embroiled in the raging political conflicts disrupting normal operation. Accompanying and at times fueling these problems was a tremendous upward surge in enrollment at all school levels. Educational expansion exacerbated shortages in facilities, materials, and personnel. Mass promotions pushed teachers up a notch on the academic status scale with primary teachers sometimes becoming secondary teachers and the latter becoming college professors and college deans. Filling each classroom with a teacher became a sizeable task but maintaining professional standards proved overwhelming. Taking advantage of the strong educational demand of the Korean people, entrepreneurial and opportunistic individuals opened many private schools, some of which flagrantly violated the qualifications set forth by the government.

Positive contributions, however, were also forthcoming. At the end of World War II the educational institutions of Korea were virtually at a standstill. The Military Government, essentially operating through the organizational structure inherited from the Japanese, quickly set the national system of education in motion. Led by a small group by competent Korean educators and laymen, a reorganization was planned and effected; textbooks were printed in the native script; a new curriculum was installed; and inservice and preservice training programs were initiated to raise the professional level of teaching personnel. The Military Government further sought to meet some of the pressing material needs by making available more adequate teaching aids, including many imported American textbooks. Attempting to promote both the general educational value of working with the hands and to alleviate the shortage of skilled labor a wider program of vocational education was encouraged. Most important of all, some attempts were made under the Military Government to widen the professional horizons of Korean educators in order that they might better compare their varied, and often authoritarian, educational heritage with American ideals and methods.

Korean Education Under the First and Second Republics, 1948-1961

All subsequent chapters discuss aspects of contemporary Korean education and often provide brief reviews of important historical antecedents. This section offers a broad overview of major educational developments in the Republic.

Educational Goals and Laws

Goals and objectives to guide the new educational system are found in the Constitution of the Republic, adopted in 1948, and in the

Education Law enacted in 1949. These statements on education were significantly influenced by the goals suggested by the National Committee on Educational Planning which had existed under the U.S. Military Government. The goals identified by this committee were:

1. Formulation of character which is realized in international friendship and harmony as well as in national independence and self-respect;

2. emphasis on individual responsibility and a spirit of mutual assistance: enforcement of a spirit of faithful and practical service;

3. contribution of human civilization by originating science and technology and by refining and emphasizing national culture;

4. cultivation of a spirit of persistent enterprise by elevating the physical standards of the people;

5. cultivation of sincere and complete character by emphasis on the appreciative and creative power of fine arts.

The Constitution of the Republic of Korea established that all people had the right to equal opportunity for education and that elementary education should be compulsory and free. The Education Law of 1949 required that compulsory education be provided for all children between 6 and 12 years of age. Article 1 of the Law described the ultimate goal of education as follows.

> Education shall aim at, under the great ideal of *hongik in gan* (benefits for all mankind), assisting all people in perfecting individual capability, developing the ability for independent life, and acquiring citizenship qualifications needed to serve for the democratic

development of the nation and for the realization of human co-prosperity.

The ideal of *hongik in gan* was an ancient notion of the general weal and had been the guiding philosophy in Korea for many centuries.

Six more specific objectives were associated with this ideal:

1. cultivation of knowledge and habits needed for the sound development and sustenance of body and of indomitable spirit;

2. development of patriotic spirit for the preservation and enhancement of national independence and values for the cause of world peace;

3. succession and development of national culture and contribution to the creation and growth of world culture;

4. cultivation of truth-seeking spirit and of the abilities to think scientifically, act creatively, and live rationally;

5. development of the love for freedom and of high respect for responsibilities necessary to lead well-harmonized community life with the spirit of faithfulness, cooperation, love, and respect;

6. development of aesthetic sensitivity to appreciate and create sublime arts, to enjoy the beauty of nature, and to utilize leisure effectively for cheerful and harmonious life.

The goals and objectives were intended as guidelines for policies, plans and reforms at all levels of the educational system. To account fully for their impact at the classroom level is an impossible task; however, there are indications that some objectives had more operational impact than others. McGinn, et al. (1980) notes that "The goal statements appear to represent an effort to blend modern concepts with traditionally approved social values" (31). Certainly the ideas of "contribution to the creation and growth of world culture," "ability to think scientifically" and promotion of "values for the cause of world peace" have a modern ring to them and suggest an appreciation for values often associated with advanced industrial societies. On the other hand references to "indomitable spirit," "harmonious life," and "the spirit of faithfulness" suggest time-honored Confucian traditions. Attention to "patriotic spirit," use of "mother tongue," and "development of a national culture" reflects the commitment to nation-building. It is, of course, possible to read contradictions into this set of goals.

The Education Law includes more specific objectives for each educational level. For example, the objectives for elementary education were:

1. to improve the child's ability to understand and use correctly the national language needed for daily life;

2. to cultivate the sense of morality, responsibility, public spirit and cooperation through understanding of the relationships between the individuals, the community and the nation, with particular emphasis upon national consciousness, self-reliance, and independence through correct understanding of the present status as well as the traditions of the national life, together with the sense of international cooperation;

3. to foster the child's ability to scientifically observe and deal with natural objects and phenomena appearing in daily life;

4. to cultivate the child's basic understanding and to deal with the relationships necessary for daily life;

5. to develop the child's basic understanding and skills for obtaining food, clothing and shelter as well as for occupations necessary for daily life, fostering the habit of hard work and the ability to lead an independent life;

6. to cultivate the child's basic understanding and skills of music, fine arts, literature, and others, enabling him to lead a cheerful, joyful and harmonious life;

7. to improve the child's ability to make harmonious development of mind and body.

The 1949 Education Law and its amendment in 1951 established the basic system of formal education which remains to this day. Many subsequent laws and presidential decrees supplemented the original law and made implementation possible. The first major reform took place during the Korean War.

War-Time Education and Reconstruction

During the two years subsequent to its establishment the Republic of Korea made significant advancement toward the stabilization of its economy and toward laying the groundwork for a system of popular education. However, on the morning of June 25, 1950 the North Korean Army crossed the 38th parallel in force and soon a three-year war had begun. By shattering the means of production, displacing large segments of the population, making casualties of many of the Republic's leaders, and destroying or damaging a high percentage of the educational institutions, the first few months of war quickly eliminated the progress the Republic had made.

The physical destruction of the war was enormous. Only two of the major cities of the Republic were not occupied one or more times by hostile troops. It was estimated, for example, that only a third of the buildings in Seoul were left standing. War-time education often meant no facilities, no textbooks and frequently no teachers. The damage to classrooms is shown in Table I.2.

Table I.2

Effect of War on Number of Classrooms

	Number of Classrooms Before 1950	Number of Classrooms Destroyed or Damaged
Elementary Schools	34,294	23,700
Secondary Schools	4,716	3,544
Colleges & Universities	3,468	1,721
TOTAL	42,478	28,965

Source: MOE. *Education Yearbook of Korea*. Portions translated by Pil Sun Lee. Seoul 1953:23.

War-time educational policies were exercises in coping rather than enforcement of the provisions of the educational law. The contribution of international aid during this period was crucial. From 1952-1960 the aid to education from USAID and UN agencies totaled approximately $100 million, of which half was spent on primary and secondary classroom construction. This external assistance became all the more important because the education budget was slashed to 2 percent of the Korean national budget during the war. In spite of the many severe problems confronted during the war the level of enrollment in primary education was maintained.

The damage of the war to higher education institutions for a brief period completely paralyzed most colleges and universities. However, an innovative plan provided for War-Time Union Colleges whereby colleges and universities whose personnel had taken refuge in a temporary location pooled their resources. These colleges were established in such cities as Pusan, Taegu, Kwanju, Chonju, and Taejon and for over a year provided basic courses to students from all parts of the country. Students attending a War-Time College could subsequently transfer credit to their original institution when it again began to function normally.

During the early part of the war a policy was developed which called for a major national higher-education institution to be located in each province. This policy partly stemmed from the desire to reduce the concentration of higher-education in Seoul and create a better regional dispersement. A second influence was to fill a void in the wake of the War-Time Union Colleges and reduce the demand for establishment of private institutions. Between 1951 and 1953 seven national higher-education institutions were created.

The period of 1951-1960 saw dozens of new public and private colleges and universities of higher learning established and the upgrading in status of a number of existing institutions. In an attempt to curb this higher education boom the Presidential Decree on the Establishment of College and University Standards was enacted in 1955. By providing standards for teaching personnel and facilities the decree slowed temporarily the creation of new institutions and forced a modest reduction of student quotas and number of departments.

The Development Decades

The decades of the 1960s and 1970s recorded many changes in Korean society and education. The Student Uprising on April 19, 1960 resulted in the overthrow of the ruling government and also focussed attention on the role of students within their institutions as well as on the national scene. Kim notes:

> . . . it (the uprising) brought forth a chance to realize the importance of students and the need for guidance of their activities. The establishment of student guidance centers and greater emphasis upon student self-government as well as student welfare services in recent

years may well be considered as the direct products of such realization . . ." (Kim J. C., 1985)

The military coup in 1961 ushered in an era of many significant national changes. The new government under Park Chung Hee, after solidifying its power and successfully resisting challenges both from within the military and within the civilian opposition groups, aggressively embarked on a comprehensive economic development policy. Immediate action included the arrest of leading businessmen who were charged with the illicit accumulation of wealth (Jin-Young Chung, 1990:40). Chung explains: "They (the businessmen) could free themselves only by 'donating' their equities of commercial banks to the state and promising to participate in national reconstruction by paying back their penalties with newly constructed industrial firm(s)." This action coupled with the creation of the National Planning Board and certain financial and fiscal reforms provided the government with needed capital and placed the state firmly in control of all levers for strategic economic planning. In a context of an absence of local resources, normalization of Korea-Japan relations, and easy access to foreign technology the Korean model of export-oriented development controlled by a strong state began to take shape.

During the 1960s the economy grew at the average annual growth rate of approximately 10 percent. This growth is attributed both to increased industrial output and to the drop in population growth rate from 2.9 percent in 1961 to 1.7 percent in 1971 (Economic Planning Board, 1971:6). No nation-state was more committed to economic development during the UNdeclared "development decade," i.e. the 1960s, than Korea.

Several major educational policies and reforms took place during the 1960s. A shift was initiated toward stronger national control of educational change. In keeping with the emphasis on state-managed, economic development education was viewed essentially as an institution developing human capital and as a process of preparing members of the corporate state. The educational slogan for the 1950s had been "one skill for one person" emphasizing the industrial and technical skills necessary to reconstruct the economy and infrastructure. The slogans for the 1960s were "education for economic development" or "nation-building through education."

Guided by the Economic Planning Board educational policies were expected to be congruent with manpower-planning goals. The universalization of elementary education and the rapid expansion of secondary education provided sources from which unskilled and semi-skilled labor could be drawn. To attain a better balance of supply and demand of high-level manpower the government made several intermittent, never fully successful, attempts at controlling the number and specialization of colleges and university students either through entrance or exit devices (see Chapter IV).

The policy of automatic promotion throughout the elementary grades supported growth at this level. Another important policy was adopted in 1968 eliminating the examination system for middle school admission and creating a system for allocating students to schools within a district by computer lottery. To supply sufficient quantity and quality of teachers the preservice and inservice preparation of elementary and middle school teachers was encouraged. As an example of qualitative improvement in the early 1960s high school level normal schools which trained elementary teachers were upgraded to two year colleges.

Several attempts at large scale revisions of curriculum were also forthcoming during this period. Particularly at issue were the content of social studies and moral education; the comparative emphasis to be placed on the individual or the nation; the time to be devoted to anti-communism; the acceptance of leadership of the state versus "individual initiative and entrepreneurship" (McGinn, et al., 1980:43, see Chapter II). Kim concludes: "especially after the Yushin declaration by the Park regime in 1972, its totalitarian ideology was positively reflected in the textbooks" (Kim, 1990:391).

Although subject to fluctuations Korean education in general continued its rapid expansion through the 1960s and 1970s. This growth is indicated not only in the increase in numbers of students at all levels but also in the accompanying expansion of teachers and facilities. The government in general encouraged growth, particularly below the college level. The people responded favorably to increased educational opportunities, and the rapid economic growth provided the necessary resources to support educational expansion.

At the higher education level the military government in 1962 initiated a national qualifying examination for college entrance, a policy to be abandoned two years later. In 1968 the Ministry of Education again initiated a national college entrance examination. However, the students who passed this examination still had to take another examination administered by the chosen university or college (Kim, S.B., 1990:387). This arrangement gave the government essential control over student selection and student quotas.

By the end of the 1960s Korea's economic strategy was in trouble. A growing trade deficit and increased competition from less developed countries in world markets led to a decision to upgrade the country's industrial structure by engaging in "industrial deepening" (Jin-Young Chung, 1990). In 1973 a heavy and chemical industrialization (HCI) plan was announced by President Park.

The 1970s were also a period of political change. The authoritarian political regime was increasingly under criticism from labor unions demanding a larger share of the economic benefits and from various middle-class businesses and professional groups seeking more autonomy. In the face of this opposition: "Park resorted to extraordinary measures to 'harden' the political regime and consolidate his personal rule" (Chung, 1990:42). Chung summarizes the results of the new economic strategy:

> The government's big push for the HCI drive resulted in rapid industrial deepening, with the HCI industries increasing its contribution to the industrial value-added from 40 percent in 1973 to 51 percent in 1979. Nevertheless, it resulted in several negative consequences. The first was a massive, rapid concentration of economic power. A handful of conglomerates became the dominant actors in the South Korean economy. The second was rapid accumulation of foreign debt. Foreign borrowing had been an essential element of South Korea's industrial strategy ever since the mid-1960s. But the magnitude of foreign borrowing requirements was increased tremendously after the oil crisis. The third was the existence of massive over-investment, putting enormous strains on the whole economy. All these factors contributed to the emergence of an economic crisis in the late 1970s, which, together with the political crisis of Park's long-term dictatorship, put an end to an era (44).

The 1970s extended the educational changes and reforms of the 1960s. The earlier abolishment of the entrance examination to middle schools opened the door to the popularization of secondary education. The vigorous competition for entrance to the middle school was now transferred to entrance to the high school. The focus on high schools led to a number of innovations designed to promote equality between institutions at this level. In higher education there was some shift in focus from control to efforts at the upgrading of quality. Examples of changes in higher education included a reduction of the credit requirements for graduation, introduction of a double-major system and recruitment of new students by broad field rather than specialized program. Another major advent in higher education was the creation in 1972 of the Air and Correspondence College--to be followed in 1974 by the Air and Correspondence High School.

Research and development activities in education received a major boost with the establishment of the Korean Educational Development Institute (KEDI) in 1972. KEDI as the R & D arm of the Ministry of Education has played a major role in national research development, training, policy and planning activities. It has also acquired a significant international reputation because of the quality of its work.

In addition to concern that the education system produce literate citizens and a sufficient supply of qualified labor, the state also sought educational support in rural development and in furthering national integration. The Saemaul Undong (New Community Movement) was launched in the early 1970s in over 35,000 villages. J. C. Kim (1985) describes this process:

> Each village was distributed with 330 sacks of cement to be used for common good of the villagers at their disposal. Rapidly it developed into a new type of rural development combining improvement of physical setting and economic standards on one hand and spiritual awakening on the other hand directed towards the spirits of diligence, self-reliance and cooperation . . . . Although government came to support the movement with both material and guidance, major decisions for development was left to villagers and their leaders.
>
> As the Saemaul Undong gradually spread to become a nationwide rejuvenization movement, it came to increasingly emphasize its educational aspect. A Saemaul Leaders' Training Institute was created in 1973 which provided short term courses for community leaders in various practical skills as well as in the spiritual meaning of Saemaul Undong, national security, and appropriate roles of individuals in national development (pp. 128-130).

Saemaul Undong may be characterized as a rural development project, an example of nonformal education, and an attempt of the state to gain further power and legitimacy. Its early influence on education was considerable, particularly in rural primary schools where many attempts were made to involve schools and teachers in community activities. Increasingly, however, the movement was criticized as sharing in the general corruption of the national government.

The 1980s may have been a watershed decade for Korea. The assassination of President Park led to a renewed struggle for power early in the decade. The emergence of the Chun regime meant a continuation of the dominance of the military over civil society. With an extraordinary concentration of power in the president, political parities and political competition had little effect on actions of the state. Any constraints, at least in economic policy making, came largely from *choebols*, the large business conglomerates.

However, the 1980s also saw considerable movement toward a private sector led, market centered, model of economic development. This transition was slow, partial, and painfully hindered by the legacy of state-led development (Jin-Young Chung, 1990:46). Responding to world economic conditions Korea experienced both economic slow downs and economic upturns. The latter part of the decade was a boom period. Chung (1990) explains:

> Extreme price stability was maintained. Large trade and current account surpluses were realized. Domestic savings came to exceed domestic investment for the first time in the contemporary Korean history. Foreign debt began to decline. An economic boom finally ensued after several years of stabilization under military authoritarian rule (47).

Accompanying economic change were social and political ferment. The benefits of economic prosperity were unevenly distributed resulting in a widening gap between rich and poor and in a hardening of social class structure. Moderate and radical political opposition grew in reaction to the repressive and sometimes violent nature of the Chun government. A broad political coalition of opposition groups with popular support forced the Chun regime to accept direct presidential elections.

A report prepared by KEDI characterizes the educational changes in the 1980s as a search for higher quality of education (KEDI, 1985:37). The changes were further described as setting:

> ... the direction of developing education for the whole person, education for spiritual revitalization, science education and life-long education. The first two [directions] refer to an ideological concern for self-realization, the instilling of right character, spiritual posture against communism and community consciousness. The remaining two give education practical orientation to equip youngsters with ability to live in a rapidly changing frame of reference. (38)

Higher education was buffeted by attempts to reduce financial and social advantages in the admittance to colleges and universities. Innovations included new constraints on private tutoring, revisions of the entrance examination, extended use of facilities, use of educational television and expansion of the Air and Correspondence College. The overall effect of these several reforms is still being evaluated; however, questions of equity, quality (and increasingly, autonomy) in higher education persisted beyond the 1980s.

The 1980s saw some stabilization in the educational system. There was a leveling off of enrollments in elementary and middle schools. The universalization of middle school education had become a reality. Expansion in high school enrollments was large but proportionately much less than in previous decades. The situation with higher education, however, was another matter.

As Korea enters the last decade of the 20th century it is facing a wide range of educational issues and difficult policy choices. Inevitably the extremely rapid enrollment growth at all levels has, in the minds of many Korean educators, sacrificed quality. The universalization of elementary and middle school education and the automatic promotion policy have perhaps made educational opportunities more equal at the lower levels of the system. But have these trends made the identification and nurturing of talent and creativity more difficult? Equity and efficiency concerns are involved in policy choices pertaining to educational finance, admissions and promotion at all educational levels, local and institutional autonomy, privatization at secondary and higher educational levels, and professionalization and democraticization of educational decision making. As such professional and ideological issues are debated the fundamental questions of purpose is also on the educational and social agenda. Can, for example, the educational system continue to focus on the function of transmission of knowledge and also develop independent, self-reliant learners?

Bibliography

Articles and Books

Abe, Shigetaka. "Education in Formosa and Korea." *Educational Yearbook 1931*. New York: Bureau of Publication, Teachers College, Columbia University, 1932.

Australia Department of Labor and National Service. *Outline of Vocational Training in Korea*. Perth, 1966.

Brandt, Vincent and Cheong, Ji Woon. *Planning from the Bottom Up; Community-Based Integrated Rural Development in South Korea*. Essex, CT: International Council for Educational Development, 1979.

Bundge, Frederica M., et al., eds. *South Korea: A Country Study*. Washington, DC: Department of U.S. Army, 1981.

Cho, Dong-Sik. "The Basic Principles of the Secondary School Reorganization in Korea." A Report submitted by the Chairman of the Sub-Committee on Secondary Education to the National Committee on Educational Planning on March 8, 1946.

Cho, Seug H. "Elementary Education in Korea." *School and Society* XLVII (January 14, 1939): 55-59.

Choi, W. P. "The Largest Women's University in the World." *Korean Survey* VIII, (October, 1959):6-12.

Choy, Bong-Youn. *Korea: A History*. Rutland, Vermont: International Press, 1926.

Chun, Tuk-Chu. "Korea in the Pacific Community." *Social Education*, 52 (March 1988):182-186.

Chung, Jin-Young. "South Korea Strategies for Dynamic Transformation 1961-88." In *Dynamic Transformation: Korea, NICs and Beyond*. 37-52, edited by Lim, Gill-Chin, and Chong, Wook. Seoul, Myung-Bo Publishing Company, 1990.

This paper describes the characteristics of Korea's development strategies for social, political, and institutional change. The achievements, the author claims, are due to the state's capacity to impose development strategies and force the private sector to comply with the government-chosen directions.

Chung, Tai-di. "Korean Education: Yesterday and Tomorrow." *Koreana*, 12 No. 3 (1970): 66-76.

Cole, David C. and Lyman, Princeton N. *Korean Development: The Interplay of Politics and Economics*. Cambridge: Harvard University Press, 1971.

Department of Education. *An Outline of Educational Administration for 1946-1947*. Seoul: Korean Government, 1947.

Deutchler, Martaina. *Confucian Gentlemen and Barbarian Envoys: The Opening of Korea, 1875-1885*. Seattle: University of Washington, 1977.

Economic Planning Board. "Major Economic Indicators, 1960-1971." Seoul, Korea, 1971.

Fisher, James Earnest. *Democracy and Mission Education in Korea*. Seoul: Yonsei University Press, 1970. (LA 1331 F5 1970)

This book was written originally in 1928 when Korea was under the Japanese colonial rule. The review covers the state of mission education, cultural and intellectual issues, and the political and economic problems of Korea, as well as a critique on missionary education.

Grajdanzev, Andrew J. *Modern Korea*. New York: John Day Company, 1944.

Hahn, Ki-Un. "Study on the Democratization of Education in Korea Based on the History of Educational Thought." *Korea Observer*, 1 (April-July 1969):11-31.

An attempt is made to trace "democratization" of education in three historical periods: democratic tradition of Korean education (before 1876), attempts to democratize Korean education between 1876-1945, and Korean education after 1945.

Han, Woo-Keun. *The History of Korea*. Translated by Lee, Kyung Shink, Seoul: Eul-Yoo Publishing Company, 1970.

Hatada, Takashi. *A History of Korea*. Santa Barbara, CA: American Biblio Center, Clio Press, 1969.

Ha, Tae-Hung. "Korea--Forty-Three Centuries." *Korean Cultural*. Series 1. Seoul: Yonsei University Press, 1962.

Henthorn, William E. *A History of Korea*. New York: The Free Press, 1971.

Hinton, Harold C. *Korea Under New Leadership: The Fifth Republic*. New York: Praeger Publishers, 1983.

Japanese Colonial Government. "Annual Report on Reforms and Progress in Choson (1910-1911)."

Japanese Colonial Government. "Annual Report of The Colonial Government (1918-1921)."

Japanese Colonial Government. "Annual Report of The Government (1926-1927)."

Japanese Colonial Government. "Annual Report on The Administration of Choson (1937-1938)."

Kim, Bun Woong and Bell, D. S. Jr. "Bureaucratic Elitism and Democratic Development in Korea?" In *Administrative Dynamics and Development: The Korean Experience*, edited by B. W. Kim, D. S. Bell, Jr. and C. B. Lee. Seoul: Kyobo Publishing, Inc., 1985.

Kim, Edward H. *Decade of Success: Korea's Saemaul Movement.* Seoul: Hyung Mun Publications Company, 1980.

Kim, C. I. Eugene. "Education in Korea Under the Japanese Colonial Rule." In *Korea Under the Japanese Colonial Rule,* edited by Andres C. Nahm. Kalamazoo, Michigan: The Center for Korean Studies, Western Michigan University, 1973.

Kim, C. I. Eugene and Kim, Han Kyo. *Korea and the Politics of Imperialism, 1876-1910.* Berkeley: University of California Press, 1967.

Kim, Jongchol. *Education and Development: Some Essays and Thoughts on Korean Education.* Seoul: Seoul National University Press, 1985. (LA 1331 K56 1985)

Part one covers various aspects of Korean education such as quantitative and qualitative growth of education, compulsory and secondary education, educational planning, manpower needs and teacher organization. Part two focuses on Korean higher education, autonomy and control, higher education policy, and higher education reforms in the 1970s.

Kim, Shin Bok. "Educational Policy Change in Korea: Ideology and Praxis." In *Dynamic Transformation: Korea, NICs and Beyond,* 383-404, edited by Lim, Gill-Chin and Chang Wook. Seoul: Myung-Bo Publishing Co., 1990.

An overview of major reform proposals in Korea (1948-1987) including the PCER reform proposals. The policies are analyzed in relation to their ideological function and extent of implementation. The author concludes that plans were always underfinanced, and had little relation to actual educational changes.

Kim, Yong Shik. "Korean Education in Historical Perspective." *Korea Journal,* 10 (October 1970):20-24.

A history of Korea and its education beginning from the "Hermit Kingdom" era to 1970. Arguing that the educational system of a country is a product of its history and culture, the author outlines the changes in Korea's educational system concomitant with social and cultural changes.

Included are some more recent educational changes such as the abolition of entrance examinations for middle schools, the promulgation of the National Education Charter, and the work of the Council for Long-Range Educational Planning in 1968.

KEDI (Korean Education Development Institute). *Korean Education 2000*. Seoul: KEDI Press, 1985. (ED 280 733)

This major report reviews the development of Korean education and suggests that the future direction of Korean education should include improvement in equality, humanization, science and technology education. This report also discusses reforming the educational system, educational administration, improving educational research, and finance. Quantitative indices include projections for the year 2001.

Korean Overseas Information Service, Ministry of Culture and Information. "Education." In *A Handbook of Korea*, 653-696. Seoul: Samholva Co., 1979. (DS902 H2864 C2)

Introduces historical development of Korea education, and brief descriptions of the formal and nonformal education system, international cooperation in education, libraries, educational research institutions, and information on collegiate studies in Korea for foreign students.

Korean Overseas Information Service, Ministry of Culture and Information. *A Handbook of Korea*. Seoul: Samhawa Company, 1982.

Lee, John-Hee. "Features of Korean History." *Social Studies*, 79 (July-August 1988).

Lee, Ki Baik. *A New History of Korea*. Translated by E. W. Wagner. Cambridge, Mass.: Harvard University Press, 1985.

Lee, S. H. "America's Missionaries' Educational Work in Korea." In *U.S. Korea Relations: 1882-1982*, 123-140, edited by T. H. Kwak, R. Chay, S. S. Cho, and S. McCune. The U.S. Korea Centennial Edition. Seoul: Kyung Nam University Press, 1984.

Lee, Won-ho. "Modern System Came Hard Way to Korea: Missionaries Gave Great Help." *Koreana*, 5 No. 2 (1991):23-29.

A review article on education in the 19th century, includes a summary of the activities of the first seminary and schooling of women. A case is made for Korea's positive commitment to adopt modern education.

Lewinski, Marcel. "Korea at the Crossroads: The Democratic Challenge." *Councilor*, 47 (October 1987):13-17.

Lovel, John P. "The Military and Politics in Postwar Korea." In *Korean Politics in Transition*, edited by Edward Reynolds Wright. Seattle, WA: University of Washington Press, 1975.

McCluskey, Dorothy. "What Shall We Export?" *Education* LXX, (1949): 166-167.

McGinn, Noel F., Sondgrass, D.R., Kim, Y.B., Kim, S.B. and Kim, Q.Y. *Education and Development in Korea.* Studies in the Modernization of the Republic of Korea 1945-1975. Harvard East Asian monographs 90. Cambridge: Harvard University, 1980. (LC 67 K6 E34)

A major reference for the period covered, this book examines the development of education since 1945 in relation to the economic development, income distribution and value changes. Alternative theoretical theses are analyzed to explain the growth of education and the pattern of human-resource development.

Meade, E.G. *American Military Government in Korea.* New York: King's Crown Press, 1951.

Morgan, Robert M. "Educational Development: The Republic of Korea 1970-1979." Paper presented at the Annual Convention of the Association for Educational Communication and Technology, New Orleans, LA, 1979.

Nam, Jin-U. "World Perspective Case Descriptions on Educational Programs for Adults." Seoul, Korea, 1989.

NIERT (National Institute of Educational Research and Training). *Education in Korea 1965-1966.* Seoul: MOE (Ministry of Education), 1966.

NIERT. *Education in Korea 1976-77*. Seoul: MOE, 1977.

Oh, Chun-Suk. *Reaffirming Conviction in the Educational Reorganization*. Seoul: Federation of Education Associations, 1959.

Park, Sun-Young. "Confucianism Molds Core of the System: Its Legacies Cost Deep Influence." *Koreana*, 5 No. 2 (1991):13-29.

   A discussion of Buddhism and Confucianism and their historical impact on Korean education since the year 372. The development of civil administration and its connection to the educational system is also examined.

Republic of Korea. *Education Law*. Seoul: Ministry of Education, 1949.

Robinson, Michael Edison. *Cultural Nationalism in Colonial Korea 1920-1925*. Seattle: University of Washington Press, 1988.

Suh, David Kwang-sun. "American Missionaries and a Hundred Years of Korean Protestantism." In *Korea and the United States*, 319-349, edited by Koo, Young-nok and Suh, Dae-sook. Honolulu: University of Hawaii Press, 1984.

   The works of American missionaries in the areas of medicine, education, dissemination of the Christian religion, theological education, and politics in modern Korea are described.

Shu, Doosu. "Korean Education Under Japanese Rule." *Korean Survey* IV (November, 1955):11-12.

Toby, Ronald. "Education in Korea under the Japanese: Attitudes and Manifestations." In *Occasional Papers on Korea*. No. 1, edited by Palais, James B. Joint Committee on Korean Studies of the America Council of Learned Societies and Social Research Council, 1974.

   This book describes major features of the educational system, the school curriculum and instructional methods in Korea during the Japanese colonial-rule period.

Underwood, Horace Horton. *Modern Education in Korea.* New York: International Press, 1926.

This book represents one of the earliest and more thorough accounts of several significant educational institutions created by the various Christian missions in Korea. The author traces the founding and growth of what have become some of the best-known secondary schools and universities in contemporary Korea. The early educational changes initiated by the Japanese are identified and the tenuous position of mission schools under the Japanese occupation is elaborated. A brief account of the Korean Independence Movement of 1919 and the response of the Japanese authorities is included.

UNESCO. The Korean National Commission for UNESCO. *Korean Survey.* Seoul: Dong-A Publishing Co. Ltd., 1960.

This survey is regarded as an encyclopedia of Korean education, science and culture. The main chapter on education gives a comprehensive review of modern education tracing its development from 1945. The descriptions include educational financing, the curriculum in the elementary, middle, high and technical schools, teacher-training and in-service training, special education, and adult education. The survey ends with a brief account of studies abroad and of parent-teacher associations.

UNESCO. *Educational Conditions in the Republic of Korea.* Pusan, Korea: Prepared by the UNESCO-UNKRA Educational Planning Mission, 1952.

UNESCO. *Rebuilding Education in the Republic of Korea.* Report of the UNESCO-UNKRA Educational Planning Mission to Korea, 1954.

UNESCO. "Republic of Korea," In *World Survey of Education.* Vol. II Primary Education. Paris: UNESCO, 1958:652-661.

The article begins with a brief historical summary of education, 1910-1955. A survey of primary school education includes policy and administration, organization, problems and trends, and a summary of school statistics for 1950-1954.

UNESCO. "Education in Asia: Reviews, Reports, and Notes." Bangkok, Thailand: UNESCO, Regional Office for Education in Asia, 1976.

UNESCO. "Education in the Republic of Korea." *Education in Asia*. Bulletin of the Regional Office, 6 (1972):99-106.

"Universities and Colleges in Korea." *Higher Education,* V (March 1949): 145-148.

United States Military Government in Korea (USMGIK). "Summation." No. 6, March 1946.

Wade, James. *West Meets East: An Encounter with Korea.* Seoul: Pomso Publishing Company, 1975.

Yang, Sung Chul. "Student Political Activism: The case of the 1960 April revolution in South Korea." *Youth and Society* 5, No. 1 (1973):46-60

Focuses on some salient attributes of students and the particular characteristics of Korean student political activism. Probes the sources of frustrations which led to the April revolt.

Yoo, Hyung Jin. "Korean-American Educational Exchange." *Korea Journal* (February 1983).

Dissertations

Bang, Hung Kyu. "Japan's Colonial Educational Policy in Korea, 1905-1930." Ph.D. dissertation, University of Arizona, 1972.

Fisher, James Earnest. "Democracy and Mission Education in Korea." Ph.D. dissertation, Columbia University, 1928.

A general survey of the conditions and major problems of mission education in Korea. Included are discussions of the relation of mission education to political and economic problems of the Korean people, the relation of mission education to indigenous Korean culture, and the growing conflict between intellectual liberalism and religious authoritarianism in Korea.

Kim, Helen Ki-teuk. "Rural Education for the Regeneration of Korea." Ph.D. dissertation, Columbia University, 1931.

This research examines the conditions in rural Korea and proposes how the educational system could better meet the educational needs of rural people. The contributions of other agencies to the education of rural people is considered. A review is included of rural development of other countries, e.g. Denmark and Russia. The author of this study became one of Korea's most distinguished educators.

Kim, Jim-young. "The Role of Christianity in the Economic Modernization of South Korea." Vol. I and II. Ph.D. dissertation, The Florida State University, 1984.

A historical study on the effect of Protestant Ethic, exploring Max Weber's theory in the Korean context and its influence on economic modernization of Korea.

Lee, Sung Hwa. "The Social and Political Factors Affecting Korean Education, 1885-1945." Ph.D. dissertation, New York University, 1958.

Park, Hyung Ko. "Social Changes in The Educational and Religious Institutions of Korean Society Under Japanese and American Occupations." Ph.D. Dissertation, Utah State University, 1964.

Rhee, Sang-yoon. "Saemaul Undong (New Village Movement) in Korea: A Strategy for Citizen Participation in Rural Community Development." Ph.D. dissertation, University of Southern California, 1985.

Evaluation of Saemaul Undong (New Village Movement) in terms of people's voluntary participation to the movement.

Rim, Han Young."Development of Higher Education in Korea During the Japanese Occupation (1910-1945)." Ph.D. dissertation, Columbia University, 1952.

Vacante, Russel A. "Japanese Colonial Education in Korea, 1910-1945; An Oral History." Ph.D. dissertation, University of New York at Buffalo, 1987.

An examination of effects of Japanese colonial education on Korean students' attitudes and behavior. Based on interviews with a sample of Koreans who were educated in Japanese colonial institutions in Korea.

Van Lierop, Peter. "The Development of Schools Under the Korean Mission of the Presbyterian Church in the U.S.A., 1919-1950." Ph.D. dissertation, University of Pittsburgh, 1955.

Yoo, Hyung Jin. "An intellectual history of Korea from ancient times, examining the impact of the west with special emphasis upon education." Ph.D. dissertation, Harvard University, 1958.

One of the most complete surveys in English of the intellectual and historical background of Korea's cultural dependence on China including the introduction of Western institutions in Korea.

CHAPTER II

The Educational System: Structure, Content and Administration

Article 81 of the Education Law of 1949 reformed education in Korea into a national, publicly funded, single-track school system, compulsory for all children between 6 and 12 years of age. Emphasizing national identity and the ideal of *Hongik in'gan* (the benefits for all of mankind), the 1949 Education Law expresses the underlying values and ultimate objectives of Korean education. The 1951 amendment to the Education Law which replaced the 6-6-4 pattern of school with a 6-3-3-4 pattern was implemented only after the Korean War armistice. Separating middle and high schools, this single-track, ladder-type schooling (shown in Figure II.1) is the current school system. The basic ladder structure looks much like that found in many westernized educational systems, adding up to 16 years of schooling.

Paralleling the basic schooling ladder are civic schools (elementary and middle) for adults or youth dropouts, trade schools (1-3 years) and higher trade schools (1-3 years) attached to businesses and factories, providing vocational and technical training.

Figure II.1 The Current Education System

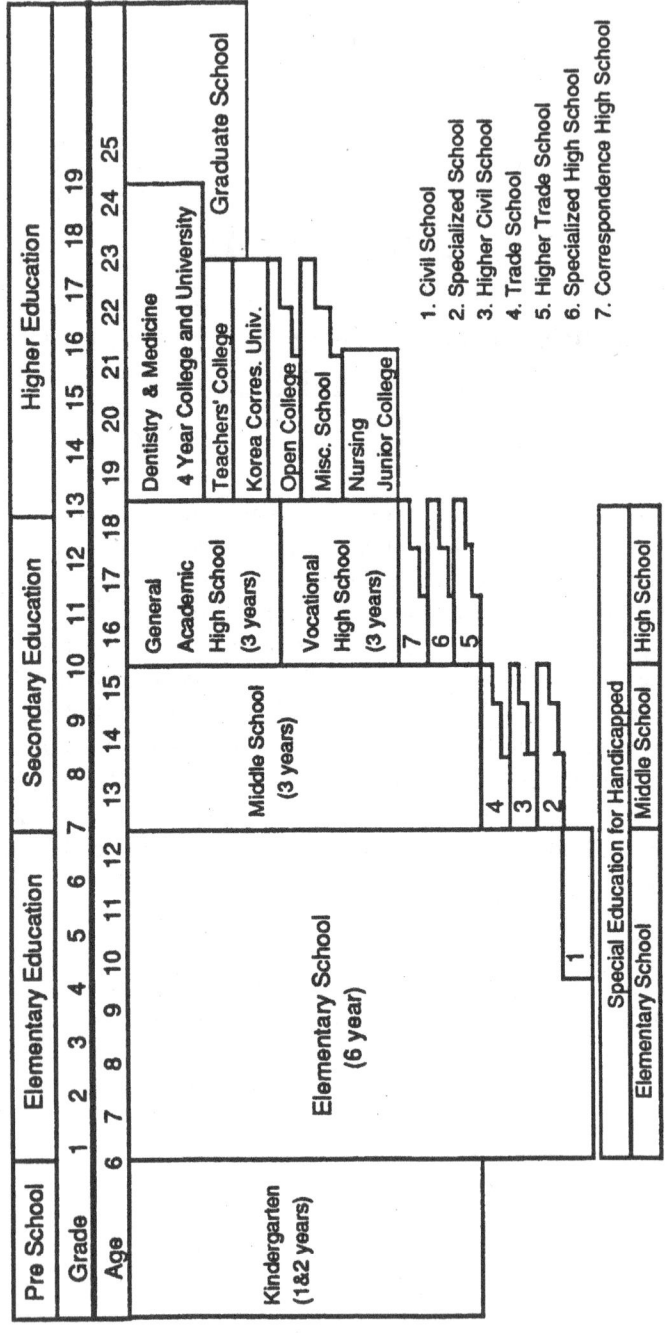

Source: NIERT. Education in Korea 1987-1988. Seoul: MOE, 1988: 41.

Formal Education

Kindergarten (Yuchiwon)

Preschool education historically has been, for the most part, under the private initiative of religious and social organizations. In 1962 the government first established facility standards, and in 1969 published a national curriculum. Recognition of the importance of preschool education was further reinforced in 1977 and 1982 through the Pre-Education Promotion Law, thus increasing enrollment (as shown in Table II.2). Between 1965 and 1990 the number of kindergartens increased over 20 times, with highest rate of increase occurring between 1980 and 1985. The growth in kindergarten education during the 1980s is shown in Table II.1.

In 1990, more students were enrolled in private kindergartens (287,388) than in public ones (127,056), even though there were more public than private kindergartens (4602 and 3751 respectively; in addition, 88 students attended four national kindergartens). However, the student/teacher ratio in private kindergartens was 20/1 in 1990 compared to 26/1 in the public kindergartens. Since preschool education is a recent development in formal schooling, achievement of more than 30 percent enrollment of the eligible age group (4-5 year-olds) in kindergartens by the end of the 1980s and a target rate of 70 percent by the year 2001 (see PCER, 1987:75-77) reflect an increased governmental commitment. An

Table II.1

Kindergarten Enrollment 1980-1990

Year	# of Kindergartens	# of Classes	# of Children
1980	901	1,906	64,433
1982	6,242	9,281	314,692
1986	7,233	11,834	354,537
1989	8,246	14,886	410,824
1990	8,354	18,511	414,532

Source: NIEE, *Statistical Yearbook of Education.* Seoul: MOE, 1990.

effort to combine this quantitative expansion with program quality is indicated by the development of a systematic educational curriculum and improvement of the overall student/teacher ratio from 56/1 in 1970 to 28/1 in 1990.

Almost all kindergarten teachers are female (99.8 percent in public institutions, 91.3 percent in the private sector). Head-start programs for children aged 3 to 4, conducted either at "child centers" or at home by volunteer mothers and regional community workers, are spreading throughout Korea as the number of employed mothers rapidly increases.

Elementary School (Kuckmin Hakyo)

Elementary education for children 6 to 12 years of age is compulsory and publicly funded. The vigor with which the plan to promote compulsory elementary education was executed is reflected in education's rapid growth: in 1945 the Korean primary education enrollment ratio was 45 percent of the 6-to-12-year-old cohort; by 1960 over 90 percent of children aged 6 to 12 were enrolled in school. Table II.2 shows the expansion in numbers of schools, students, and elementary school teachers. Out of the grand total of 6,335 elementary schools, 76 schools are private and 17 national and the remainder are public schools accommodating 98.2 percent of all students. By 1990, the enrollment ratio of elementary school age children (6-12) was 98.7 percent. The massive shift of rural population to the cities often left rural schools under sized and urban schools crowded. Only during the 1980s, when student numbers decreased due to declining birthrate and the number of teachers continued to increase (by 114 percent between 1980 and 1990), did the student/teacher ratio improve, from 47/1 in 1980 to 35.5/1 in 1990. Facilities have greatly improved, yet out of a grand total of 7,969 elementary-school classes in 1990, 13.3 percent operated under a double-shift system.

Table II.2

Expansion of Elementary Education, 1945-1990

Year/ Classification	1945	1960	1970	1980	1989	1990
Schools	2,834	4,496	5,961	6,487	6,396	6,335
Index	100	158	210	229	226	223
Teachers	19,729	61,605	101,095	119,064	134,898	136,800
Index	100	312	512	603	684	693
Students	1,366,024	3,622,685	5,749,301	5,658,003	4,894,262	4,868,520
Index	100	265	420	414	358	356

Source: NIEE. *Statistical Yearbook of Education*. Seoul: MOE, 1990.

The main objective of elementary education is to provide basic skills and general education in support of Korean culture and national integration. All instruction is carried out in the Korean language. The Ministry of Education provides general standards for the curriculum, and has established definite educational objectives, specifying subjects, time allocation, teaching materials and all textbooks. Table II.3 shows the elementary school curriculum.

As in most countries, the national language occupies more time in the schedule than any other subject. Also typical is the significant level of attention given to science, arithmetic, and social studies. The social studies curriculum includes such subjects as Moral Education, Anti-communism, Education for Peace, and National Ethics.

Korean schools differ from schools in many other countries in their emphasis on health and physical education, music, crafts, and moral education. As can be seen in Table II.3, these four subjects account for approximately one-third of the class hours per week in elementary school. The quality of Korean elementary education was subjected to considerable criticism by foreign as well as Korean observers during the 1960s and 1970s. The conditions receiving most attention were the large pupil-teacher ratios, poor facilities, and shortage of equipment. The system was further criticized for emphasizing rote memorization in classroom instruction and uniformity in student behavior within and outside the classroom. Critics also noted the lack of intellectual interaction among students and between students and teachers, and the absence of student creativity in problem-solving.

Table II.3

Primary School Curriculum

(Unit: Teaching Hours)

Subject/Classification	1st Year	2nd Year	3rd Year	4th Year	5th Year	6th Year
Moral Education			68(2)	68(2)	68(2)	68(2)
Korean Language	330(11)	374(11)	238(7)	204(6)	204(6)	204(6)
Social Studies			102(3)	102(3)	135(4)	136(4)
Arithmetic	180(6)	204(6)	136(4)	136(4)	170(5)	170(5)
Science			102(3)	136(4)	136(4)	136(4)
Physical Education			102(3)	102(3)	102(3)	102(3)
Music			68(2)	68(2)	68(2)	68(2)
Fine Arts	180(6)	238(7)	68(2)	68(2)	68(2)	68(2)
Crafts			----	68(2)	68(2)	68(2)
Extracurricular Activities	*30(1)	*34(1)	68(2)	68(2)	68(2)	68(2)
Grand Total	790(24)	850(25)	952(28)	1,020(30)	1,088(32)	1,088(32)

*The hours shown on this table represent the minimum school hours allotted for 34 weeks per year.
*One teaching hour in this table represents 40 minutes.
*Extracurricular Activities in the 1st and 2nd year are the principal's optional subjects.
*Figures in parentheses are hours taught per week. Source: NIERI. *Education in Korea 1989-1990*. Seoul: MOE, 1990:54.

The government has made four large-scale curriculum revisions since 1953, mostly through the changing of textbooks. Examination of elementary school social studies textbooks indicates that the curriculum in the 1960s emphasized social ethics and problems of group participation, but with texts published in the 1970s, focus shifted to the individual's contribution to the welfare of the nation (see Cole, 1975). All curriculum revisions gave priority to social studies revision, and remained "education by textbook" (Hyonki Paik, 1969:61-2). During the 1973 curriculum adjustments the government formally acknowledged that anti-communism, nationalism and patriotism were emphasized over individual initiative and enterprise. In addition to changing textbooks, the curriculum revision of 1973, promoted as the "new education system," introduced new instructional methods and materials in elementary and secondary education (KEDI's E-M project) and a new school management system (see Chapter IV).

The curricular revision of 1983 also included a new program in moral education, but emphasized mathematics and science education and the provision of experiment-centered instruction (KEDI, 1985:166). Since 1987 computer education has been introduced, and the distribution of computers to all schools has begun.

Middle School (Chung Hakyo)

Middle school education for students 12 to 15 years of age comprises the first tier of secondary education. Until 1985 middle school education was noncompulsory and tuition costs were borne by the students. Since 1985 middle schools in remote rural and isolated areas have been made compulsory and free of charge. "Middle school education in other areas will be made free and compulsory on an incremental basis" (NIERT, 1990:56).

Following the abolition of the entrance examination to middle school (in 1968), all candidates from elementary school were assigned to a school in their residential district through lottery. This system eliminated the fierce competition for entrance to prestigious middle schools, and freed elementary education from drill and preparation to pass the entrance exam. Rates of advancement to middle school rose immediately in 1969 to 62 percent and to 70 percent in 1970. By 1990 the national advancement rate was 99.7 percent (99.9 percent in Seoul). In effect, nine-year universal education was achieved by the mid-1980s (Kim Jong-Chol, 1985:32-39).

The expansion of middle school education can be seen in Table II.4. Student enrollments have steadily increased, with a peak of 2.7 million in 1985. Since then the absolute number of students has decreased due to falling birthrate, while the number of schools and teachers has continued to increase. Consequently the student/teacher ratio has been reduced from 58/1 in 1960 to 40/1 in 1985 and to 26/1 in 1990.

Table II.4

Middle School Expansion 1945-90

Year/Classification	1945	1960	1970	1980	1989	1990
Schools	166	1,053	1,608	2,121	2,450	2,474
Index	100	634	968	1,277	1,476	1,490
Teachers	1,186	13,053	31,207	54,858	81,699	89,719
Index	100	1,100	2,631	4,625	6,889	7,565
Students	80,828	528,593	1,318,808	2,471,997	2,371,215	2,275,751
Index	100	654	1,631	3,058	2,934	2,816

Source: NIEE, *Statistical Yearbook of Education*. Seoul: MOE:1990.

In 1990, 28.5 percent of the middle schools were private. Female students made up 45.3 percent of the student body at this level and in 1990 almost 50 percent of the graduating class were female students. Female teachers make up 46.4 percent of the teaching force in middle schools, compared to 50.1 percent at the elementary school level.

The objectives of middle school are to "develop the skills and attitudes essential for citizenship in a democratic society, respect for work, the proper code of conduct, initial vocational training, self-discipline, good health and physical fitness" (MOE, 1988:7). As can be seen from Table II.5, in addition to the continuation of subjects offered at the elementary school level, the middle school curriculum introduces the first foreign languages, English and classical Chinese, vocational skills for boys and home economics for girls. Since 1987, in addition to a new science education program and use of computers, emphasis has been placed on writing skills and English as a foreign language.

Table II.5

Middle School Curriculum

	(Unit: Teaching Hours)		
Subject/Classification	1st Year (7th Grade)	2nd Year (8th Grade)	3rd Year (9th Grade)
Moral Education	68(2)	68(2)	68(2)
Korean Language	136(4)	170(5)	170(5)
Korean History	-----	68(2)	68(2)
Social Studies	102(3)	68-102(2-3)	68-102(2-3)
Mathematics	136(4)	102-136(3-4)	136-170(4-5)
Science	136(4)	102-136(3-4)	136-170(4-5)
Physical Education	102(3)	102(3)	102(3)
Music	68(2)	68(2)	34-68(1-2)
Fine Arts	68(2)	68(2)	34-68(1-2)
Classical Chinese	34(1)	34-68(1-2)	34-68(1-2)
English	136(4)	102-170(3-5)	102-170(3-5)
Vocational Skills (Boys) Home Economics (Girls)	Se 1 102(3)	Se 1 136-204(4-6)	-----
Agriculture, Technical, Commerce, Fisheries, Housekeeping	-----	-----	Se 1 136-204(4-6)
Elective	0-68(0-2)	0-68(0-2)	0-68(0-2)
Extracurricular Activities	68(2)	68(2)	68(2)
Grand Total	1156-1224 (34-36)	1156-1224 (34-36)	1156-1224 (34-36)

*The hours shown on this table represent the minimum school hours alloted for 34 weeks per year.
*One teaching hour in this table represents 45 minutes.
*Se: Select
*Figures in the parentheses are hours taught per week.
Source: NIERI. *Education in Korea 1989-1990*. Seoul: MOE, 1990.

Middle school learning is driven by the need to prepare for entrance examinations to high school. However, the middle school automatic promotion policy, by which all students pass from grade to grade, helps sustain the belief that every student is capable of passing, and poor performance is viewed more as evidence of inadequate application by the student than as indication of low ability. The problem of poor performance is addressed through home instruction by parents or by use of private tutors. The impact of high school and university entrance examinations, even after the various attempts at reform (see Chapter IV), continue to be felt both inside and outside the school system. Middle school teachers emphasize those aspects of the curriculum relevant to the students' upcoming examinations. The presence of a parallel education system, mostly involving one-on-one instruction (either by parents or private tutors), may help to account for the high achievement of Korean students in science and mathematics compared to those of other countries.

High School (Kodung Hakyo)

High schools are of two kinds, academic and vocational. The three grades of high school are noncompulsory, with tuition costs borne by students and parents. In 1990, 97.7 percent of all middle school graduates (96.6 percent of all female middle school graduates) applied for high school admission.

As seen in Table II.6, high school enrollment quadrupled between 1970 and 1980. The number of students fell slightly between 1989 and 1990 in both academic and vocational high schools. In high school education the share of private education is much larger than in elementary or middle school education. In 1990 50.5 percent of all high schools were private, accommodating 61.6 percent of the students (MOE, 1990).

Table II.6

High School Expansion, 1951-90

Year/Classification	1951	1960	1970	1980	1989	1990
Schools	307	640	889	1,353	1,672	1,683
Index	100	208	289	435	545	548
Teachers	1,720	9,627	19,854	50,948	87,277	92,683
Index	100	559	1,154	2,962	5,074	5,389
Students	40,271	273,434	590,382	2,696,792	2,326,062	2,283,806
Index	100	678	1,466	4,213	5,776	5,669

Source: NIEE. *Statistical Yearbook of Education*. Seoul: MOE, 1990.

The objectives of high school education are to promote both advanced general studies preparing for higher education and vocational education. Until 1988 the objectives of high school education remained constant. Every year MOE's *Education in Korea* has reprinted the following specific objectives:

1. To cultivate in students the character and capability necessary as a sound citizen . . .

2. To develop the understanding and healthy criticism in students toward the country and society . . .

3. To instill in students an awareness for the mission of the nation, to develop their physical capacity, to enable students to choose their own future career appropriate to their own aptitude, to increase students' grasp of general knowledge and to develop their occupational skills. (MOE, NIERT, 1988:55)

The Ministry of Education in 1989-1990 identified new specific objectives for high school education:

1. Improvement and extension of the results of middle school education.

2. Improvement of the student's capacity to understand and form judgments about nature and society.

3. Improvement of the student's physical well-being and of his ability to plan and manage his own life. (MOE, NIERT 1990:56)

The new discourse may signify a shift from a more indoctrinating approach to education, and the need "to instill" the right values, to a new, more democratic conceptualization of educational objectives in line with the Presidential Commission's "General Goals and Aims of Education" (see PCER 1987:35-41).

Since 1965 it has been government policy to promote vocational education over academic secondary education. As seen in Figure II.2, vocational education has grown rapidly, expanding from 312 schools in 1965 to 635 schools in 1985. The years 1984 to 1986 were the peak years for vocational school enrollments. Since then, enrollment has dropped (to 810,000 in 1990), and the number of schools has fallen to 587 (1990), whereas the number of academic high schools has continued to grow from 967 schools in 1985 to 1,096 in 1990.

The economic plans and incentives for developing vocational high school education have not been realized, with only 35.4 percent of students enrolled in vocational education schools in 1990 compared to a target of 70 percent established by planners in 1965. Some of the reasons for this unfavorable turn in the development of vocational education are mentioned in KEDI's *Korean Education 2000* (1985). In addition to "rigidity of operation, the inferior educational conditions, and under-qualified teachers," vocational education suffers from having been designed "for children from needy families" (p. 189). The report recommended viewing vocational education as part of the general education offered at academic high schools.

Figure II.2 Changing Trends of Enrollment in High School, 1979-1989

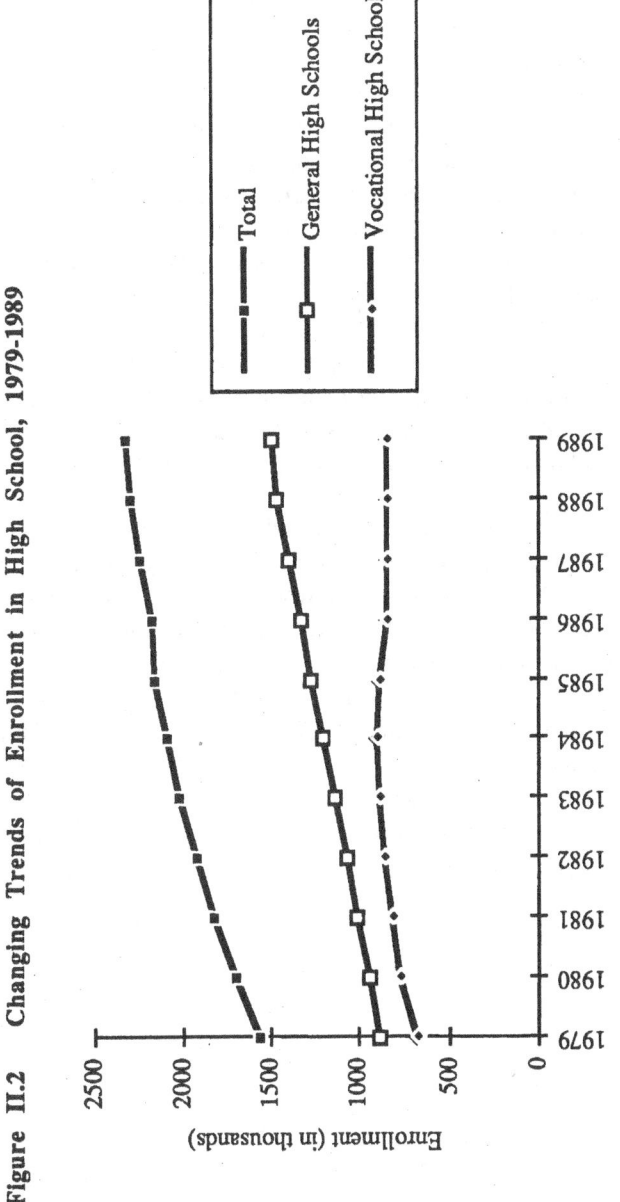

Source: NIERT. *Education in Korea 1989-1990*. Seoul, MOE, 1990: 57.

Academic High School

The excessive competition for admission to prestigious high-schools, which persisted as long as each school developed and administered its own entrance examinations (until 1972), was curbed in 1973 by a lottery system of allocation of places. In 1974 the entrance system was modified again so that the entrance exam for vocational education is now administered before the general eligibility test for high schools. Those who fail to gain admission to vocational schools can apply to academic high schools admission if they pass the test.

The academic high school curriculum is shown in Table II.7. The continued heavy emphasis on mathematics and science at the high school level should be noted. Military training under the Student Defense Corps is a requirement. In addition to English, students elect another foreign language which they study up to 10 hours a week in the second and third years of high school. At the end of the first year, students select between humanities and natural science majors as preparatory courses for entrance to college.

Out of 1,096 academic high schools in 1990, 1 percent (11 schools) are national schools, 52.6 percent private schools, and the rest public schools. The advancement rate from the national schools to higher education was the highest (60 percent) from public schools the advancement rate was 46.7 percent, while from private schools it was 47.2 percent. In 1990, 85.9 percent of all graduates of academic high schools (a total of 419,463 students) applied for higher education. Of these applicants 47.1 percent succeeded directly in entering higher education institutions, 32.5 percent of those selected were accepted to junior colleges, 64.9 percent to colleges and universities, and 1 percent to teachers' colleges.

Table II.7
General (Academic) High School Curriculum

Classification	Subjects	General Curriculum			
		Required Subjects Units (10th Grade)	Students Select One of Three Majors		
Moral Education	Moral Education	6			
Korean Language	Korean Language	10			
	Literature		8	8	
	Composition		6	4	4
	Grammar		4		
Korean History	Korean History	6			
Social Studies	Political Economy	6			
	Geography	4			
	World History		4	4	
	Social Studies/Culture		4		4
	World Geography		4		
Mathematics	Mathematics	8	10	18	6
Science	Science (1-2)	10	8		
	Physics			8	
	Chemistry			8	4
	Biology			6	
	Earth Science			6	
Physical Education	Physical Education	6	8	8	8
Military Training	Military Training	12			
Music	Music	4			2
Fine Arts	Fine Arts	4			
Classical Chinese	Classical Chinese		8	4	4
Foreign Language	English (1-2)	8	12	12	8
	German				
	French				
	Spanish				
	Chinese				
	Japanese				
Industrial Arts & Home Economics	Industrial Arts (Boys)				
	Home Economics (Girls)				
	Agriculture				
	Technology				
	Commerce				
	Fisheries				
	Housekeeping				
Electives			2	2	2
Extracurricular Activities		12			
Grand Total		204-216			

Source: NIERT. *Education in Korea 1989-1990*. Seoul, MOE, 1990: 58.

Vocational High Schools

Vocational high schools include technical, agricultural, commercial, fishery, and marine training schools. Figure II.3 identifies the distribution of vocational school students among the different types of schools. Out of the grand total, 54 percent of vocational high schools are public (including three national schools), and the rest are private high schools.

Commercial high schools. In 1989, 45.2 percent of all vocational high school students were enrolled in 204 commercial high schools. With the advent of information-processing technology, commercial education underwent a drastic change, training high school graduates for roles in the information society. Managerial skills, competence in foreign languages, and information-processing skills make up the main vocational curriculum.

Comprehensive high schools. One hundred ninety-five schools in 1990 were comprehensive high schools offering both academic and vocational courses. These schools are located in rural areas or small and medium-sized cities, where the choices at the high school level are limited. Out of the 195 schools, 123 were coeducational, while 22 were for boys only and 49 for girls only. The largest number of comprehensive high schools were located in Kyonggi and Kyongbuk provinces, and only 11 of them in Seoul (NIEE, 1990:328).

Technical high schools. Technical education has changed with industrialization. In the early 1960s technical education catered to the needs of light industries. As Korea moved into heavy and chemical industries in the 1970s, there was a lag in the focus of technical education. By the time it had caught up with the manpower needs of the 1970s, those needs had already shifted again, with the new high-tech industries of the 1980s calling for advanced technological training. In 1990, technical high schools offered 38 courses in chemistry and "heavy industry," and 13 in what is called "light industry," including applied electronics, electronic communication, and information processing. Technical high schools, more than the other vocational high schools, are actively seeking to establish cooperative relations with industry (MOE, NIERT, 1990:59).

Fishery and maritime high schools. There are nine fishery and maritime high schools located along the coast of the Korean peninsula. The curriculum includes six-month on-the-job training in such fields as

Figure II.3   Distribution of Students in Vocational High Schools by Major Field, 1989

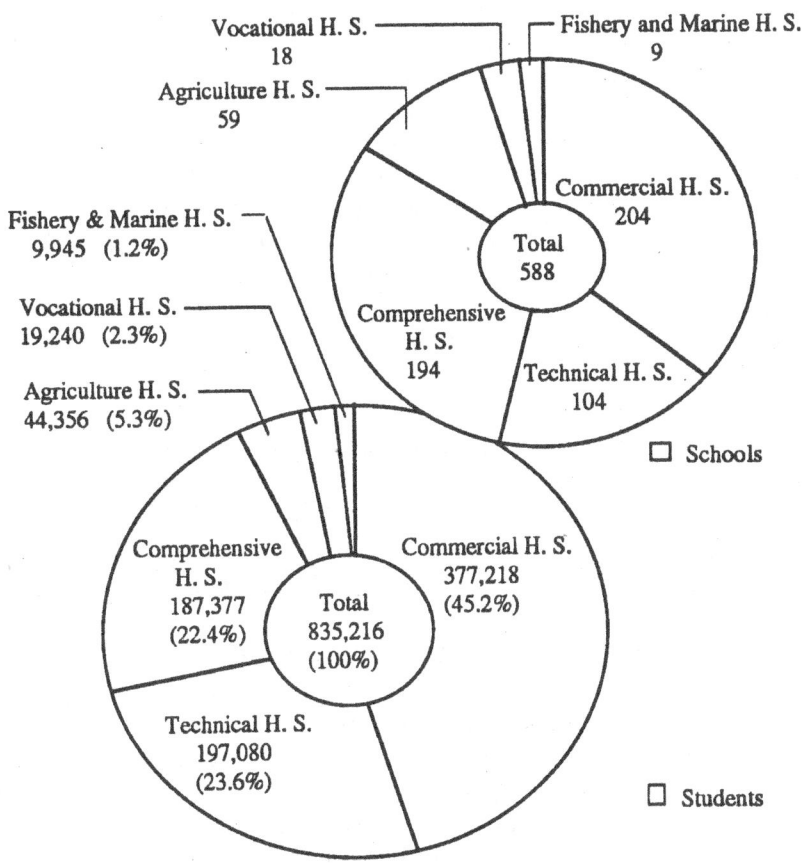

Source: NIERT, *Education in Korea, 1989-1990*, Seoul, MOE: 1990:60.

fishery industry management and ship construction. Students in these schools receive government scholarships, tuition exemption and free accommodation to encourage vocational preparation in this field.

Agricultural high school. Agriculture is a field of study that is not generally attractive to high school students, even to those in rural areas. The program for promoting high school agricultural education focuses on scientific mechanization of farming. The twelve agricultural high schools offer curricula in self-managed farming, scientific management of farming, agricultural planning, and mechanization. Students in agricultural high schools also receive scholarships, tuition exemption, and free accommodation as incentives for studying agriculture.

During the 1980s, special measures were adopted to broaden the instructional goals and programs and to improve the quality of learning in vocational high schools, with special attention given to writing skills and foreign language proficiency. In addition, practical training facilities were improved (see Lee, Key-Woo 1983:39). In 1990 there were slightly fewer students in vocational high schools than in 1989 (810,651 compared to 835,216). Of the vocational high-school graduating class of 1990 (a total of 274,150 students), 76.6 percent found employment upon graduation, while 22 percent applied for higher education. However, only 8.2 percent of those who applied for higher education were accepted, over half of them (14,489 students) to junior colleges, and the rest to colleges and universities or teachers' colleges.

Special Education (T'uksu Hakyo)

Special education in Korea includes programs for gifted and handicapped students. Limited special education opportunities for handicapped children are available to students in kindergarten, elementary, middle and high school levels. A total of 104 schools, mostly private, in 1990 accommodated 19,971 physically handicapped students (as shown in Table II.8.) In addition, 32,262 less severely handicapped students are enrolled in 3026 classes in regular schools; efforts to mainstream handicapped children have just begun. Special education curricula strongly emphasize living skills and vocational education. Teacher-student ratios in special education schools are kept low (1/8 in 1991).

A few recently established high schools are devoted to special fields such as science, arts, and physical education, with gifted students being recruited throughout the country. In 1990 there were 11 art high schools, nine of them private, one public, and one national, accommodating 10,009 students, most of them (87.7 percent) female. Eight physical education high schools (seven of them public, one private) accommodate 3,248 students, most of them (80.5 percent) male, and six science high schools, all public, accommodate 744 students, 83.9 percent of them male. The reform outlined in *Korean Education 2000* (1985) forecasts newly developed programs sufficient to serve all gifted youth in operation by the 21st century (pp. 414-15).

Table II.8

Schools for Handicapped Students, 1990

Classification	Schools				Classes	Students
	Total	National	Public	Private		
Blind	12	1	2	9	143	1,416
Deaf & Dumb	19	1	5	13	399	4,508
Mentally Retarded	60	4	19	40	899	11,768
Physically Handicapped	13	---	3	10	183	2,279
Total	104	3	29	72	1,762	19,971

Source: NIERT, *Statistical Yearbook of Education.* Seoul: MOE, 1990.

Higher Education

Higher education in Korea includes: a) colleges and universities, offering four-year undergraduate programs, professional programs, and graduate programs; b) teachers' colleges and colleges of education; c) junior colleges, and d) miscellaneous schools. As in shown in Table II.9, the number of higher education institutions more than doubled between 1980 and 1990, and enrollment reached almost a million and a half students in 1990 (of which 30.4 percent were female).

Table II.9

Expansion of Higher Education, 1945-1990

Year/Classification	1945	1960	1970	1980	1989	1990
Schools	19	85	168	236	536	556
Index	100	450	890	1,240	2,821	2,926
Teachers	1,490	3,808	10,435	20,900	39,950	41,920
Index	100	260	700	1,400	2,681	2,813
Students	7,819	101,041	201,436	601,994	1,434,259	1,490,809
Index	100	1,290	2,586	7,700	18,343	19,066

Source: NIERT, *Statistical Yearbook of Education*. Seoul: MOE, 1990.

According to the Educational Law, all higher education institutions, both public and private, are under the direct supervision of the Minister of Education. The Ministry of Education established yearly student quotas for each institution, qualifications for faculty and staff, and curriculum and degree requirements. The president of Korea appoints deans and presidents of national and public universities, following recommendations by the MOE. Presidents of private universities are elected by their respective boards of trustees, subject to approval by MOE. Seventy-nine and three-tenths percent of all institutions of higher education in 1990 were private. All teachers' colleges are national, while most junior colleges (86.3 percent) are private. The various categories of higher education, private, public and national, and the numbers of their departments are shown in Table II.10.

Table II.10

Korean Higher Education by Category, 1989-90

Classification	Total	By Time			By Sex			# of Departments
	1990	Day	Eve.	Day & Eve.	Men	Women	Co-Edu.	1990*
Grand Total	556	244	141	151	5	49	482	8,725
National	111	64	19	21	2	4	98	2,445
Public	4	1	1	1	---	---	3	52
Private	441	179	121	129	3	45	381	6,228
Junior College	117	56	---	61	3	24	90	1,264
National	16	16	---	---	2	4	10	143
Private	101	40	---	61	1	20	80	1,121
Teachers' College	11	4	---	7	---	---	11	346
National	11	4	---	7	---	---	11	346
College & Univ.	107	63	1	40	1	10	93	4,009
National	23	21	---	1	---	---	22	1,156
Public	1	---	---	1	---	---	1	25
Private	83	42	1	38	1	10	70	2,828
Graduate Sch.	298	108	140	30	1	15	262	4,287
National	61	23	19	13	---	---	55	1,227
Public	3	1	1	---	---	---	2	34
Private	234	84	120	17	1	15	205	3,027
Miscellaneous School	23	13	---	13	---	---	26	109
Private	23	13		13	---	---	26	109

Source: NIERT, *Education in Korea 1998-1990*. Seoul: MOE, 1990:62.
*NIEE, *Statistical Yearbook*. Seoul: MOE, 1990.

Junior Colleges

Junior colleges offer two or three years of post-secondary education. Of the 117 junior colleges (as of 1990), some had, prior to 1979, been two-year "junior technical colleges" while others had been five-year "professional high schools." In 1990 a total of 378,384 students applied to junior colleges, of which 34.5 percent were admitted upon passing the standard entrance examination for higher education. Enrollment in junior colleges has steadily increased from 165,000 in 1980 to 323,800 in 1990.

The main objective of junior colleges is vocational training for middle-level technicians. Courses are grouped into the following specializations: technical, agricultural, nursing, fishery and sanitation, commercial and business, home economics, and arts and athletics. The curriculum is 80 percent professional subjects, including laboratory and practice. The emphasis on practical training is made possible by cooperative arrangements involving the colleges and industry. In addition to on-the-job training, this cooperation facilitates exchange of new technological information and joint research projects.

Junior colleges are, in the 1990s, in the process of making two major adjustments, the first in response to changes in industrialization and technological development in Korea, the second in response to the increased number of female high school graduates who apply to junior colleges (41.6 percent of all 1990 applicants) with the intention of joining the professional work-force. Both these adjustments will entail program diversification.

As can be seen in Figure II.4, in 1989 53.9 percent of all students enrolled in junior colleges studied in the 589 natural science departments, which included programs in engineering, architecture,

Figure II.4   Students in Junior Colleges, 1989

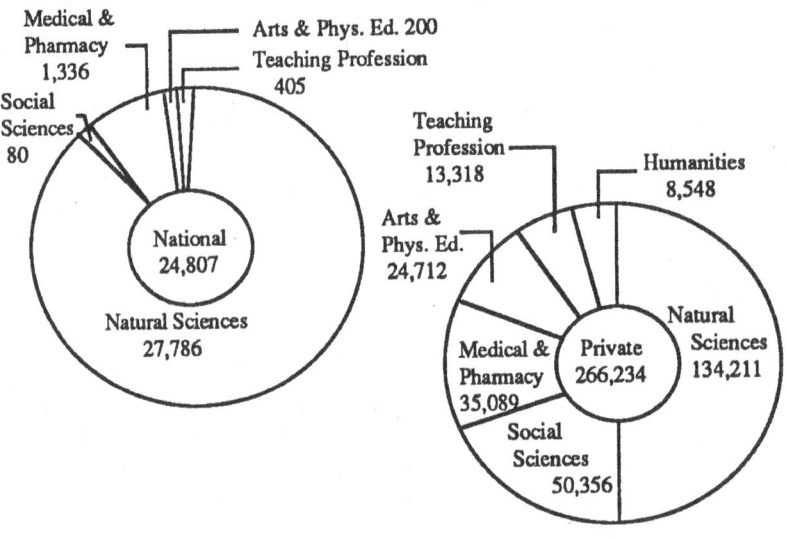

Source: MOE, NIERT. *Education in Korea, 1989-1990*. Seoul: MOE, 1990:68.

industrial management, railroad maintenance, and chemistry applications. The second largest proportion of students were enrolled in the 262 social science departments, including business administration, insurance management, public health administration, and office automation.

Although junior vocational college graduates are employable as middle-level technicians, a junior vocational college degree is not necessarily terminal, and junior colleges provide a second chance for higher education at universities. Graduates can continue to study in university day or evening programs or at open, air and correspondence universities. In 1990, out of the 87,131 graduates from junior colleges, 54 percent found employment and 17 percent enlisted in the army.

Colleges and Universities

According to the Educational Law, a university must have at least three component colleges, one of which must be a college of liberal arts, while another must be a college of science. Undergraduate programs are usually of four years' duration; medical and dentistry programs are usually six years.

To earn a bachelor's degree, a student must complete 140 academic credit units (where a credit unit equals 16 class-hours per term). Bachelor's degrees are offered in 25 fields. In each field, the curriculum is composed of general and professional courses. In addition to their major field of study, students are required to choose a minor field with the aim of "foster[ing] a broader perspective cutting across disciplines" (MOE 1990:65).

The entrance examination system has been changed several times. Until 1968, colleges and universities administered their own entrance examinations. From 1969 to 1979 a preliminary national college entrance examination (PECE) was introduced; candidates who passed this hurdle then went on to take the entrance examinations of individual institutions. The PECE was replaced in 1980 by a scholastic achievement examination (SAE). This test is taken after applicants have made their selection of a university or college. In 1985, in addition to the SAE, high school scores and an essay administered by the individual institutions began to be taken into account in university admissions procedures.

As seen in Table II.10, there were 107 colleges and universities in 1990 (83 of them private institutions), with 4009 departments. The total number of students in 1990 was 1.04 million. Out of a total of 904,306 applicants, 196,397 were accepted for enrollment in 1990 (28.4 percent of them female), an acceptance rate of 21.7 percent. Of the accepted applicants, 60.9 percent were 1989 high school graduates, while 36.8 percent were graduates from previous years who had been re-examined. In 1990, 165,916 students (36.9 percent of them female) graduated from colleges and universities. The highest number of graduates were produced by departments of natural sciences (34.6 percent of 1990 graduates), social sciences (27.1 percent) and engineering (18.4 percent). 48.2 percent of all 1990 graduates (37.3 percent of all female graduates) found employment in 1990.

Measures to raise the quality of higher education have included reducing the number of students per class (which stood at 35 in 1990) and encouraging faculty development. The number of Ph.D. holders among faculty increased from only 10 percent in 1967 to 40 percent in 1983; by 1990 a Ph.D. had generally become the minimum prerequisite for teaching in all 4-year institutions of higher education. Governmental support for faculty further education at Korean universities and overseas has been increased, and leaves of absence have been institutionalized for professors conducting research (NIERT, 1990:65).

Graduate Schools

In 1949 the master's degree was introduced by Seoul National University. All other universities have followed suit, establishing an American-style sequence of degrees. The Education Law stipulates that every university must have a least one graduate school. The graduate divisions of Korean universities are divided into academic and research-oriented degree programs, and professional graduate schools. In 1990 there were a total of 298 graduate schools, 234 of which were located in private institutions. In these graduate programs, 27 different master's degrees and 19 doctoral degrees are offered. Out of a total of 86,911 graduate students, 83.3 percent were enrolled in master's programs, and 16.6 percent in doctoral programs. The natural sciences and engineering fields accounted for about 13.8 percent of the students in graduate programs in 1990. In 1990, 19,788 students were awarded master's degrees (23.7 percent female), and 2,481 received doctoral degrees (13.3 percent female). Forty-eight percent of all doctoral degrees conferred in 1987 were earned at four institutions: Seoul National University, Yonsei University, Korea University, and Kyungbuk University (NIERT, 1988).

Higher education in Korea is moving from an elite system to a mass system. Increasing economic demand for higher education graduates in preference to high school graduates has influenced educational planners to modify high school curricula in the direction of preparation for higher education (see Chapter IV). Planners have also sought to upgrade vocational instruction and learning, and to promote programs at universities and colleges, which respond to the demand for the highly trained manpower required by high technology and the new industries being introduced in the 1990s.

Teachers and Teacher Education

Until 1962, elementary school teachers were trained at secondary-level normal schools. Selected normal schools were upgraded to two-year post-secondary education institutions in 1962. During 1981-4 these two-year training institutions were upgraded to four-year colleges, granting the first degree (B.A.) to graduates preparing to become elementary school teachers. Secondary-school teachers have historically been prepared at the college or university level. At present, five kinds of institutions prepare teachers in Korea, as shown in Table II.11.

Kindergarten teachers are trained at four-year colleges, junior vocational colleges, and air and correspondence colleges. In 1990 13,654 students (all female) were enrolled in early childhood education programs at 3-year junior colleges. Six thousand five-hundred seventy-four graduated that year, and 80.1 percent found employment.

Enrollment in the 11 national teachers' colleges expanded from 7,300 in 1979 to 21,100 in 1985, and has decreased since then to 15,900 in 1990. The percentage of female students in teachers' colleges was 69.1 percent in 1990, somewhat higher than the 50.1 percent of females in the elementary school teaching force. In 1990, 3,220 students were accepted to the 11 teachers' colleges and 4,965 graduated (61.5 percent of them female); of the graduates, 94.3 percent found employment.

The largest number of elementary school teachers are trained at the 11 national teachers' colleges. Enrollment in university and college education departments was 67,837 in 1990. Of the total number of university and college graduates in 1990, 10 percent received degrees in teaching (16,586 graduates in all, 63.6 percent female). 40.8 percent of these graduates found employment, and 5.7 percent continued on to graduate school.

Table II.11

Teacher Education Institutes, 1989

Institutions	Qualification (2nd Grade)	Courses	Departments
College and University	Secondary School	College of Education	403
		Department of Education	53
		Course of Teachers' Education	82
		Educational Graduate School	40
	Elementary School	Primary Education	1
	Kindergarten	Nursing Teacher	13
Teachers' College	Elementary School	Teachers' College	11
Air & Correspondence College	Elementary School	Primary Education	1
	Kindergarten	Child Rearing	1
Junior College	Kindergarten	Child Rearing	55
Miscellaneous School	Kindergarten	Child Rearing	3

Source: NIERT. *Education in Korea 1989-1990*. Seoul: MOE, 1990:86.

Graduate studies in education are offered by 40 departments in national universities, and 44 departments in private universities. Graduate studies in education are intended to upgrade the profession, and to prepare researchers and evaluation specialists. In 1990, 3,587 students received degrees from graduate schools in education; 86.9 percent of them found employment in the same year. Only 35 percent of the graduates were female, indicating that the highest positions in the education field remain male-dominated.

Four types of teacher certification are offered for those preparing for careers in elementary and secondary education. Figure II.5 shows the types of certificate and the promotion system. The higher type of certification is obtained by inservice professional training and graduate studies at colleges and universities.

Figure II.5 Teachers Promotion System

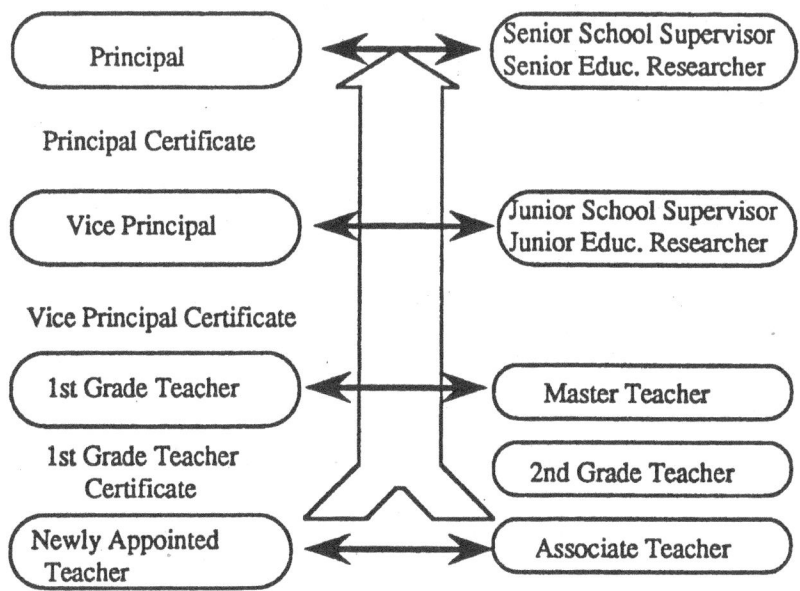

Source: NIERT, *Education in Korea, 1989-1990*. Seoul: MOE, 1990:84.

In-service and re-training programs not only provide instruction in new teaching skills and methods but also offer "spiritual or ideological education to heighten a sense of commitment to the teaching profession, together with a strong sense of mission and concern for the nation" (KCUE, 1990:76). A 60-hour course in moral education is a required part of in-service training for all teachers seeking additional certification, and is offered by municipal and provincial boards of education. Teachers may also be sent overseas for training and to observe new teaching methods. Foreign language teachers are sent to relevant host countries to improve their language skills.

Korean teachers are placed on the national salary schedule according to their academic degree. Although there is only one scale for all teachers, graduates from a college of education enter one step higher on the scale than graduates from a general college. Military service, central or local government work, or research at a university also affect initial placement on the salary scale. Advancement up the scale is achieved through years of teaching experience or additional study. A graduate degree in education adds two steps on the scale.

Teachers' Organizations

The Korean Federation of Education Associations (KFEA) is the largest teachers' organization, its membership comprising about 80.7 percent of all teachers. The Korean Teachers' Mutual Funds and the Teachers' Pension Fund, as their names imply, are organizations for teachers' welfare and financial security. After nearly 45 years of campaigning, the National Educators' Labor Union (NELU) was formed in May 1989. One of its main goals has been to reform the authoritarian administration of education and to work toward greater teacher participation in decision making.

Nonformal Education

By 1948 more than one million adults were enrolled in "civic schools" for literacy programs and basic education. Illiteracy among adults over 19 years of age was reduced from 78 percent in 1945 to 41 percent in 1948 and to 27.8 percent in 1960 (female 39.8 percent; male 15.8 percent; see Chapter V). UNESCO (1980) gives the 1970 illiteracy rate as 12.7 percent; however, the Korean census places the rate for that year at 11.6 percent. Since 1980 the illiteracy rate may be assumed to be minimal. It is difficult to evaluate literacy statistics in South Korea, since the criterion of literacy could be either knowledge of the Korean alphabet (*Han'gul*), which has only 24 characters, or knowledge of about 1,000 additional Chinese characters, without which it is impossible to read many publications in South Korea. Unlike South Korea, North Korea chose to eliminate entirely the use of Chinese characters in order to make all reading materials more widely available. This may partly explain how North Korea could report achieving full literacy as early as 1956 (Byung, Soon Song, 1984).

Enrollment in civic schools, offering adult elementary education, had declined from 53,000 students in 1947 to 15,400 students in 1975. By 1990, civic schools had been replaced by higher civic schools, offering the equivalent of middle school education.

Trade schools and higher trade schools offer vocational education programs which prepare for examination for certification developed by the National Skill Certification System, instituted in 1973. Through work experience and nonformal vocational courses of various durations (1 month to 3 years), skilled workers can prepare for three different grades of technicians' degrees and four different grades of skilled-worker degrees (Park, C.Y 1982). By the late 1970s enrollment in trade schools had dropped due to universalization of school education, high unemployment among high school graduates, and the growing sophistication of job-related skills. Since 1985 enrollment in higher trade schools has also dropped sharply. Due to the lower income returns on nonformal certificates as compared with returns from formal school certification, the demand for nonformal vocational education is diminishing, while the demand for schooling with certificates equivalent to that of formal education is increasing.

Adult education of a different kind is provided by voluntary organizations such as the Young Mens' Christian Association (YMCA), Korean Mothers' Association (KMA), and the Korean Association of Women College Graduates (KAWCGA). The KMA claims to have made the most significant contribution to the decline in birth rate through conducting literacy programs and dissemination of birth-control information.

As can be seen from Table II.12, the correspondence high school enrollment is down, and the enrollment in the Korean Air and Correspondence University up only slightly. The Open College greatly increased its enrollment between 1987 and 1990, reflecting perhaps its ability to give its students the same opportunity to advance to the next higher level of education as that received by graduates of formal schools.

The government promulgated the Promotion Law of Continuing Education in 1982 to encourage life-long educational opportunity, to realize the "schooling of the society," and to establish criteria for the recognition of nonformal educational equivalents of formal education. Life-long education includes the nonformal education described above as well as the educational offerings of youth organizations, cultural programs and libraries.

Table II.12

The Institutions of Nonformal Education, 1987-1990

Classification	Schools		Students		Teachers/Professors	
	1987	1990	1987	1990	1987	1990
Correspondence High School	51	46	48,067	35,212	2,139	---
Korea Air & Correspondence Univ.	1	1	146,990	148,650	78	136
Open College	6 (Nat'l. 3) (Priv. 3)	6	28,823	51,970	626	855

Source: NIEE, *Statistical Yearbook of Education.* Seoul: MOE, 1990.

Administration of Education

The organization of educational administration consists of three layers of administrative authorities, namely the Ministry of Education (MOE), the provincial or municipal "Board of Education" (not to be a confused with an American-style elected board), and the District Office of Education. Figure II.6 shows the chain of command from the MOE to the 15 Boards of Education to the Offices of Education in each town.

The Ministry of Education

The MOE is the central authority responsible for discharging the constitutional mandates for education. It formulates policies, directs and coordinates subordinate agencies for planning and policy implementation, reforms institutions, curriculum and instructional methods, publishes and approves textbooks, provides supports and supervisors to local educational administrations and national colleges and universities, and plans and implements the educational budget.

Figure II.6   The Education Administration System

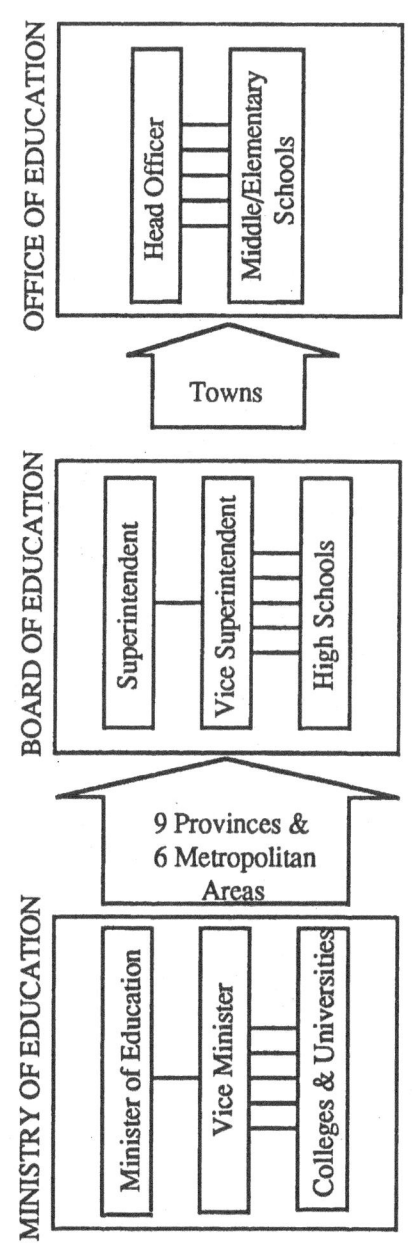

Source: Moon, Yong-lin. "Facts about Education Present No Shangi-La: Korea's Examination Hell Mars Schooling." *Koreana*, 5, no.2, 1991: 33.

The Ministry of Education is headed by the Minister of Education who, as a cabinet member, represents the President. The Ministry consists of three branches, five bureaus, and 25 sections. In addition, 20 directors are responsible for professional affairs which do not belong to any of the branches or bureaus (See Figure II.7).

The local administrative bodies were reorganized in 1964. Five metropolitan and nine provincial Boards of Education were created in response to the need for local educational administration, since the system had become too diverse to be administered from one central office. Each board has two ex-officio members, the superintendent and the provincial governor or mayor. At present the other 11 or 13 members of the Board are appointed by the local government authorities or by the Minister (MOE, 1990:39); see Figure II.8 for the organization of a Board of Education. The 1985 Presidential Committee for Education Reform envisions a democratically elected body with advisory power for policy making and oversight of administration (MOE, 1990:36).

Schools at the elementary and middle-school levels are under the direct administrative responsibility of town Offices of Education. The local education officers are nominated by the Superintendent and appointed by the Minister of Education. See Figure II.9 for the organization of a District Office of Education.

With regard to higher education, the Minister of Education still directs and supervises the establishment of new institutions and departments, facility standards, enrollment quotas, appointment of the faculty, curriculum, and academic credits and degrees. The presidents and deans who are recommended by the board of trustees of the college or university are subject to the approval of the Minister. In 1982 the Korean Council for University Education (KCUE) was established. Composed of the presidents of all four-year colleges and universities, KCUE's objectives include "enhanc[ing] autonomy and accountability in the management of colleges and universities" (KCUE, 1991:5), inter-university cooperation in research and higher education development, and advising the MOE on policy formation with respect to autonomy for higher education. KCUE hopes to develop into an advisory and research body.

Figure II.7 Organization of the Ministry of Education (Munkyo-Bu)

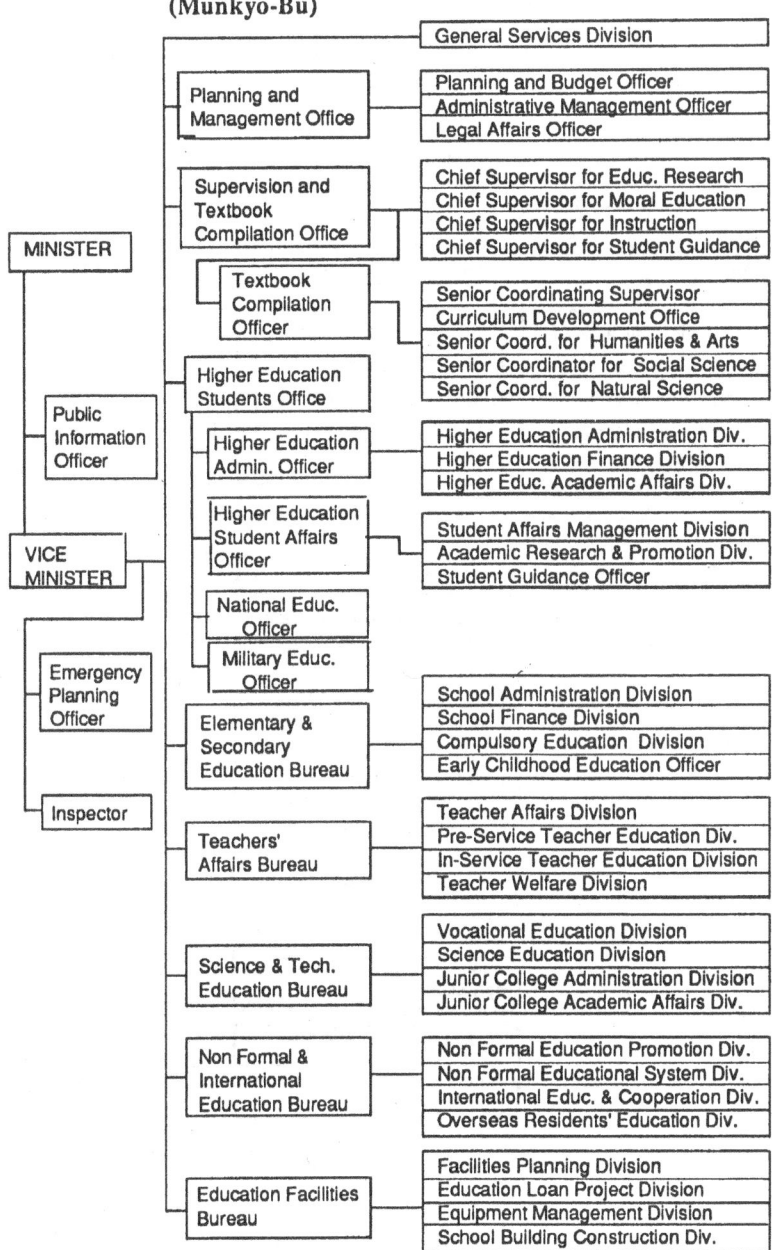

Source: NIERT. *Education in Korea 1987-1988*. Seoul: MOE, 1988: 41.

Figure II.8   Organization of a Board of Education

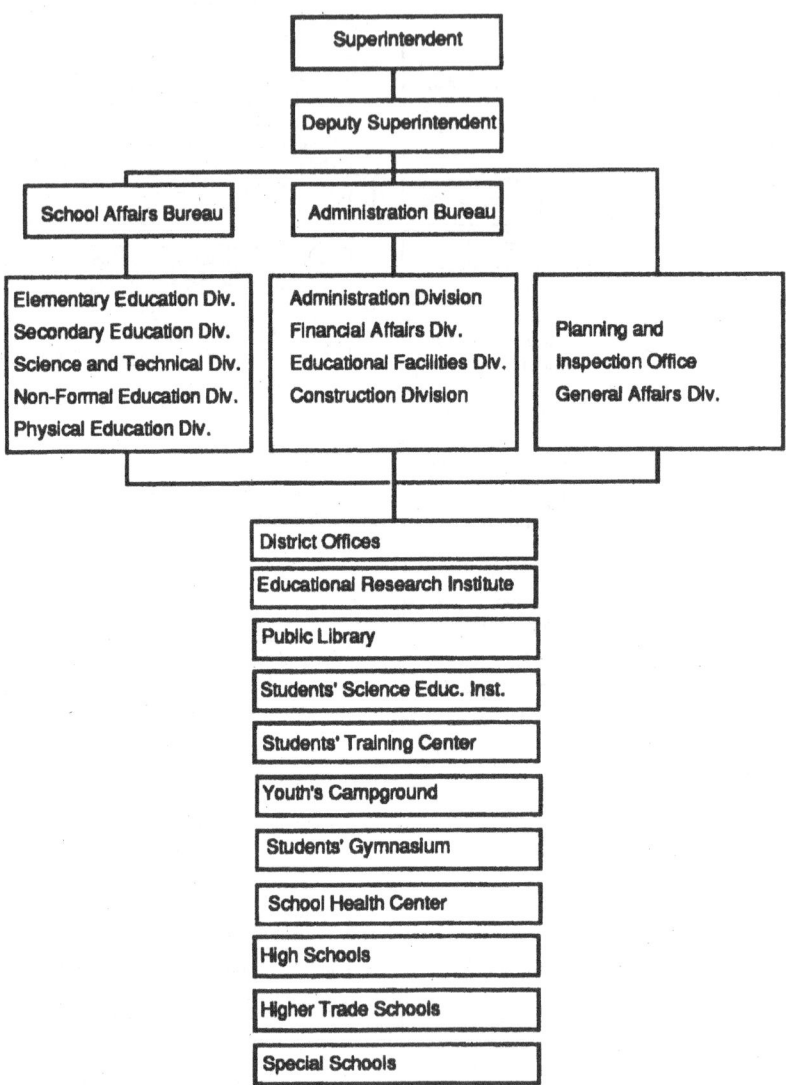

Source: NIERT. *Education in Korea, 1989-1990*. Seoul: MOE, 1990: 38.

Figure II.9   Organization of a District Office of Education

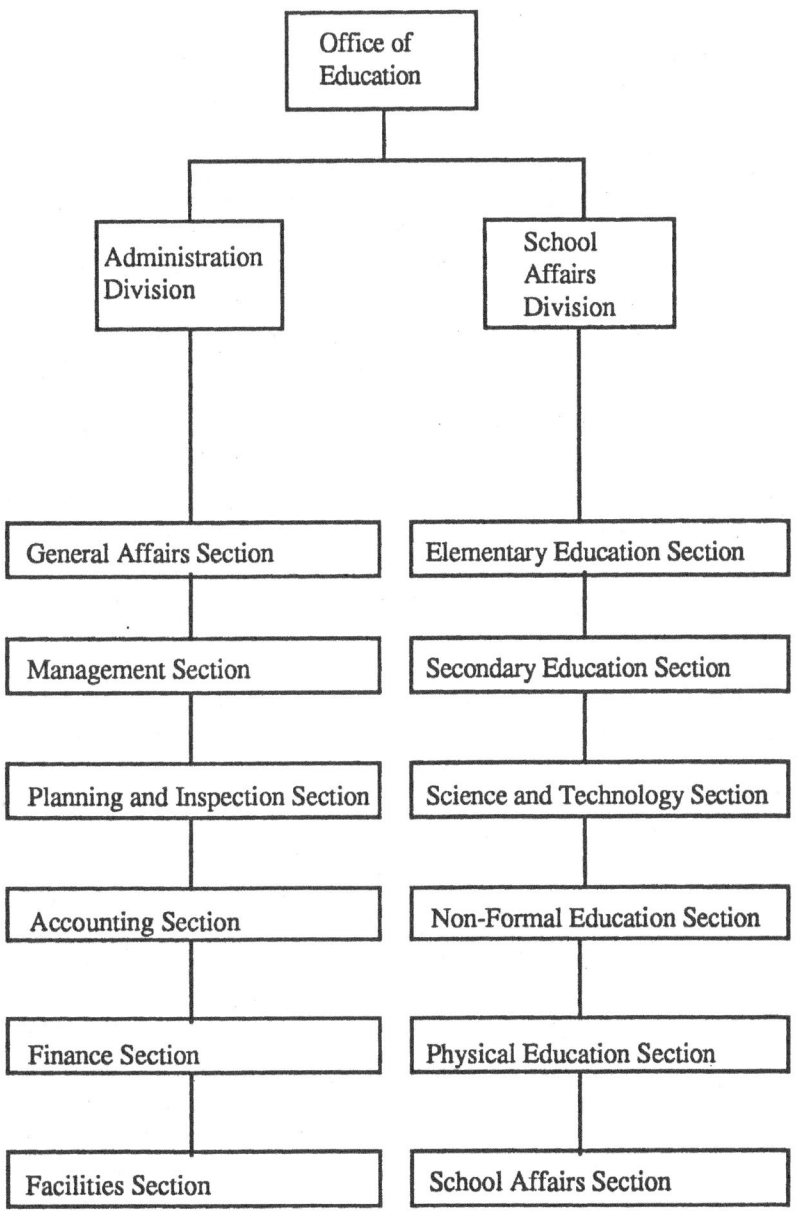

Source: NIERT. *Education in Korea 1989-1990*. Seoul: MOE, 1990: 39.

Finance

The educational budget comprises the revenue and expenditures of the Ministry of Education, the boards of education and local district offices, and the state and public schools, as well as the PTA accounts of each school and student government accounts of universities. The Ministry of Education's budget is divided into general accounts and special accounts. General accounts include the recurrent operational costs, such as grants for local educational organizations, grants and subsidies for national universities, and finances for public schools. Special accounts, i.e., the development budget, include specific expenditures, such as investment in educational facilities and support for national university hospitals.

The financial system is organized into four levels: 1) the Ministry of Education, recipient of annual governmental appropriations for education and the major dispenser of both general and special funds; 2) the 15 "Boards of Education," each with a financial affairs division responsible for financial management of secondary education; 3) the 179 district offices of education, each with a financial accounting section responsible for the financial matters of elementary schools; and 4) individual schools, each of which is allocated its own operational budget from the educational office, supplemented by the PTA's collections.

The Boards of Education and Offices of Education formulate budget drafts which are reviewed and approved by the Ministry of Education. Major sources of finance are derived from government grants and subsidies, self-earned incomes and transferred funds. The educational expenditures of the National Government are classified as follows: 1) direct expenditures for national schools, including national colleges and universities; 2) subsidies for the Boards of Education, private schools, and research institutes; and 3) grants for balancing the local budget to compensate for financial deficits of local administrative authorities. The local educational expenditures include the direct expenses of educational programs carried out by the Boards of Education, and payment of salaries of personnel employed in elementary, secondary, and special schools. Parents also pay tuition for schooling beyond elementary education, expenses for instructional materials and transportation fees. But public elementary education is financed almost entirely by national taxes (NIERT, 1978:45-7).

The major sources of revenue for each local education administration are grants from the Ministry of Education, entrance fees and tuition from middle school, high school, and higher education students, sales of properties, and local education taxes. Local sources have provided between 20 percent and 25 percent of the total amount of local education expenditures for elementary education (McGinn et al., 1980:17). Students' families are the source of approximately one-third of in-school expenditures on education. In addition, families fund out-of-school expenditures in the form of books, school supplies, transportation, extracurricular activities, and, in the case of higher education, room and board (see Table V.2).

Revenues for education come from three major sources: parents and students, the government and private foundations and industry. The original local education tax was abolished in 1961, and the law of educational funds for compulsory education was enacted. This law increased the dependence of local educational finance on the national treasury through the general accounts of the MOE. To meet the shortfall in the financing of public education, the government in 1968 enacted another law supporting secondary education. In 1971, the two laws were integrated in a single "law to support elementary and secondary education." Unlike the tax abolished in 1961, a local tax for local use, the new law earmarked 11.8 percent of national internal taxes for educational expenditures. Revenue raised by this tax is part of the annual MOE budget, and is disbursed by the central administration as grants for local education finance. This new tax law further centralized educational administration in the hands of the MOE, but its distribution to the Boards of Education gave MOE an opportunity to equalize funds among provinces and cities. As the Korean economy grew steadily during the 1980s, this fund provided stable income for education. During the oil crisis of the early 1970s, the law was suspended, causing deficits to accumulate.

The revival of the Education Tax as a percentage of income tax in 1981 has significantly increased the revenues for education. This additional contribution, amounting to about 12 percent of the total educational budget, was earmarked for improving facilities (Kim, Shin-Bok, 1990). Originally imposed for a five-year period, the new education tax has been repeatedly reimposed, most recently in 1986.

As the government is promoting a plan to create a local education tax to replace the existing tax, the major source of education financing will shift in 1992. Creating an educational account in the budget of local government while maintaining the percentage of total government budget, has increased educational funds by 20 percent in 1992 (Lee, C.J., 1992). The Presidential Commission has not only projected the financial requirements of their proposed reform but also suggested the following measure: "In order to meet the total requirement of education finance, the share of MOE's budget to GNP should increase at an annual rate of 0.1 percent over the present 3.34 percent, until it reaches 4.7 percent in 2001" (PCER, 1987:212).

Most private schools rely heavily on public support and tuition as their main source of revenue. The direct financial contribution of students through registration and tuition fees made up 11 percent of the total revenue in 1990 (MOE, *Statistical Yearbook*, 1990:754). This relatively large contribution by students is the cause of official concern. "The more pressing task at this point is to reduce the share of students to an appropriate level and hold the other two [government and industry] responsible for greater shares of financing" (MOE, 1990:40). Recently the government has lowered the tax rate on school foundation funds and intensified financial monitoring of school organizations.

The Ministry of Education's budget in 1990 was 5,062.4 billion *won* 1,003.1 billion more than in 1989, and 2,570.1 billion more than in 1985. However, as a percentage of total governmental budget, the educational budget has grown by 2.2 percent from 1989 to 1990, and by 3.5 percent from 1985 to 1990. Throughout the 1980s, financing compulsory education amounted to between 52 percent and 62 percent of the MOE budget. The 1990 percentage was the lowest, 52.2 percent, reflecting declining enrollment in elementary and middle schools. The highest percentage of expenditures for compulsory education occurred between 1957 and 1967, the period in which universal elementary education was achieved, reaching a peak of 80.9 percent in 1960. The expenditures of the Ministry of Education's budget in 1989 are shown in Table II.13.

As might be expected, the financing of educational institutions takes up the largest share of the budget. The share of expenditures by level of education have changed in accordance with the expansion of the system from a high of 72.3 percent for elementary education and a low of 1.4 percent for higher education in 1965 to a more balanced division in 1985: 50 percent on elementary education, 33.2 percent for secondary education and 10.3 percent for higher education. Out of the total general accounts in 1990, expenditures for elementary education were 58.4 percent, secondary education 23.7 percent, with higher education expenditures 17.7 percent.

Although the Ministry of Education has tried to expand the revenues for education its efforts have seldom had satisfactory effects (Kim, S.B., 1990). Enrollment increases, often exceeding planners' targets, were not followed by corresponding increases in facilities and teachers, due to lack of funding. Inadequate financing by the central government budgeting authorities for this continually expanding system can be depicted as one of the most serious constraints on qualitative achievement.

Table II.13

MOE'S Expenditure Classified by Items, 1989

Item	% of Total
Local Education Finance	77.36
Development Expenses	7.78
Educational Organization	7.39
H.Q. of MOE	3.52
Special Account	3.3
Academic and Artistic Research Institutes	0.37
Hospital Management	0.18
Incomes by Substituted Expenses	0.08

Source: NIERT, *Education in Korea, 1989-1990*. Seoul: MOE, 1990:43.

Bibliography

Articles and Books

Adams, Don. *Higher Educational Reforms in the Republic of Korea.* Washington, DC: Office of Education, U.S. Department of Health, Education and Welfare, U.S. Government Printing Office, 1965.

This study focuses on the changes in organizational structure and instructional programs in the field of higher education of the Republic of Korea since the fall of the First Republic in the spring of 1960. The following headings describe the coverage: Higher Education Prior to World War II; Higher Education Under the U.S. Military Government, 1945-48; Progress and Problems Under the First Republic, 1948-59; Reorganization and Later Modification, 1960-64; A Comparative Review.

Bae, Chong-Keun. "The Mobilization of Additional Funding for Higher Education in Korea." A paper presented at the Regional Seminar of Mobilization of Additional Funding for Higher Education, UNESCO. Bangkok, Thailand, August 22-27, 1988.

Barro, Steven M. and Suter, Larry. *International Comparisons of Teachers' Salaries: An Exploratory Study.* Washington, DC: National Center for Education Statistics, 1988. (ED 296988)

A survey report in which elementary, middle and high school teachers' salaries in Korea are compared with those of teachers in United States, Canada, United Kingdom, Federal Republic of Germany, Netherlands, Sweden, Denmark, Japan, and New Zealand.

Chin, Hai-Sool. "Science and Technology Development Strategies: Experience of the Republic of Korea." In *Proceedings of the International Workshop On Formulation of Science and Technology,* November 19-28, 1986. Seoul: Korea Advanced Institute of Science and Technology, 1988.

Chong, T'ae-Si. "Twenty Years of Korean Education Through Statistics." *Korea Journal,* 8 (August, 1968): 4-13.

This article surveys 20 years of Korean education from 1945-1967 through statistics increase in number of various kind of schools, annual increase in the number of students, annual ratios of school age children entering school, ratio of male and female students, and annual increase in the number of teachers. No interpretations are drawn from data.

Cho, Sung-Ok., ed. *Higher Education in Korea, 1984*. Seoul: Korea Research Foundation, 1984.

Chung, Chan-Young, et al. *A Study on the Autonomy of Educational Administration*. Seoul: KEDI Press, 1988.

Analyzes the advantages of allowing more autonomy in educational administration at the provincial and local levels. Reports the results of a survey of teachers and administrators which suggests the need for more local initiatives, evaluation and control.

Chung, Il Hwan. "Decentralization of Educational Administration and Strengthening of Local Educational Planning in Republic of Korea." Paris: UNESCO, 1990.

An overview of what many observers describe as an excessive centralized statewide administration of public affairs and educational administration. A discussion of a conceptual model of local governance system of educational administration and some policy suggestions for decentralization of education in Korea and local planning, based on future prospects of changes in educational administration.

Chung, Kyung Ae. "A Comparative Study of Principals' Administrative Behavior." *Journal of Educational Administration*, 27 (1989):45-57.

An attempt to analyze similarities and differences in the managerial behavior and beliefs of Korean and American secondary school principals.

Eversull, Frank L. "Some Observation on Higher Education in Korea." *School and Society*, LXV (January 25, 1947):51-53.

Hakwon-sa, Ltd. "Education." In *Korea: Its Land, People and Culture of All Ages*, 365-403. Seoul: Hakwon-sa Ltd., 1963. (DS902 K841)

　　An introduction to the history of Korean education, the education system, education at various school levels, curriculum and textbooks, financial management and facilities, teacher training and group activities of teachers, extra-curricular activities, education of the general public, and the education of Korean students abroad.

Hwang, Hamil Jong-Gon. "Adult Education: Imperative for a New Society." *Korean Journal* (July, 1966):7-12.

Kalakicha, Bimala. "Nature and Functions of the Regional University." In *Roles of Universities in Local and Regional Development in Southeast Asia*, edited by Yip Yat Hoong, Singapore: Regional Institute of Higher Education and Development, 1973.

Kang, Moo Sub and Im, Chon Sun. *The Current Status and Prospect of Vocational Education and Training*. Seoul: KEDI Press, 1983.

KCUE (Korean Council for University Education). *Higher Education in Korea*. Seoul: KCUE, 1990.

KCUE. *Korean Higher Education: Its Development, Aspects and Prospect*. Seoul: KCUE, 1988.

KCUE. *Current Issues in University Education in Korea and Japan*. Seoul: KCUE, 1987.

KEDI. *The Long Term Prospect For Educational Development 1978-1991*. Seoul: KEDI Press, 1979.

　　A parallel document to Korean Development Institute's long-range economic prospect published in 1978, covers all aspects of education and assesses the quality and relevance of education to a society on the threshold of higher industrialization. New educational objectives are recommended and specific quantitative targets are projected.

Keyes, Charles F. "Summary of Themes." In *The Growth of Southeast Asian Universities: Expansion and Consolidation*, edited by Amnuay Tapingkae. Singapore: Regional Institute of Higher Education and Development, 1974.

Kim, Byung Ha and Yeo, Kwang Eung, eds. *Special Education in Korea*. Daegu: Korea Social Work College, Research Institute for Special Education, 1976. (ED 138 026)

Discusses the situation and future direction of special education in Korea. Includes four sections: history of special education, current status of special education, the special education plan of the Young Kwang Educational Foundation, and listings of schools and classes for exceptional students.

Kim, Jong-chol and Koo, Byung Rim. "Higher Education Expansion in Korea: Its Process, Problems and Prospects." In *Higher Education Expansion in Asia*, 96-107. Reports of the International Seminar on Higher Education in Asia. January 28-31, 1985. Hiroshima, Japan. (ED 264787)

The authors describe the major causes and problems of the expansion of higher education in Korea and suggest future prospects and policy directions. Comment on the paper by a Japanese professor is attached.

Kim, Jong Su. "Survey on Illiteracy." In *Survey Report*, Vol. 5. Seoul: Central Educational Research Institute, 1959.

Kim, Shin Bok. "Educational Policy Change in Korea: Ideology and Praxis." In *Dynamic Transformation: Korea, NICs and Beyond*. 383-404, edited by Lim, Gill-Chin and Chang, Wook. Seoul: Myung-Bo Publishing Co., 1990.

Kim, Young-chul, Kong, Eun-bae and Lee, Yun-sik. *Educational Investment and Optimum Unit Cost*. Seoul: KEDI Press, 1983.

A report on the criteria of educational resource allocation in Korea, financial requirement of education, total educational expenditure including opportunity cost, and the optimum educational cost per unit, by school level. Comparison of private educational expenditures is made between public and private schools, by school level and region.

Ko Hwang-Kyung. "Korean Women's Education." *Korea Journal* (February 1964).

KIRI (Korea Industrial Research Institute). "R & D in Korea." *Electronics Korea* (April 1989).

Korean Central Education Research Institute. *Report of Korea/Seadag Seminar on Non-formal Education.* Seoul, 1971.

Kwang Myong Publishing Company. "Education." In *Korea: Past and Present*, 229-250. Seoul: Kwang Myong Publishing Company, 1972. (DS902 K547)

A brief introduction to the various levels of Korean education, including liberal arts education, high school, and technical education, special education, academies for higher education and research institutes.

Leavitt, Howard B. and Klassen, Frank H., eds. *Teacher Education and National Development.* Washington, DC: International Council of Education for Teaching, 1979.

Lee, Chong Jae. "A Diagnostic Analysis Of the Organization and Development Tasks Of Educational Administration in Korea." A paper submitted to Regional Technical Cooperation Programme for Increasing Efficiency in Education Through Improved Management and Planning, July 1984. (LB 2831.626,K6 L44)

The author describes the educational administration system and supervision at various levels. The professionalization of educational administrators and potential future directions of Korean education and educational administration are suggested.

Lee, Chong Jae. "A Korean Model of Educational Development." Paper presented at the Conference on the Second Twenty-five Years Educational Planning in Indonesia. January 21, 1992, Jakarta, Indonesia.

    A summary of the Korean educational system with a critical overview of major issues and problems. The paper concludes with an overview of the educational reform proposed by the Presidential Commission on Educational Reform, 1987.

Lee, Kye-Woo. *Human Resources Planning in the Republic of Korea: Improving Technical Education and Vocational Training.* Washington, DC: World Bank, 1983.

    Summarizes the policies and strategies of the Fourth Economic Development Plan (1976-1981) and describes the problems of Fifth Plan period (1982-1986). Renewed national commitment to human resources development and major structural changes in the Korean economy are seen as fundamental to Korea's future.

Lee, Kwan. "Past, Present, and Future Trends in Public And Private Sectors In Korean Higher Education." In *Public and Private Sectors in Asian Higher Education Systems: Issues and Prospects*, 49-70. Reports from the International Seminar on Higher Education in Asia, November 25-28, 1987, Hiroshima, Japan. (ED 291329)

    This report describes the historical development of higher education and higher education policy, autonomy and control of higher education, the financing of higher education and general issues and prospects of higher education in Korea.

Lee, Sungho. "Higher Education Research Environments in Korea." In *Scientific Development and Higher Education*, 31-82, edited by P.G. Altbach, et al. New York: Praeger, 1989.

Lee, Sungho. "The Korean Education System." Unpublished paper, Seoul: Yonsei University, Department of Education, July 6, 1991.

A set of tables, comparable to the ones published yearly by MOE, describing the educational system and statistical data on all levels of education including the educational budget and expenditures, as of 1989.

Lee, Sunhwa and Brinton, Mary C. "The Expansion of Secondary and Higher Education in South Korea, 1965-1988." Paper presented at the CIES Annual Conference, March 13-15, 1991, Pittsburgh, Pa.

An analysis examining how educational access and selection policies have affected differently Korean men's and women's educational attainment and participation in the work force.

Lee, Yung-dug. *Educational Innovation in the Republic of Korea*. Paris: UNESCO, 1974. (ED 109767)

The author describes eight education policy changes during 1963-1972, including upgrading of elementary school teacher training, enforcement of preliminary college entrance examinations, abolition of middle school entrance examination, and three instructional innovation projects such as Mastery Learning.

McGinn, Noel F. et al. *Education and Development in Korea*. Studies in the Modernization of the Republic of Korea, 1945-1975. Cambridge: Harvard University, 1980.

Miller, Harry G. and Lee, Hyon Chong. *Adult Education in Korea*. Carbondale and Edwardsville: Southern Illinois University, 1980.

Nam, Jin-U. *World Perspective: Case Descriptions on Educational Program for Adults Korea*. Battle Creek, MI: Kellogg Foundation, 1989.

NIEE (National Institution of Educational Evaluation). *Statistical Yearbook of Education, 1988*. Seoul: MOE (Ministry of Education), 1988.

NIEE. *Statistical Yearbook of Education, 1989*. Seoul: MOE, 1989.

NIEE. *Statistical Yearbook of Education, 1990*. Seoul: MOE, 1990.

Published yearly, a comprehensive set of tables on all levels and aspects of education in Korea. All titles and subtitles are in Korean as well as in English.

NIERT (National Institute of Education Research and Training). *Education in Korea 1983-1984*. Seoul: MOE, 1983.

NIERT. *Education in Korea 1985-1986*. Seoul: MOE, 1985.

NIERT. *Education in Korea 1987-1988*. Seoul: MOE, 1987.

NIERT. *Education in Korea 1989-1990*. Seoul: MOE, 1989

Each of these monographs presents a short historical overview of the educational system as well as a detailed description of school organization and curriculum at all levels. Chapters on teacher education and teachers' organizations, research institutes, life-long education, and data on Korean students abroad is also included. The 1989-1990 volume identifies a new set of educational objectives by educational level, as well as highlights educational change in the 1970s and 1980s.

Noble, G. A. "Science Education in Korea." *Science* (January, 1948): 32-33.

Oh, Chae-Kyong. "Education." *Handbook of Korea*, 147-172. New York: Pageant Press, Inc., 1958.

A brief survey of the organization of education and a description of the different levels of the system.

Park, Kyung-sook and Park, Hyo-jung. *A Study on the School Education of Korean Autistic Children*. Seoul: KEDI Press, 1986.

Paik, Hyun Ki. "The Present Status of Education." *Korea Journal*, 3 (April 1963): 4-15.

Paik, Hyun Ki. *A Content Analysis of Elementary School Textbooks and a Related Study for Improvement of Textbook Administration*. Seoul: Central Education Research Institute, 1969.

Pathmanathan, Murugesu. "University Autonomy and Academic Freedom in the Context of Changing Conditions in Asia." In *The Role of Asian Universities In A Changing World*, edited by K. S. Nijhar. Kuala Lumpur: Academic Staff Association, University of Malaya, 1972.

PCER (Presidential Commission on Educational Reform). *Korean Educational Reforms Toward The 21st Century*. Seoul: MOE, 1987.

The commission's report takes a broad historical perspective of Korea's current educational conditions and problems. All in all it suggests 44 reform proposals, in various levels and functions of the educational system. In general the approach is critical of the existing situation, and the radical changes proposed by the PCER support Korea's economic and social-political reforms toward the 21st century. For each major reform a set of strategies is identified.

Public Information Office, The Kia Corporation. "The Selection of Students for the Program of Industry-Institution Cooperation Scholarship." *KIA Monthly*, 72 (May-June 1989).

Rhee, Tae-Yung. "Special Education and Welfare Activities for the Handicapped in Korea Spearheaded by Taegu University and Its Affiliated Institutions: Let's Make the Handicapped the Light of the Global Village." Paper presented at the Annual Convention of the Council for Exceptional Children, Chicago, 1987. (ED 291 212)

UNESCO. *Higher Education in the Asian Region*. Bangkok: UNESCO, 1972.

UNESCO. *Review of Educational Studies in Korea*, No. 1. Seoul: Korean National Commission for UNESCO, 1972.

Abstracts of research papers presented to the Korean National Commission for UNESCO. Chapters 1-4 and 16-19 are a particularly important source of empirical studies on Korean education.

UNESCO. "Administration of Education in the Asian Region." *Bulletin of the Regional Office for Education in Asia*, No. 15. Bangkok: UNESCO, 1974.

UNESCO. "Education in Asia." *Reviews, Reports and Notes*, No. 5. Bangkok: UNESCO, 1974.

UNESCO. *Social Change and New Profiles of Educational Personnel: National Studies--India, Nepal, Philippines, Republic of Korea*. Bangkok: UNESCO Regional Office for Education in Asia and the Pacific, 1981. (ED 237 264)

UNESCO. "Towards Universalization of Primary Education in Asia and the Pacific." *Country Studies--Republic of Korea*. Bangkok: UNESCO Regional Office for Education in Asia and the Pacific, 1984. (ED 274 455)

Veramu, Joseph. "Past, Present, and Future of Literacy Education in Korea." In *Literacy for Peace and Human Rights*. Canberra, Australia: Asian South Pacific Bureau of Adult Education, 1990. (ED 328 711)

Yi, Yongdok. *Educational Innovation in the Republic of Korea*. Paris: UNESCO, 1974. (LA1331. Y56)

A description of major national educational policies in the 1960s, such as upgrading of elementary school teacher training institutions, abolition of middle school entrance examinations and establishment of Korea Education Development Institute. Some KEDI projects are also mentioned.

Yi, Gouzeh. "Moral Education in Korea." *Journal of Moral Education*, 8 (January 1978): 5-23.

Introduces moral education in terms of background, goals, teacher education and training, method, and evaluation. The author argues that moral education in Korea aims to reinforce such desirable aspects of the Korean value system as self-control, sincerity, and freedom.

You, Injong. "Primary and Secondary Education in Korea." In *Basic Education For The Real World: International Perspectives On Human Resource Development*, 131-134. Washington DC: International Council on Education for Teaching, 1981. (ED 212597)

Identifies problems encountered by primary education such as overcrowded classes in provincial cities and urban centers resulting in impersonalized relationships between teachers and students, and a lack of emphasis on speech skills and mathematical concepts. The increase in the number of middle school students increased the need for additional teachers and new systems for evaluating students' achievement.

Yun, Chung Il. "Education Finance in Korea." In *Comparative Study of University Finance in Asia*, edited by Korean Council for University Education (KCUE). Seoul: KCUE, 1986.

Dissertations

Adams, Donald K. "Education in Korea, 1945-1955." Ph.D. dissertation, The University of Connecticut, 1956.

A descriptive analysis of the educational goals, organizational structure, administration and teaching practices in South Korea. The major educational developments are discussed in the context of the changing Korean society.

Bae, Cheon Ung. "A Comparative Study of the Open University of Britain and the Air Correspondence College of Korea." Ph.D. dissertation, Michigan State University, 1984.

The comparison includes issues important to open college education, organizational cooperation between regional study centers and central organization, instructional material preparation and provision, aims and objectives, and common problems such as low completion rate.

Choe, Won Hyung. "Curricular Reform in Korea During the American Military Government, 1945-1948." Ph.D. dissertation, The University of Wisconsin-Madison, 1986.

Based on a Neo-Marxist conceptual framework, this study investigates the curricular reform activities of the American military government. Analysis is based on historical documents stored at the U.S. National Archives. The study concludes that the curricular reform was the result of complex interaction of the ideological, material, and historical conditions during the occupation.

Choi, Joon Yul. "A Comparative Study of Teacher Salary Structures and Trends of Teachers' Economic Status in Korea and the United States of America From 1960 To 1986." Ph.D. dissertation, University of Iowa, 1989.

Chung, Sol Gu. "The Political Socialization of Selected Elementary and Middle School Students in the Republic of Korea: Political Knowledge, Political Trust and Political Efficacy." Ph.D. dissertation, Florida State University, 1973.

Hong, Ki Hyung. "Prevention of Dropout in the Air and Correspondence High School in Korea." Ph.D. dissertation, University of Alberta, 1982.

Kim, Mahn Kee. "A Study of Organizational Strategies for The Development of Interorganizational Relationships: The Case of KEDI." Ph.D. dissertation, University of Pittsburgh, 1978.

The case of KEDI serves to examine the impact of an R&D center in its efforts to make basic changes in a national education system. Fourteen external organizations perceived as having multiple linkages with KEDI were studied. The results suggests that KEDI depended on informal and ad hoc activities as much as on formal and planned activities for dissemination of information.

Kim, Myung Hee. "Factors Affecting Teacher Turnover in Korea." Ed.D. dissertation, Boston University, 1987.

Kim, Young Man. "The Relationship of Principals' Instructional Leadership to Student Achievement in Academic Private High Schools in Seoul, Korea." Ed.D. dissertation, University of Southern California, 1988.

Kim, Yongchu. "The Academic Environment of Korean Graduate Education: Perceptions of Graduate Students and Faculty of Four Universities." Ph.D. dissertation, Kent State University, 1988.

A study of the difference between students' perception on their graduate school's academic environment and that of faculties in Korea.

Kim, Young Shik. "Education of Elementary School Teachers and Administrators in the Republic of Korea, 1958-1964." Ph.D. dissertation, George Peabody College for Teachers of Vanderbilt University, 1968.

Kim, Sooil. "A Comparative Study of Adult Education in Indonesia, The Republic of Korea and Japan." Ph.D. dissertation, Florida State University, 1981.

Lee, Kyung Woo. "Conceptual Curriculum Models for Early Childhood Education in South Korea." Ed.D. dissertation, Temple University, 1980.

Lee proposes two conceptual curriculum models based on both cognitive and affective needs of young children. These models try to take into account the local value system, individual needs, and national needs of the Korean society.

Lee, Kohn Man. "The Characteristics of Students Served by Different Types of High Schools and Some Consequences of Academic Differentiation: A Study of the Secondary School System in South Korea." Ph.D. dissertation, University of California-Los Angeles, 1988.

Park, Chong Yul. "Impact of Nonformal Vocational Education on Occupational Mobility in Korea." Ph.D. dissertation, University of Pittsburgh, 1982.

A comparison of occupational status attainment of vocational educational graduates, and workers with nonformal education. The Korean National Skill Certification system is critically reviewed since it confirms formal education rather than nonformal education or work experience. Long term nonformal education is more influential on occupational mobility than short term nonformal education.

Park, Hun. "The Relationships Between the Principal's Rating of Teacher Effectiveness and Certain Selected Teacher Variables in Korea." Ph.D. dissertation, University of Southern California, 1972.

Song, Bokjoo. "Education of Elementary School Teachers in the Republic of Korea: Present Status and A Proposal For An Alternative Approach." Ph.D. dissertation, George Peabody College for Teachers of Vanderbilt University, 1983.

    A descriptive study of elementary teacher training in Korea which proposes an alternative teacher-training system based on the number of teachers needed for the different school levels, and the knowledge and skills required for each level.

Whang, Hichul Henry. "The Tasks of Public Education As Perceived by The Public in The Republic of Korea." Ph.D. dissertation, The University of Wisconsin-Madison, 1972.

Yun, Whidug Chung. "An Assessment of the Development of Higher Education in the Republic of Korea from 1945 to 1988." Ed.D. dissertation, Pepperdine University, 1989.

Yu-Tull, Ducksoon. "An Investigation of Attitudes and Perceptions of Educators in Korean Higher Education Towards Job Performance Ability of Women in Korean Higher Education." Ed.D. dissertation, George Washington University, 1983.

CHAPTER III

Transnational Transfer Of Knowledge And Its Influences On Korean Education

What has been the overall impact of the various contemporary external influences on Korean education? What was the impact of the American occupation of 1945-1948? Has economic dependence on the United States been eliminated? What have been the consequences of the unique, extensive interaction of Korean students and scholars with United States educators and the international scientific community? Have too many ideas, organizational arrangements, and professional roles been borrowed?

Korean educators are now asking these questions. There is an uneasiness about becoming too American or too Western and inadvertently losing important cultural institutions and traditions. Thus, Korea in the last few decades has experienced both increased use of United States and Western knowledge and increased doubts about the side effects of using this knowledge. The utility of the technical knowledge from the West in fueling Korea's economic growth is apparent and usually appreciated; however, in education, theories, models and methods for academic or practical purposes have been borrowed from the United States which sometimes share little with Korea in terms of cultural heritage, historical experience, developmental stage, or economic and political conditions. Some scholars have argued that Korea has become increasingly dependent on importation of knowledge and that, in effect, Korean education is linked to the United States as part of a transnational knowledge system in which the pace-setting countries (United States, Japan, and some of the European countries) are engaged in producing new knowledge while peripheral countries, such as Korea, are mainly consumers of knowledge produced elsewhere.

The Transnational Knowledge System

Transnational transfer of knowledge involves the exchange of theories, models, and methods for educational, scientific, or industrial purposes among countries. The predominant model of knowledge exchange between advanced Western industrialized nations and the Third World nations during the 1950s and 1960s was one of intervention and imitation based on an explicit or implicit assumption of the universal applicability of Western knowledge. In a world system of knowledge transfer, the advanced industrial countries, led by the United States, are major producers and disseminators of knowledge while the nations peripheral to the central knowledge system are "importing knowledge." Social sciences and educational theories and reforms are among the "goods" circulated by the world knowledge system. Linkages, both formal and informal, keep educational systems in the periphery tied to those in the center of the knowledge system. Educational structures, curricula and reforms, academic standards, and modes of applying research programs and legitimating educational institutions are all formulated and disseminated by the "pace-setting" countries. Peripheral systems are tied to the center through the education of their scholars and scientists at universities in the central countries, through professional organizations based in the core countries, and through pressure on local scholars to publish their research in international (mostly English-language) journals. Funding agencies such as USAID and the World Bank and foundations such as the Rockefeller Foundation and Ford Foundation actively support the dissemination of scientific, technical, and professional knowledge throughout the world.

Korea's educational development has not escaped the asymmetry of the world knowledge system in general. In particular, it has been drawn within the orbit of a system centered on the United States, with its institutionalized networks of influence. These United States-centered networks include the leading universities, research institutions, book- and journal-publishing enterprises, and the bulk of the world's research and development funds and of its discoveries and patents. Thus the higher education system of the United States has acted as the source of acceptable technical and professional knowledge to many Koreans.

United States Influences On Educational Theory and Practice

Although a relationship and some educational transfer has existed between the United States and Korea since 1882 (the late Yi Dynasty; see Chapter I), large-scale knowledge transfer dates only from 1945. Japanese colonialism before 1945 had two important effects on Korean education. First, the Japanese destroyed *Dong To Suh Ki*, the dominant frame of reference of Korean scholars during the late 19th and early 20th centuries with regard to intercultural exchanges. *Dong To Suh Ki* contained the core precept that Koreans should import Western learning for its technology or utility (*Suh Ki*), while maintaining oriental learning as educational content. The destruction of Dong To (oriental learning) meant discarding cultural tradition and self-awareness, and may be viewed as a preparatory stage for the massive importation, without great resistance, of American knowledge after 1945. Second, many of the Koreans who later became national leaders fled colonized Korea between 1910 and 1945 and were educated in the United States. Both of these factors contributed to the formation of a Korean knowledge system influenced by the United States.

The 1945-1948 period of the United States Military Government in Korea (USMGIK) was the educational bridge between Japanese imperialism and the introduction of several institutions and processes in Korea based on United States models (Kim, D.K. 1974). During this period, at least three types of new or expanded transnational networks between the United States and Korea emerged: (a) institution-building through United States technical assistance, (b) direct technical assistance by United States advisors, and (c) higher education of Koreans in the United States.

The United States' presence in Korea and the expansion of transnational networks fostered the following conditions which contributed to the growth of a knowledge system in Korea that is at least partly United States-dependent:

(a) a change of leadership in academic activities and recruitment of United States-educated Korean scholars into leadership positions;

(b) the development of a social and academic reward system organized to favor United States-educated Korean scholars;

(c) the introduction of a new educational frame of reference based upon the ideological superiority of Western science and technology, and including the adoption of English as the international scientific medium;

(d) the creation of new research institutions and university programs based upon United States models, which created new social roles for scholars; and

(e) the emergence of new social roles dominated by the United States-educated Koreans (Lee, J.G., 1986).

Gradually after 1945 United States educational and social-science theories came to provide the only concepts by which Korean educational scholars conceived, planned, and evaluated educational innovations and change (Kim and Lee, 1980). As particular educational theories waxed and waned in popularity in the United States, so with some time lag did they in Korea. This process was reinforced by continuing cycles of Korean students who were increasingly predisposed to go to the United States for higher education.

Another early influence on Korean education was a series of education missions to Korea underwritten by the United States State Department and contracted by the Unitarian Service Committee, Inc. during 1952-1955. The first mission's contribution was in introducing a life-centered curriculum movement, advising on the establishment of a democratic education administration system, and guiding or reforming teaching methods. The second mission concentrated on in-service training, exposing teachers to Western professional educators and to new ways of teaching. Yoo noted, that "Almost all Korean leading educators at this time participated in these workshops" (Yoo, Hyung-Jin, 1983:9). The work of the third mission included assistance in (1) the development of instruments to measure the scholastic achievement of Korean students; (2) curriculum planning and textbook preparation; (3) planning in-service teacher training programs; and (4) designing programs for upgrading the professional knowledge of administrators. "The mission members actually taught in schools, advised classroom teachers, and assisted school administrators both in schools and in government. (Yoo, Hyung-Jin, 1983:9). Between 1956 and 1962 a faculty team from George Peabody College of Education continued to provide technical aid to reform teacher education and to the professional preparation of educational administrators. One recommendation of the Peabody team was to convert the normal schools into two-year teachers colleges.

The Case of United States Teaching Methods in Korea

In order to illustrate how the Korean educational system has been structured and continues to operate under the influence of United States educational theories, Lee, J. G. (1986) examined one large-scale innovation, identified as the "inquiry teaching method" (ITM).

Two characteristic operations of the Korean knowledge system were elaborated by Jong Gag Lee. First, regardless of its potential relevance, Western knowledge attracted large numbers of Korean scholars. Educators in the mid-1980s remembered the early promotion of ITM as "a newly introduced method which was assumed to be the best and most important of possible innovations," and reflected that Korean scholars were often "enraptured by new theories imported from the West." Although by 1973 there had been little accumulation of knowledge about its effectiveness, ITM faced little opposition. In the absence of arguments raised against ITM there was no need for an elaborate justification of its introduction in Korea; moreover, there was at this time a lack of competing social studies curriculum theories or instructional methods. Secondly, the selection process of ITM was disconnected from past experiences in Korea because of the lack of concern with indigenous problems, a result of the attraction to new foreign theories. For example, no study had been carried out on the effectiveness of the existing expository method of teaching. Further, those involved in the ITM selection process did not consider the reasons why past reform activities in social studies education influenced by United States concepts had failed. And, theories newly imported from the United States were usually perceived as stronger than theories previously imported and therefore could be accepted as legitimate replacements.

The immediate context for the transfer of new teaching methods from the United States was the new national elementary and secondary social studies curriculum of 1973. This curriculum employed the notion of a "discipline-centered curriculum" as its basic philosophy. In the development and implementation of the new curriculum a commitment was made by KEDI to "apply the most current learning theories and instructional technologies" (Masoner and Klassner, 1979:117 in Lee et al., 1988:238).

The first model of ITM developed by the Unit of Social Studies Education (USSE, a special unit of KEDI) was a combination of three United States models. The resulting instructional model focused on teaching/learning processes intended to foster the acquisition of social knowledge and values, and clarification of values and attitudes. ITM underwent a process of "reality testing" by the developing unit. USSE members reviewed the relevance and usefulness of ITM in the Korean context. Members of USSE as well as the members of KEDI in general recognized the need to adapt ITM to the Korean context. Interviews with USSE founding members reveal that the most important question raised both during the selection period and as implementation began was whether the United States-originated ITM would have any utility in Korea. Interview data by Lee (1986) also show that the founding members conjectured about potential problem areas pertaining to Korea's "passive political culture, authoritative human social relations, oversized classes, rote-memory education for examinations, etc." (Chung, S.G., 1977:55). However, they failed to review systematically available cases of experiences with ITM use in Korea schools.

Although most USSE members were optimistic about the utility of ITM, agreement was reached on an experiment utilizing two fifth-grade classes (designated as experimental and control) (Chung et al., 1973). In the experiment, "applicability" of ITM in a Korean situation was interpreted as "effectiveness" by the research team. The experiment verified that ITM improved the students' conceptualization ability, inquiry skills and value-clarification skills. "Effectiveness" was measured by "high scores" on summative pencil-and-paper tests constructed by the researchers.

In addition to this evaluation, a survey of teachers was conducted which resulted in the identification of 18 problems (Chung, 1974) which may be summarized as follows: lack of knowledge of the theories and methods of ITM; teacher-student ratios (one teacher to 70-80 students) which made ITM application difficult; difficulties of controlling lesson progress because of the time-consuming nature of ITM; extensive and burdensome teacher preparation; lack of inquiry and participation skills in students; and lack of confidence in the effectiveness of ITM in terms of student preparation for the crucial university entrance examination. However, the results of the survey were only discussed in one published article (Chung, 1973) and in one unpublished report (Chung et al., 1974). These discussions were positive about the potential applicability of inquiry teaching in the Korean context but recognized that ITM's effectiveness in preparation for the university entrance examination depended on the exchange of existing memory-type examination items for inquiry-type examination items.

From an analysis of the "reality testing" of ITM a number of conclusions may be reached. First, the tests were conducted within a range of problems earlier anticipated and identified by USSE members. The problems identified through the teachers' survey, for example, were only superficially examined. Moreover, problems uncovered in the two reality testings were not subjected to extensive analysis. Finally, other important actors were not invited to participate in any of the review and evaluation processes pertaining to ITM. In sum, the reality testings conducted by USSE seemed to be focused more on defending ITM than on seeking information to better adapt ITM to fit the Korean social and cultural context.

The limited testing of ITM in the Korean context generally offered positive findings in terms of ITM's application in Korea. However, informal external criticisms from ministerial curriculum specialists and teachers influenced USSE to consider possible modifications. Changes resulting from a three-year trial process of ITM included the addition of "remembering facts" (rote memory) to the cognitive inquiry process; the addition of "value exposition" (value indoctrination) to the value-clarification process; and a redefinition of the inquiry teaching classroom from one in which more than "two-thirds of the students" are involved to one in which more than "one-third of the students" are involved in inquiry learning. One informant called this modified approach "Koreanized inquiry teaching."

Experience with ITM led to modifications but did not lead to a comprehensive examination of new questions or issues related to importation of educational reforms. For example, although Korean teachers and Korean students are clearly different from their American counterparts in many ways, this difference was not a subject for intensive analysis or debate. Researchers did not ask how Korean teachers could deal with passive Korean students who are not used to inquiry approaches to learning and do not communicate freely their thoughts and feelings in the classroom. Instead teachers' roles in the inquiry classroom were prescribed by proponents of ITM essentially as United States scholars had originally proposed. Korean experiences with ITM did not find their way into the general Korean knowledge system in education; modifications and adjustments in ITM remained largely unanalyzed, unshared, and unused. Books and articles published in Korea still explain ITM according to United States theories (Shin, S.H., 1984; Chung, S.G., 1985).

The difficulties in this case of knowledge transfer raise questions about the roles of the recipient knowledge mediators as gatekeepers in the importation of foreign knowledge. In retrospective self-criticism, these mediators have commented on the superficiality of their efforts. Some of them have stated that most of the articles and books they produced were only mosaics of United States sources. The USSE members also pointed to their inability to initiate widespread dialogue and criticism among Korean educational scholars, an action which might have uncovered a range of potential problems. They understood but failed to respond satisfactorily to the fact that Korea represented a different social context, a different tradition, and a different cultural environment from the United States.

In the Korean context, knowledge accumulation is restricted, and its direction influenced, by (a) the perceived status of theories and (b) prevailing patterns of communication. The status of a theory in Korea tends to be determined by the status of the theorist and the absence of competing theories. It is not uncommon that those who have higher degrees from the United States automatically become recognized authorities and consequently gain high status. Thus, in Korea the status of a theorist, often legitimized through the importation of external knowledge, is maintained through two strong internal factors: the rigidly hierarchical nature of Korean society and, particularly until very recently, that society's lack of resources to create new theoretical knowledge. The status of a theorist depends on the novelty of the knowledge he or she is importing; thus the scholar who imports the newest trend from the central knowledge system will displace scholars associated with older trends.

The status of scientific knowledge in Korea may also be determined by the lack of commensurate competing knowledge. In the case of ITM, this method was only one among many available in the United States context, and it achieved its meaning, prestige and relative recognition in that context through competition with other methods. When ITM was transferred to Korea, by contrast, its prestige was determined in a context virtually devoid of competing theories. Within Korea's centralized society the high status attained by ITM seems to have been maintained and reinforced by its support from KEDI, a powerful institution affiliated with the national government. Thus another determinant of the status of a theory derives from control of valued imported knowledge. Knowledge imported into the Korean education system tended to come under the control of United States-educated Koreans for at least two reasons: (a) the inability of local scholars to operate freely in English (the current international scientific medium), and (b) the access of United States-educated scholars to international information sources. Yet another determinant of the status of a theory is the tendency to replace a previously imported theory by a newly imported theory because such a theory is assumed to represent an advance over the old and because the new theory has acquired disciples. With some time lag, the new theories and instructional methods from the United States eventually become part of the educational planning process in Korea. Korean returnees and United States academic advisers are like an extension of a conveyor belt, transporting new theories (Lee, Adams, and Cornbleth, 1988).

The difference in the transfer of educational reforms is mainly in the implementation phase: whereas in the United States diversity, decentralization, and the sheer size of the country may militate against universal acceptance of many new theories, in Korean hierarchical social relations, the Korean seniority system, and patterns of communication characterized by an absence of interactions and criticisms serve to maintain the status of an imported social-science theory. Seniority in terms of age interrupts scholarly exchanges and interactions, effectively eliminating Western types of argument across age groups of scholars. Further, the absence of criticism in the periphery is influenced by the knowledge-legitimating and status-allocating functions of the center knowledge system. The imported knowledge is perceived as already legitimized internationally, requiring no further elaboration or systemization by scholars in the periphery. Moreover, in a rigidly hierarchical society, lower-status academics and teachers do not want to risk argument with higher-status, United States-educated scholars. In the absence of any serious challenge, imported knowledge passes as truth.

Koreans Studying in Western Countries

Another major index of Western influence on the development of the Korean knowledge system is the number of Korean students studying abroad. As early as 1956 MOE established an Advisory Committee on Study Abroad in order to provide testing, guidance, and scholarship assistance for students. Opportunities for Koreans to study abroad during the 1950s and 1960s were largely limited to those students who had received scholarships from the United States government, private foundations, or directly from United States institutions. During the 1970s, a policy change on the part of the Korean government allowed students to study abroad at their own expense. Between 1953 and 1979, 15,206 Korean students studied abroad (85.1 percent of them in the United States, 3.9 percent in West Germany, 2.1 percent in France, and the rest in other countries, [MOE, 1979]). As a result of the new policy, the number of students seeking graduate study outside Korea expanded considerably.

In 1980 the Korean government not only eased the qualification test for study abroad but also opened the way for undergraduate study overseas. Nevertheless, according to Yoo (1983), out of 13,113 students studying abroad in 1983, most studied in graduate schools (72 percent studied in the United States). The number of Korean students in the United States in 1988, as seen in Table III.1, was a total of 17,907, with the largest number of students in California. By 1988 Korean undergraduate students were also found in significant numbers in United States universities. For example, at the University of Wisconsin-Madison in 1988, out of 481 Korean students, 128 were undergraduate students (Hwang, Bo-Sung, 1990:44).

The Korean government continues to support outstanding college graduates with government scholarships for study abroad, yet the number of government-supported students is very small compared to self-supporting students (597 compared to 26,500 in 1987; OPM, 1987:98). Not only do students and university professors study abroad, but the government also sponsors various continuing inservice training programs for career civil servants. Most candidates for higher echelon positions in the civil service are sent to graduate programs abroad. During 1977-1988, the largest number, 1,875, were sent to the United States, followed by 348 to Great Britain and 334 to Japan, with 186 going to all other countries.

Table III. 1

Korean Students in the United States, 1988

Top 5 States		Top 10 Universities	
1. California	(2,356)	1. University of Texas-Austin	(406)
2. New York	(1,743)	2. University of Wisconsin-Madison	(363)
3. Illinois	(1,259)	3. Ohio State University	(351)
4. Texas	(1,153)	4. University of Michigan-Ann Arbor	(325)
5. Michigan	(927)	5. University of Southern California	(324)
		6. University of Illinios-Urbana	(319)
Last State		7. Michigan State University	(279)
		8. University of Minnesota-Twin Cities	(249)
West Virginia	(7)	9. University of California-Los Angeles	(239)
		10. Iowa State University	(235)

Source: The Fulbright Student Advisory Service. "Korean Students in USA.," *The Monthly Recruit*, No 7 (July 1989):114.

Although the knowledge transfer system mainly operates from the center of the system (the core industrialized countries) to its periphery, Korea increasingly has been making efforts to disseminate knowledge to the Western countries, reversing the usual direction of the transfer "flow." The Korean government encourages and supports the development of Korean studies at overseas institutes of higher learning by providing grants for staff development and lectures, facilitating the exchange of academics, financing research and publication and supplying materials. By 1990, 173 universities and research institutes, representing 36 countries, had developed Korean studies programs. The Korean government has bilateral agreements with some 60 countries on educational exchange programs. Between 1965 and 1986 a total of 1,222 foreign students studied in Korea and the government continues to actively support programs of international exchange of professors and researchers. From 1978 to 1988, a total of 2,119 professors were the beneficiaries of 21.9 billion *won* of scholarship through this program.

Building An Indigenous Knowledge System

What changes need to occur if the Korean knowledge system is to become more successful in accumulating local knowledge? Possibilities include (a) the development of more self-sustaining academic communities; (b) the modification of the roles of knowledge mediators to include responsibilities not only for knowledge transmission but also for knowledge construction; (c) the creation of a system which better supports reality testing of Western knowledge as well as studies of indigenous educational concerns; and (d) the encouragement of critical and competing Korean educational theories.

Suggestions such as those above are supported by international scholars who call for non-Western models of development and aspire to create a new international order based on such principles as independence, sovereign equality, and reduction in economic inequities between developed and developing countries. The structural constraints imposed on educational and social groups in peripheral nations by international relationships are real and powerful. Indeed, some scholars have concluded that the poorer of the developing nations are becoming more, rather than less, peripheral in their knowledge relations with the West, since research and development funding is still dominated by the pace-setting countries.

But caution is in order. Korean and other internationally oriented scholars raise a number of questions. Can national knowledge capabilities be generated without creating a climate of intellectual ethnocentrism? Appropriate recognition of cultural diversity is one thing but protectionist strategies which attempt to wall off national cultures from external influences are quite another. (After all, the history of nations which sought to exclude foreign ideas is rife with experience of economic and social as well as educational stagnation.) There is, moreover, a widely accepted premise that some knowledge, at least scientific knowledge, should be transnational. Indeed, perhaps universal? And what of the practical problems of the conditions and resources necessary to produce original research-based knowledge? Large investments in educational research tend to be found only in a handful of rich nations. Even in the rapidly industrializing country of Korea, scholars tend to play multiple roles and are afforded less time and fewer resources for specialized, original research than their counterparts in the large, highly industrialized nations.

However, Korea is rapidly acquiring world-class universities and research institutes and other knowledge-producing institutions which are counteracting the one-way flow of knowledge. The Korean higher education system has expanded rapidly (see Chapter II), with enrollment in higher education institutions in 1990 exceeding one-third of the 18-to-21-year-old cohort, a higher ratio of enrollment than among any of the other newly industrialized countries (NICs), e.g. Taiwan, Singapore,

Malaysia, and among many of the European countries. Responding to the growing demand for highly advanced research scholars in the various science and technological fields, full-scale graduate schools have developed during the 1980s. The Korean Institute of Science and Technology (founded in 1966) and the Korean Advanced Institute of Science (founded in 1961) were reorganized in 1981 to advance applied research and to provide local leadership in scientific and technological research and development. KAIST provides eight graduate programs, including mathematics, physics, chemistry, biological science and engineering. KAIST had graduated 5,200 students, including 495 Ph.Ds, as of July 1988 (Lee, SungHo, 1989).

Korea has done more than most other NICs to entrench local language as the scientific medium of communication. There is a range of postsecondary textbooks available at the undergraduate level, as well as established scholarly journals in Korean. Korean academic journals in English (e.g., *The Korean Journal of Policy Studies*) and research reports translated into English (such as economic and policy study reports) have a significant international circulation (see list of Korean publications in English in the Library of Congress). Nevertheless, Korean professors who expect to be promoted at top universities must publish their research abroad. The use of the indigenous language for higher education, combined with reliance on English for advanced scientific work, has been successful in the development of a strong local educational system and the emerging research community (Altbach, P. 1989:3-25). Compared to the other NICs, Korea has one of the most successful scientific infrastructures, including scientific materials in the indigenous language, forming a strong base for the development of a local knowledge system.

Such knowledge centers by themselves or as reinforced by regional knowledge networks may substitute for, as well as interact with, local and global knowledge networks. Indeed, Korea, particularly with respect to many less developed countries, is now playing a central role in the transnational knowledge system, producing and disseminating knowledge and technical assistance to several Asian and African countries.

Differing capabilities in the production and dissemination of knowledge will continue to exist in a system where resources are unequally distributed. Some nations, usually the older industrialized countries joined by a few of the newly industrialized countries, inevitably will be larger producers than others.

The lesson from the experiences of Korea in its interactions with the United States suggests that the focus should be placed not only on the source of knowledge but also on its critical acceptance. At minimum, a critical posture implies an attempt to understand the limitations of the knowledge in question, including its technical quality, the assumptions underlying its production, and the extent of local utilization. It also implies consideration of the comparability of environments in which the production and utilization of the knowledge take place.

*This Chapter has drawn heavily from Lee, Adams, and Cornbleth (1988).

Bibliography

Articles and Books

Adams, Don. "Cultural Pitfalls of a Foreign Educational Advisor." *Peabody Journal of Education*, 36 (May, 1959):338-344.

Using Korea as a case in point, Adams describes some of the cultural pitfalls facing an American working in that country. Differences are identified between Western and Korean value orientation in: (1) time orientation, (2) man-nature orientation, and (3) power and status orientation.

Adams, Don. "Problems of Reconstruction in Korean Education." *Comparative Education Review*, 3 No. 1 (February, 1960):27-32.

A historical review of major developments in Korean education with emphasis on conditions since 1945. The constraints on progress toward an education supportive of a modern industrial state are identified.

Altbach, Phillip G. and Selvaratnam, Viswanathan, eds. *From Dependence to Autonomy: The Development of Asian Universities*. Norwell, MA: Kluwer Academic Publishers, 1989.

This collection of descriptions of Asian higher education systems and universities includes a paper on the evolvement of contemporary Korean universities, and their influence on higher education.

Altbach, Phillip G. "Higher Education and Scientific Development: The Promise of Newly Industrializing Countries." In *Scientific Development and Higher Education*, 1-27, edited by Phillip G. Altbach, et al. New York: Praeger, 1989.

The opening chapter of a collection of case studies of newly industrializing nations. The world academic and research networks and their influence on the Third World scientific growth is explored in relation to contextual aspects such as industry, government, and multinational transfer of knowledge.

Bark, Dongsuh. "The American-Educated Elite in Korean Society." In *Korea and the United States,* 264-280, edited by Young-nok Koo and Dae-sook Suh. Honolulu: University of Hawaii Press, 1984.

The writer describes the activities of students who studied in United States after their return home and the contributions they had made to Korea's national development in the Chosun period, Japanese Colonial period, and the post colonial period to 1960.

Chung, S. G. "Theoretical Background and Practical Consideration on the Improvement of Instructional Method of Social Studies." *Journal of Social Studies Education,* 18 (1985):12-26. (in Korean)

Chung, S. G., Han, M. H., Song, Y. U. and Han, K. J. "Social Studies Instructional Model." In *Instructional Design* II, 80-98, edited by S. H. Shin and Y. G. Byun. Seoul: KEDI Press, 1973. (in Korean)

Chung, S. G. et al. *An Experimental Research on the Effect of Inquiry Teaching: An Application of the KEDI General Instructional System Model to Inquiry Teaching in Social Studies.* Seoul: KEDI Press, 1974. (in Korean)

Fulbright Student Advisory Service. "Korean Students in USA." *The Monthly Recruit,* 8 (July 1989).

Han, Myun-hee, Song, Yong-yi and Yoo, Kyeu-soo. *Social Studies Teaching in the Korean Elementary School.* Seoul: KEDI Press, 1986.

Huh, Unna. "Designing Education for the 21st Century: The Korean Experience." Paper presented at the Conference Learning for All, sponsored by U.S. Coalition for Education for All. October 30, 1992, Alexandria, Va.

A descriptive paper explaining KEDI's new instructional reform of 1973, includes the model design, objectives, flow chart describing the implementation processes and results of the follow up research.

Kang, S. P. "Cultural Interchange Between the US and Korea." In *Korea and America: Past, Present and Future*, 5-11, edited by Koo, Y.R. et al. Seoul: Pakyongsa, 1983. (in Korean)

Kim, Hyung Chan. "American Influence on Korean Education." *Educational Perspectives*, 21 (Winter, 1982):27-32.

Discusses American influence and cooperation on Korean education through via American Protestant missionaries and the American military government.

Kim, C. S. and Lee, H. W. "Curriculum and Instruction in Korean Schools As Observed By Foreign Specialists." *Kyoyukhak Yanku*, 18 (1980):82-99. (in Korean)

Kim, J. C. "The Influence of US Culture on Korean Educational System and Administration." *Journal of Asiatic Studies*, 10 (1967): 91-106. (in Korean)

Kim, Oaksook Chun. "Lessons for Korean Studies in the 80s and Beyond: Korean Studies Programs at UCLA." In *Dynamic Transformation: Korea, NICs and Beyond*. 452-466, edited by Gill-Chin Lim and Wook Chong. Seoul: Myung-Bo Pub. Co., 1990.

Kim observes that the renewed interest in Korea and Korean studies stems from the wish to uncover the so-called "extraordinary formula" for economic development. Caution is to be taken not to repeat arbitrary compartmentalization and over simplification of Korean history and cultural complexity. Innovative and collaborative work among all social scientists is Kim's concrete idea for ending the reductionism in Korean studies.

Kim, Seong-Jin. *Korea-USA Centennial 1882-1982*. Seoul: Yonhap News Agency, 1982.

Kim, Young-Chul. "Culture and Achievement." In *Factors in Achievement*, 61-85, edited by B. Chung and S. Lee. Seoul: Kyoyukchulpansa, 1985. (in Korean)

Korean Publishers Association. *Books and National Development*. Seminar Report, Academy House, Seoul, April 27-29, 1968. (ED 038145)

The following topics are presented by various authors: Role of books in developing Korea; Role of books as a tool of national development; Publishing in Korea; A historical survey; Problems of Korea's publishing industry; Textbooks in national educational development; and Development of the publishing industry.

Lee, Jong Gag, Adams, Don and Cornbleth, Catherine. "Transnational Transfér of Curriculum Knowledge: A Korean Case Study." *Journal of Curriculum Studies*, 20 no. 3 (1988):233-246.

The article reports on a qualitative research project, investigating the designation of inquiry teaching methods in connection with the national curriculum reform of 1973. The conclusion suggests modifications in the role taken by knowledge mediators, reality testing of Western knowledge in local context, and the development of a more self-sustained Korean academic community.

Lee, Sungho. "The Emergence of the Modern University in Korea." *Higher Education*, 18 (1989):87-116.

Masoner, Paul H. and Klassen, Frank H. "Analytical Case Study of the Korean Educational Development Institute." American Association of Colleges for Teacher Education, Final Report, University of Pittsburgh, 1979. (ED 207976)

This USAID-sponsored evaluation reviews the purposes, development and scope of activities of KEDI. The efficiency of KEDI as an organization is examined, major projects undertaken are reviewed and the overall impact of KEDI is assessed.

McGinn, N. R. "International Social Science or Cultural Imperialism?" *Harvard Educational Review*, 52 (1984):209-214.

NIERT (National Institute of Educational Research and Training). *Education in Korea 1979-1980*. Seoul: MOE, 1979.

Morgan, Robert M. "Instructional Systems Development in Third World Countries." *Educational Technology Research and Development*, 37 (1989):47-56.

Within the context of educational reform in developing countries attention is given to a project to improve the efficiency of Korean education. The project focused on a model of instructional systems design.

Morgan, Robert M. and Chadwick, Clifton B. "Systems Analysis for Educational Change: Republic of Korea." Final report, Department of Educational Research, Florida State University, Tallahassee, Florida, 1971. (ED 119374)

Korea's future manpower needs, cost-benefit of Korean education, and strategies for instructional and technology innovations are analyzed. Based on a system analysis, a number of changes and the creation of a major educational R&D unit (KEDI), intended to provide more relevant education at a lower unit cost, are recommended.

Moskowitz, Karl, ed. *From Patron to Partner: The Development of U.S.-Korean Business and Trade Relations*. Lexington, MA: Lexington Books, 1984.

Office of Planning and Management. "The Educational Sector Plan." In *The Sixth Five-Year Economic and Social Development Plan, 1987-1991*. Seoul: MOE, 1987.

Shin, Se-ho. *Studies on Impact of E-M Project on Korean Education*. Seoul: KEDI Press, 1984. (ED254533)

Describes the background, process, and effect of the Korean Elementary-Middle School Development Project, the major curriculum reform which was designed and carried out by KEDI, between 1973-1983.

Steinberg, David I. *Foreign Aid and the Development of the Republic of Korea: The Effectiveness of Congressional Assistance*. Washington, DC: Agency for International Development, 1985.

A USAID evaluation report on its aid to the Republic of Korea. The report describes ethnicity and culture, land reform, education, and the meritocratic state as the factors affecting economic growth and equity of Korea. The report concludes that the process of economic growth has been efficient but the process promoting equitable development is still flawed.

Unitarian Service Committee. "American Education Mission in Korea." Final Report, United Nations Civil Assistance Command Headquarters, Seoul, Korea, June 1953.

Werth, Richard. "Educational Development Under the South Korean Interim Government." *School and Society*, 69 (April 30, 1949): 305-309.

A brief survey of conditions and problems during the period when educational policy making was strongly influenced by the U.S. military presence in Korea.

Witherell, Ronald A. et al. *Korea Elementary-Middle School Pilot Project*. Washington, DC: US Agency for International Development, 1981.

USAID evaluation report on Korea's major curriculum reform, including project setting, objections, implementation and impact.

Yoo, Hyung-Jin. "Korean-American Educational Exchange." *Korea Journal*, (February 1983).

Dissertations

Chang, Duck Soo. "A Comparative Study of the Service Academies of Korea and the United States." Ph.D. dissertation, University of Pittsburgh, 1984.

Historical descriptive research on the influence of the service academy in the United States on the service academy of Korea. The study concludes that there were less influences from the U.S. than from Japan and that the great cultural gap between the U.S. and Korea led the same type of educational system to function in different ways.

Hwang, Bo Sung. "The Role of Higher Education in the Development in Korea: Planning, Ideology, and Problems (Social Capital Theory)." Part I and II. Ph.D. dissertation, University of Wisconsin-Madison, 1990.

A very wide coverage of the history of the whole educational system and economic development, with special detailed description of higher education. Documentation of the educational attainment of first and second generation of owners, corporate heads and managers of main industrial and commercial companies attempts to show a linear relation between higher education and industrial development.

Kim, Dong Koo. "American Influence on Korean Educational Thought During the Period of US Military Government, 1945-48." Ph.D. dissertation, University of Connecticut, 1974.

Examines the transfer of American educational thought to Korean education. Kim argues that although American ideology was applied in the areas of educational aims and objectives, instructional processes and educational administrative policies, some areas, including centralized administrative structure and formal types of instruction, experienced little change under American influence.

Kim, Hyun Soon. "A Cross-Cultural Study of Korean and American Teachers' Perceptions of Behavior Disorder as Related to Value Concepts." Ed.D. dissertation, Teachers College, Columbia University, 1982.

This empirical cross-cultural study of teachers' perceptions of children's behavior concludes that there were significant correlations between value concepts held by the teachers and their perceptions on children's behavior disorders.

Kim, Ji Soo. "Postgraduate Science and Technology Education in LDCs A Case Study of Korea." Ph.D. dissertation, Stanford University, 1984.

An investigation of the relationship between establishment of advanced science and engineering education institutions and industrialization. A cost-benefit analysis of investing in advanced education is also included.

Kim, So Oak. "Design of an Instructional Systems Development Process for Korean Education in Harmony with Korean Culture." Ph.D. dissertation, Ohio State University, 1983.

    Kim describes the Korean's way of thinking as deductive and the Western scientific thinking as inductive. A new instructional system proposed by this study considers both ways of thinking so as to meet the Korean cultural needs.

Lee, Gil Sang. "Ideological Context of American Educational Policy in Occupied Korea, 1945-1948." Ph.D. dissertation, University of Illinois at Urbana-Champaign, 1989.

Lee, Jong Gag. "Trans-national Knowledge Transfer: The Case of Inquiry Teaching Method in Korea." Ph.D. dissertation, University of Pittsburgh, 1986.

    A qualitative research of the transfer of instructional methods, as part of the "new educational system" (1973-1983), in particular, inquiry learning, from the U.S. to Korea. Theories of knowledge transfer are used to consider the U.S. knowledge systems' influence on Korean educational development.

Lippia-Tenney, C. "A Comparison Between the Perceived Needs of the Republic of Korea and Graduate Programs at United States Institutions." Ph.D. dissertation, University of Connecticut, 1981.

    Analyzes the perceived educational needs of high level manpower in Korea in eight selected discipline areas, and compares the needs with curriculum content of graduate programs in the same discipline areas in the U.S.

Nam, Byung Hun. "Educational Reorganization in South Korea Under the United States Army Military Government: 1945-1948." Ph.D. dissertation, University of Pittsburgh, 1962.

    A historical descriptive study on educational reorganization activities under the United States Army Military Government.

Park, Young Youl. "Education in South Korea: Schools in Transition." Ed.D. dissertation, University of California, Los Angeles, 1967.

This dissertation includes a description of education prior to 1945, postwar trends in Korean education, and the implications of education reform in the 1960s.

CHAPTER IV

Educational Policy Making and Planning

Korea since the establishment of the First Republic has been committed to centralization of institutions and processes of policy making and planning. Although there have been many proposals for decentralization, and a few experiments in decentralized planning, the political and bureaucratic power of the center has typically pervaded all branches of government.

Organization of Planning and Policy Process

Planning

Educational planning as part of the educational administration in Korea has existed since 1948, but it was not until 1953, in the wake of the Korean War, that more formalized, national, short- and mid-term planning became fully institutionalized.

The first national educational plan in the post-war period was a six-year plan for expansion of compulsory elementary education. From 1960 the government moved to implement centralized national planning by establishing a planning coordinator's office under the Prime Minister, an office of planning and management in each ministry and the new formal mechanism for comprehensive national planning--the Economic Planning Board (EPB). Since 1962 educational sectoral plans have been drawn up by MOE and the Economic Planning Board (EPB). The systematic five-year economic plans are drafted by the EPB with research and technical assistance provided by the Korean Development Institute

(KDI). The mechanism of educational planning has been closely linked with national and economic planning. Officials of the relevant ministries, especially the Ministries of Finance and of Home Affairs, as well ad hoc committees and outside experts, all participate in the educational planning process.

Since 1966, proponents of long-range educational planning have used publications, seminars, and lectures as means of motivating governmental agencies to participate in long-range planning activities. One of the more conspicuous attempts to shift responsibility for strategic educational planning away from the administrative arm was the establishment of the Council for Long-Range Educational Planning (CLEP) in 1968. CLEP, under the direct chairmanship of the Prime Minister, was designed to give high political visibility to comprehensive educational planning. The CLEP planners cooperated with agencies such as EPB, with liaison ministries of various departments, and with national and provincial education authorities (see Kim, J.C., 1971:6-8). Although many of the most distinguished educators of Korea were involved in its development, the CLEP educational plan was not adopted, partly because of financial limitations, but also more generally because there was an apparent gap between what the professional education planners intended and the feasibility of the plan in the view of the administrators responsible for plan implementation (Kim, Jong-Chol, 1985:82). The incumbent Minister of Education discontinued CLEP and in 1971 nominated in its place the 50-member Council of Educational Policy.

A few former members of CLEP worked for MOE on the first "Five-Year Educational Development Plan 1972-1976." However this plan, in contrast to the CLEP's plan, was less ambitious in terms of educational reform. Since 1972 MOE's educational development policies and planning processes have been supported by a new R&D unit, the Korean Educational Development Institute (KEDI). Similarly to KDI, which provides the Economic Planning Board (EPB) with research and technical assistance, KEDI provides MOE with research and educational development assistance and has the responsibility of producing mid-term and long-range educational plans.

The structure of national planning is shown in Figure IV.1. As may be inferred from the organizational chart the President and his immediate staff make a large proportion of important decisions. The President's advisers function as auditors of the performance of the cabinet.

Probably the most important of all advisory bodies is the Economic Planning Board (EPB) headed by a deputy to the Prime Minister. The EPB has been for the past 30 years the major influence in formulating economic and social policies including education.

Since 1982 some economic functions have been transferred to the ministries while EPB is still in charge of inter-ministerial coordination. The EPB's technical capabilities are supported by the Korean Development Institute (KDI), a research organization funded by the government but with considerable independence in operation.

Educational planning is built on multiple relationships among the President, his direct advisory staff on education at the "Blue House," the EPB and KDI, the Minister of Education, the senior staff of MOE, and KEDI.

Figure IV.1. Organizaton of National Education Planning

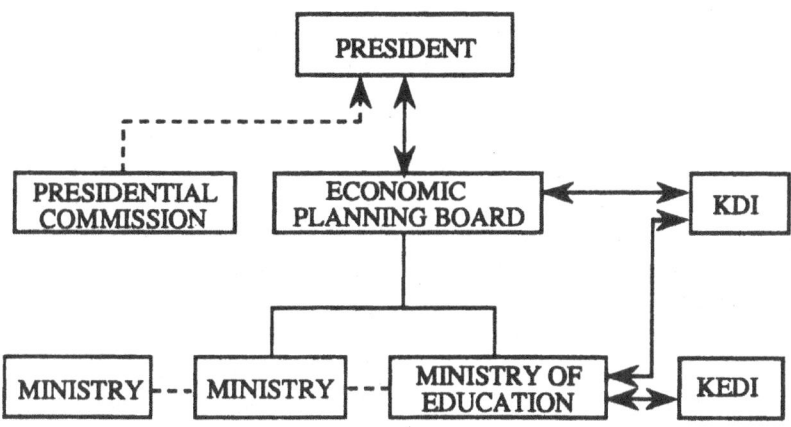

Advising MOE on policy and reform matters are various "Consultative Bodies." Created to extend professional and public participation in educational decision making, the first of several such bodies was organized in 1971. The Council for Educational Policy (CEP), an appointed body of 60 members, consists of seven subcommittees, which cover different sectors such as: private education, teachers' education, science education, and life-long education. By its charter, CEP's purpose is "to assist and advise the Minster of Education in regard to educational policies and development" (MOE, 1990:40). The difficulty in involving large consultative bodies in the setting of educational priorities is suggested by the fact that the Council has failed to "reach a consensus and [has] rarely received the necessary cooperation from other sectors," and as a result has had little effect on policy formation (Kim, Shin-Bok, 1990:394).

Within the Ministry the organization of planning is well established, and the process of planning routine operations is effective. As can be seen from the organizational chart of the MOE (Chapter II), the Bureau of Planning and Management is an integral part of the centralized educational adminstration. The bureau consists of three officers: a Legal Affairs officer, a Planning and Budget officer, and an Administrative Management officer. Within the scope of Ministry activities these three officers are the major planning actors. They translate laws, decrees and legally mandated educational plans into action, develop budget requests, and establish budget guidelines. On the Provincial and Metropolitan level, each "board of education" has a "Planning and Inspection Office," and each school district has a "Planning and Inspection Section." Coupling planning with inspection means that lower administration levels are mainly concerned with the implementation of educational planning.

The establishment in 1985 of the Presidential Commission for Education Reform (PCER), an ad hoc committee, constituted a renewed effort to move toward wider public and professional participation in planning and educational reform. The work of the PCER as an advisory body under direct Presidential oversight has again (as in the earlier case of CLEP) given prominence to the idea of strengthening the educational planning process by associating it with national priorities of economic development under Presidential leadership.

For the three years of the Commission's existence it has engaged in a number of activities such as surveys of educators and students, organization of conferences, and public hearings. The work of the Commission has involved wide participation of the executive and legislative branches as well as the public at large through extensive media coverage. The result was the publication of a major reform proposal (PCER, 1987).

One of the PCER's recommendations in their document, *Korean Education Reform Toward the 21st Century* (1987), pertains to the process of educational planning itself: "It is recommended that the process of policy formulation be open to ensure across-the-board participation." The Commission's own work on the educational reform proposals was "a significant departure from the earlier mode of policy formation, when it was limited to a handful of persons;" the Commission "allowed opportunities for educational practitioners to have their voices heard in the process of conceptualizing specific reform tasks" (PCER, 1987:230-231).

In 1989 the Government created the Presidential Commission on Education (PCE) as a permanent advisory body to the President and created the National Commission of Education (NCE) as a standing advisory committee to the Minister of Education. Lee Chong-Jae (1992) is critical of the latter but positive on the work of the former: "The NCE has been nothing more than a nominal commission, but PCE [has] proposed important policy developments. So far PCE [has] submitted 30 proposals" (p. 12). The Commission is "composed of 15 distinguished members representing various walks of life, 12 professional members, and five specialists" (MOE, 1990:41).

Policy Making

Formal education policies may take the form of legislated laws, Presidential decrees, or Ministerial orders. Evidence of the direction of educational policy may also be found in Presidential addresses and ministerial plans which translate policies into objectives and targets. Policies such as admission procedures, student quotas, tuition and fees, qualification criteria for elementary and secondary school teachers and higher-education faculty, revenue and expenditures, and equipment and facilities are all stipulated by law.

Organs of centralized administration were formed under the First Republic. The specific nature of planning and policy making mechanisms have continued to evolve. The governance of education is shared by the three branches of government: the executive, the congress and the courts. Under the executive branch, the Ministry of Education (MOE) is responsible for administration as well as policy making, planning and implementation.

As noted in Chapter II, local school districts were created in 1952, with limited authority to administer primary schools. At that time the Ministry of Education had not yet developed adequate control functions; therefore, even individual schools and universities could exercise some measure of autonomy. In the 1960s the government centralized educational administration further by abolishing the local Education Tax (1961) and enacting the "National Grant for Local Education Finance" law, whereby most local expenditures for education are allocated by MOE's general accounts. In 1964 MOE transferred what little authority the local "Boards of Education" had exercised to the newly created Provincial and Metropolitan Boards, appointed by MOE. Since then, centralized policy making and a top-down national planning approach has left little room for autonomy at the provincial or city level, let alone at the school level (Lee, C.J., 1992).

President Park not only consolidated policy making in the hands of his central government and made implementation mandatory, he also attempted to control the development of education, under the pressure of high social demand for higher education. Policy was couched in terms of maximizing educational investments through reduction of illiteracy and improvement of the quantity and quality of primary education. The internal efficiency of education also became a major policy concern and was translated into a campaign against corruption, imposition of a higher level of student discipline, and establishment of means for choosing students most likely to contribute to economic development (Kim, 1961:19).

The law of Temporary Exception in Education (1961) authorized the government to execute control policies in all national public and private institutions, such as fixing enrollment quotas and tuition, reorganizing schools and departments, introducing degree registration (all degree holders had to be nationally registered), and reappointing teachers and faculty. Although these policies were greatly modified by the Educational Policies Reappraisal Council under the Supreme Council for National Reconstruction (1964), the mechanisms of central control of higher education have been institutionalized since then.

The Private School Law (1963) finally brought this sector also under government supervision by strengthening controls over the private schools. Under the new law, private schools had to obtain government approval of budgets and appointments, and were made subject to central administrative control.

The most recent reform recommendations call for new local autonomy in educational administration. In early 1988, the National Assembly passed several acts concerning the realization of local autonomy in the near future. The amended Education Law stipulates that the local board of education should change its role and status from an executive body to a decision making body, and that the local assembly should appoint the board members who would then have the power to elect the superintendent. The Law also provides for considerable delegation of authority from the central government to local authorities, especially in the spheres of financial and personnel administration.

Under the Sixth Republic a greater tolerance of criticism and a better flow of information to the public has led to the growing importance of interest groups (e.g. Korean Federation of Trade Unions and Teachers' Union), and improved communication channels for influencing policy making. Also under the Sixth Republic more authority was transferred to the local people. Between 1961 and 1990 officials of the local councils were appointed. Since 1990, however, new legislation provides for election of local councils. Local autonomy presumably will extend to education for the amended education law seems to provide a legal base for a new policy of securing greater autonomy of educational administration at the local level. Election of board members is scheduled for April 1992.

Educational changes and reform have been dominated by three sets of policies which have persisted across the successive planning periods. These are (1) access and selection policies; (2) educational content and methods policies; and (3) administration and management policies. These policies can best be understood within the context of national educational planning.

Sequential Middle-Range Plans

Plans translate policies into objectives, targets, and programs to be implemented. Plans may be classified as short-term yearly plans, or as middle- and long-range plans. Yearly plans, largely the responsibility of MOE and the educational bureaucracy, are not reviewed here.

The 1954-1959 Planning Period

The first of the middle-range educational plans was the *Six-Year Plan for Completion of Compulsory Education (1954-1959)*. Its main objective was to implement the free compulsory education policy at the elementary school level; the target was a 96 percent level of enrollment of school-age population. The plan was mostly concerned with quantitative growth to be accomplished by building an additional 30,000 classrooms. It included, in addition to classroom expansion plans, an enrollment plan, a teacher demand plan, and a financial plan.

By the end of the planning period, 80 percent of all children 6 to 12 were enrolled in school. Most children who entered primary school finished in the prescribed time, reflecting a policy of automatic promotion. Education was largely allowed to expand in response to social demand. Despite a shortage of teachers and of accommodation facilities, resulting in crowded classrooms and double-shift schools, the three R's were successfully taught (see Adams, 1990). This ambitious plan was underfunded from the beginning, and secured only 38 percent of the funds requested by planners (McGinn, et al., 1980:37). However, in 1958 a law for educational funds for compulsory education was enacted to support the implementation of this plan.

The major educational outcomes by the end of the 1954-1959 planning period were: 1) provision of compulsory elementary education to children aged 6-12 and to adults through literary courses in "civic schools;" 2) further consolidation of control in order to bring all educational institutions under the administration of MOE, including the 12 provincial normal schools, and colleges of commerce and agriculture previously under the jurisdiction of other ministries; 3) transfer of the management of the education budget from the Ministry of Home Affairs to MOE; 4) creation of a preferential salary schedule (3 percent higher) for teachers (compared with other public servants); 5) re-education of teachers and principals in national ideology and military affairs, and 6) the establishment of patriotic youth movements in all secondary and tertiary education institutions.

At the secondary level a pragmatic educational policy was pursued which emphasized industrial and technical education under the slogan "one skill for one person." However, the low status of manual or blue-collar work made the policy impossible to implement throughout the 1950s. Parents and teachers continued to regard white-collar positions such as public administration and academic and political appointments as the more desirable professions, while resisting commerce, manual labor and agriculture as appropriate pursuits. As a result, emphasis continued to be placed on academic education which better prepared students for the entrance examinations to higher education than for manual work (McCune, 1966).

Higher education during this planning period was not controlled. While intensive planning activities took place on the lower level of education the consequences of the laissez-faire policy toward higher education in the 1950s created the basis of modern Korean higher education.

The 1962-1966 Planning Period

The first five-year *Educational Reconstruction Plan, 1962-1966* was prepared by the Ministry of Education under the Park Military Government. Since 1962 the educational five-year plans have been published in conjunction with the Five-Year Economic Development Plans.

In addition to compulsory education, this plan covered secondary and higher education. The problem of high numbers of unemployed college graduates and lack of skillful high school graduates was addressed by 1) fixing promotion rates to higher school levels and allowing for only a natural increase of enrollments resulting from expansion of school-age population, and 2) establishing secondary-level trade schools and five-year senior trade high schools, thereby reinforcing the commitment to vocational education and early preparation for work.

The annual policy statements of the President and Ministers of Education restated the major educational goals. The highest priority was economic development; second priority was given to national defense, followed by national unity and Korean cultural development (Kim, Jin-Eun, 1973:108).

These goals were translated into concrete policy measures through the design of a new curriculum for elementary and secondary education. Social-studies textbooks were revised, with a view to increasing the number of lessons devoted to anticommunism, nationalism, and patriotism.

At the higher education level the so-called "rearrangement plans" cut back the number of the 4-year institutions from 71 to 44 and reduced student quotas. These plans also increased the number of two-year junior colleges from 12 to 27, and replaced the normal schools (in 1962) with junior teachers' colleges.

Among the outcomes of this plan were a high school enrollment which exceeded predicted levels by almost 30 percent, and increase in the total number of higher-education students by 40 percent over 1960 figures.

The 1967-1971 Planning Period

The second five-year educational plan focused on improving the quality of education. In addition the plan also included 1) a plan for renovating the school system, and 2) a plan for promoting science and technical education.

On the elementary school level MOE submitted a school investment plan for classroom construction which was incorporated and budgeted through the Second Economic Development Plan (1967-1971). Facility expansion was designed to solve the "double-shift" problem, and to enable the achievement of the target of 95 percent enrollment in elementary education. The enrollment climbed above the target, reaching 98.1 percent in 1971.

The secondary education plan called for the increase of promotion rates from elementary to middle school to 51 percent, and from middle to high school to 75 percent.

In accordance with the Charter of National Education (1968), the open-door policy in education was extended in 1968 when the government cancelled the entrance examination to middle school. Under the new admissions policy, every student who completed primary education could advance to middle school, and would be allocated to a school within his/her district by computer lottery. Implementing the new policy meant increased enrollment in middle schools in excess of the planned targets.

With regard to higher education, the control of access by use of restrictive enrollment quotas did not produce the expected outcome. In order to control student selection more effectively, and in the name of quality control enforcement, MOE in 1968 decided to institute (as the military regime had done between 1962-1964) a national qualifying exam for college entrance. The "Preliminary Examination for College Entrance" was taken by high school graduates prior to the entrance examination given by the institution. The Ministry also imposed guidelines on curriculum development in colleges and universities, and initiated a series of policies, including government grants for expansion of scientific and technological facilities.

To develop technology and science in general, and scientific education in particular, a new Ministry for Science and Technology and a Bureau of Science Education within MOE were established in 1967. The establishment of a national science foundation and the increase of student quotas in science fields reflected a new commitment to the "scientification of the whole nation" in the interest of economic development.

The 1972-1976 Planning Period

The goal of the next plan, the so-called *First Five-Year Educational Development Plan (1972-1976)*, focused again on qualitative improvement of elementary and secondary education.

In 1972 the Minister of Education issued six directives, mandating 1) intensification of the system of national security education, 2) establishment of a new value education program, 3) implementation of science and technical education, 4) promotion of health and physical education, 5) introduction of earlier specialization in education, and 6) establishment of local adult schools to promote rural development (Hwang, B.S., 1990). This last directive was the most important, since the economic plan (1972-1976) called for strategies to balance economic growth between urban centers and rural areas. One such strategy was the promotion of "Saemaul Gyoyuk," new village and community education (see Chapter I).

Abolition of the entrance examination to middle school (1968), MOE control of high school entrance exams (1973) and assignment of students to high schools in their home localities by computer lottery made the system less exam-driven. However, from a school-management point of view the new access policy created classrooms with students of heterogeneous abilities, and generated further instructional problems (Kim, Shin-Bok, 1990). This condition gave impetus to the new curriculum and instructional methods reform, the "New Educational System."

The reform of instructional methods was directed by the newly established (1972) Korean Educational Development Institute (KEDI), following a national educational needs assessment carried out by an advisory team including experts from Florida State University. KEDI's first project was an elementary and middle-school curriculum design, known as the E-M Project (see Chapter III). This Project included (a) a wholly new curriculum; (b) a new instructional system emphasizing learner-centered instruction; (c) improved administration and management systems; (d) a continuing evolution plan; (e) new programs for teacher education and staff development; and (f) a follow-up and an evaluation plan (Unna Huh, 1991).

Additional programs were designed to improve effectiveness in the teaching/learning process and efficiency of delivery systems. A new management system was launched predicated on the slogan, "plan rationally, practice efficiently, and evaluate scientifically."

This plan, like the two preceding plans, seems not to have taken into account the manpower demands set out by the Five-Year Economic Plan (1972-76). All the estimates in the Educational Development Plan were based on demographic projections of population and aggregate labor-force requirement models (see Kim, S.B., 1973). Although statistics on population employment, labor force, and education are included in the Economic Plan, according to the Office of Planning and Management they did not receive proper attention in educational planning (Office of Planning and Management, 1972).

The 1977-1982 Planning Period

The next *Five-Year Educational Development Plan, 1977-1981* included the perennial goal of integrating educational planning more closely with manpower development needs. Both quantitative and qualitative development at the secondary and tertiary levels of the system received priority. Implementation of both KEDI's "New Educational System" and the "Pilot University Program" were implemented throughout the system.

Not a part of the original 1977-1982 educational plan, the so-called "July 30, 1980 educational reform" (see Table IV.1), was formulated under the new military regime in the transition period after the fall of Park's government.

During this planning period, the severe competition for higher education entrance and excessive use of private tutoring emerged as major social problems. To cope with the ever-growing high demand for advanced education the government took the following actions:

(1) The various technical and trade schools were reorganized into 2-year junior colleges. Their number increased to 128 in 1980, with a dramatic increase in junior college enrollment, from 62,000 in 1975 to 242,000 by 1985.

(2) The Preliminary Examination for College Entrance was replaced by the Scholastic Achievement Examination for College Entrance, abolishing the additional exam by individual institutions. In addition the new system assigned 30 percent-50 percent weight to the students' scholastic record from high school as part of the entrance criteria.

(3) Private tutoring was prohibited except in the arts and music.

(4) A new "Graduation Quota Policy" was introduced in 1980 in order to ease demand while continuing to control the number of graduates. Colleges could admit an additional 30 percent of applicants, but the number of students graduating had to be maintained at the same level as before.

Table IV.1

Chronology of Major Korean Education Policies and Reforms

1948 Establishment of MOE
 First national curriculum reform
1949 Promulgation of Education Law
1952 Establishment of free and compulsory elementary school education
1953 Second major curriculum reform
1961 "Rearrangement" plans: establishment of new standards for 4-year institutions; lowering of student quotas; establishment of new technical trade schools
1962 Abolition of normal schools; replaced by junior teachers' colleges
1963 Third major curriculum reform and textbook revision
 Establishment of 5-year senior vocational schools
1964 Discontinuation of national qualifying examination for entrance and graduation from colleges and universities
1965 Setting of new college and university quotas
1966 Inauguration of mandatory state registration of bachelor and master's degree holders
1968 Promulgation of the Charter of National Education
 Establishment of preliminary college entrance examination, administered by MOE, to be taken prior to entrance exam administered by colleges
 Abolition of middle school admission exam
1972 Establishment of 2-year Correspondence College
1973 Reform of high school admission system ("Equalization of High Schools"): all students to take a state qualifying exam, and to be assigned by lottery to a regional high school
 Implementation of "New Educational System:" elementary and secondary curriculum reform; school management reform
1979 Reorganization of all 2- and 3-year institutions into junior colleges

Table IV.1 continued

1980 "Educational Reform of July 30": abolition of individual college exams, replaced by national Uniform College Entrance Pre-examination; weight to be given to high school academic records in college admission procedures; establishment of college graduation quotas; ban on private tutoring
1981 Teachers' colleges upgraded to 4-year programs offering B.A. and B.Ed. degrees
Correspondence College upgraded to 5-year Korean Air and Correspondence University
Establishment of open colleges
Establishment of new Scholastic Achievement Examination for college admission
Fifth national revision of educational curriculum
1985 Establishment of the Presidential Commission for Educational Reform
1987 Publication of *Korean Education Reform: Toward the 21st Century*
1988 Reorganization of the Advisory Council for Educational Policy
Establishment of the Presidential Commission on Education as a permanent advisory body to the President
Reform of college admission procedures: students to apply first for college, then take exam
Abolition of college graduation quotas
Teachers' new recruitment and promotion program
1989 Private tutoring by college students is permitted, but the ban on private tutoring by school teachers continues

The 1982-1986 Planning Period

The *Five-Year Education Development Plan, 1982-1986* was developed to implement the July 30, 1980 reform proposals. This reform included three major plans: 1) reform of higher education; 2) establishment of the education tax to provide supplementary revenue; and 3) upgrading of teachers' education.

The Fifth Economic and Social Development Plan, 1982-1986 is the first plan that actually includes "social development" in its title. Reflecting a growing recognition of inequities in income and standards of living, this educational plan included the following measures: 1) Incremental implementation of compulsory free middle school education, starting with remote rural areas; 2) expansion of pre-school education and "head start" plans for disadvantaged rural and large urban student populations; 3) an increase in the number of comprehensive high schools.

The plan proposed a decentralization of the educational administration system by reorganizing the local "boards of education," linking them to a new more powerful elected local government. The upgrading of teacher education was successfully accomplished through changing the 2-year teachers' colleges into 4-year, first-degree granting programs. New inservice programs for teachers took effect, leading to an academic degree for a larger proportion of the teaching force and consequent improvement of teachers' professional status. Air and correspondence universities expanded, both in term of number of students and in terms of total share of broadcast educational programs, in accordance with the new "life-long education" plan. One of the most important events of this planning period was the establishment of the Presidential Commission for Educational Reform (1985).

The 1987-1991 Planning Period

The *Sixth Year Plan* emphasizes economic balance and adjustment, as well as growth. The EPB projects the move from a "medium" to a "large" economic power, expanding into new markets in Europe and in other developing countries. Internally, more attention was given to small and medium industry, and the development of industry outside the great urban centers. Sang-mok Suh (1987) popular demands have forced more attention to a greater balanced growth among economic sectors and among people of various income levels. A minimum wage was established in 1988, and a national pension program and extension of medical insurance to the entire population in 1989.

A major goal of the Sixth Five-Year plan is the "internationalization" of Korea, both through economic measures involving treater trade liberalization and through educational programs augmented foreign language instruction designed to increase the people's global awareness (Suh, 1987:15).

The Presidential Commission's report, published in 1987, had an impact on MOE planning during this period. MOE proposed:

(1) to improve school facilities in elementary and secondary education (as was earlier proposed in the 1982-1986 plan);

(2) to train 116,000 teachers at the elementary and secondary levels in new teaching methods (including "the teacher as a researcher" program);

(3) to reform completely basic science education (two percent of all science teachers would be sent overseas for refresher training, and one experiment assistant would be assigned to every six classes, instead of one to every 19 classes);

(4) to increase financial support for developing instructional materials and teaching aids;

(5) to strengthen computer education, including supplying 300 computers to each school;

(6) to implement changes in teacher recruitment and promotion policy (implementation was carried out with a certain urgency, in the face of teachers' moves to organize their new free union in 1988);

(7) to reform high school education in order to cope with ever-growing demand for higher education (this reform included reduction of enrollment in academic high schools, expansion of technical and vocational education programs, and expansion of vocational guidance for earlier career choice, as was earlier proposed in the 1972-1976 plan);

(8) to reform college admissions by requiring candidates first to apply to college, then take the entrance examination;

(9) to implement a new system of local educational autonomy.

A draft of the Republic's *Seventh Five-Year Plan* (1992-1996), published in the Fall of 1989, put primary emphasis on high-teaching industries in line with the reorientation of Korea's basic development policy. This new policy was influenced by three forces: first, the increased resistance of industrialized countries to Korea's exports; second, competition from other developing nations with cheaper labor; and third, growing popular pressure for improvement in the quality of life and expanded social welfare.

Policy/Planning/Practice: The Example of Vocational Education

Some observers hesitate to say that there has been considerable discrepancy between manifest policy statements and practice in education. Shin-Bok Kim (1990), however, has observed that

> though the government has promoted education as fundamentally contributing to economic development, major trends have not been toward skill acquisition and developmental values so much as toward the identification of students with the future of Korea as a corporate state. Korean education seems to have played a greater role in national political integration than in the development of skills and individual creativity. (p. 385)

Coping with the ever-growing demand for academic high school education remains a continuing problem in the beginning of the 1990s. Access policies and the student-selection system for high schools have been the target of governmental control throughout the past four decades. Policy statements throughout the 1960s, the 1970s and the 1980s, and all the five-year plans since 1962 have emphasized vocational education at the secondary level. Yet as we have seen in Chapter II, the balance in enrollment between vocational education and academic education never came close to achieving the targeted 70-30 ratio for 1980 (Paik, Hyun-Ki, 1963).

Since 1974, entrance examinations for vocational education candidates have been administered before the general eligibility test for high school entrance. Those who fail to gain admittance to vocational high schools are permitted to take the entrance examinations for academic high schools, and if they pass are assigned a high school within their residential district. As were earlier attempts, this policy was geared to encourage the better students to opt for vocational education.

An analysis of high school enrollments in 1990 exemplifies the distance between official policy and practice. The freshman quota for vocational education was 278,678 students, compared to 490,116 for academic education. In the same year, however, the number of candidates for the two kinds of high school education were 407,693 for vocational education, and 538,579 for academic education. This means that only 66.9 percent of applicants for vocational high school were accepted, compared to 90.9 percent of applications for academic education. Thus, although the government's long-standing policy has been to give priority to vocational education over academic education, access to vocational education continues to be highly restricted and the demand apparently is higher than the schools can supply.

Long-Term Educational Planning

Not until the Korean Development Institute (KDI) documents of the late 1970s and 1980s do there appear comprehensive long-range (10-15 year) national development plans. The first of KDI's long-range planning documents are *The Long-Term Prospect for Economic and Social Development 1977-1991* and *Korea Year 2000: Prospects on Issues for Long-Term Development*. These KDI national economic plans include sections on education. However, elaboration of the educational plans in these reports was undertaken by KEDI in two reports paralleling the KEDI reports: *The Long-Term Prospect for Educational Development 1978-1991* and *Korean Education 2000* (1985).

Another long-range educational plan also appeared in the 1980s, prepared by the Presidential Commission on Education Reform (PCER). This plan is contained in the document *Korean Education Reform Toward the 21st Century* (1987).

The 1977-1991 economic plan was stimulated by the belief that the country in the mid-1970s was on the threshold of a "new stage of industrialization." Although the focus of the Plan was clearly on economic changes, it also established long-term goals for technological and social development and social welfare. Fifteen-year projections and forecasts were set for the achievement of each goal. Considerable specificity was attempted, even to the description of the futures of major industries.

The KDI document *Korea Year 2000*, published in 1986, is remarkably different from the *Long-Term Prospect for Economic Development*. Though the two plans cover the same span of time, the later document, *Korea Year 2000*, makes no direct reference to the earlier one. Moreover *Korea Year 2000* has a minimum of forecasts, projections, or other quantification, and takes a very broad view of the institutional and sectional changes assumed to be necessary to bring Korea into the club of "advanced" industrialized countries.

Ad hoc presidential commissions produce important future-oriented documents which may be considered quasilong-term plans. The report *Realizing Korea's National Priorities for Economic Advance* (1988) looks at the need for economic restructuring through a more international development strategy, and societal change with emphasis on more social equity and higher quality of life. The recommendations and broad vision of the future found in this report are congruent with those found in *Korea 2000*.

KEDI, acting as the research, development and planning arm of the Ministry of Education, prepared *The Long-Term Prospect for Educational Development (1978-1991)*. This document does not formally identify itself as a parallel planning or policy document to *The Long-Term Prospect for Economic and Social Development*, but its complementary function is clear. Recognizing that Korea is "at the threshold of a highly industrialized society," the KEDI document assesses the current quality and relevance of education, recommends new goals, specifies changes in the educational system and sets specific quantitative targets.

Both KEDI and the Presidential Commission for Education produced reports looking toward the 21st century. KEDI's volume was called *Korean Education 2000*, and the Commission's volume was titled *Korean Education Reform Toward the 21st Century*. The Commission's report takes a broad, historical perspective of Korea's current educational conditions and problems. It proceeds to suggest reforms in various levels and functions of the educational system. For each major reform a set of strategies is identified (see Chapter VI).

The long-range plans serve (a) to inform and educate decision makers, bureaucrats, private sector leaders and, through media coverage, interested citizens and (b) to offer general, but not detailed, direction to the 5-year planning process, but (c) do not serve as a general reference for public servants and scholars as to ongoing educational change.

The plans give considerable attention to external and international contexts. Korean planners are very conscious of Korea's status among the countries of the world. Many of the educational research projects include a review of world trends in major European and North American countries, comparing and analyzing background, form, content and achievement of these reports, so that they can serve as points of reference for comprehensive planning in Korea (e.g., Kim, Yoon Tai, 1980).

The plans produced in the 1980s, looking forward to the year 2000 and beyond, give more attention to the need to improve quality of life than do earlier plans. Equity concerns are openly and extensively addressed for the first time. The recent long-term and medium-term planning reflects a higher level of participation by scholars, officials and citizens. Increasingly, long-term and medium-term planning is viewed by planners as indicative planning rather than "command" planning. Both long- and medium-term national planning over time has become more qualitative and less qualitative in the interpretation of needed educational changes.

Summary

Like most developing and newly industrialized countries, Korea has had varying levels of commitment to national planning and policy making. The faith in, and commitment to, formal centralized national educational planning peaked perhaps in the 1970s. The tradition of national five-year educational plans continues, but the discourse of policy makers increasingly emphasized decentralization in decision making (particularly for primary and secondary education) and institutional autonomy (particularly in higher education).

Although the trend toward decentralization and autonomy is apparent, there are also countervailing forces giving new recognition of the importance of national educational policies. Long-term (perspective) plans depicting the characteristics and national needs of Korea to the end of the 20th century and beyond describe the transformation of Korea from an industrial society to an information society. Such a change implies that information and knowledge are becoming the core of economic activities with a corresponding shift in employment to information industries.

Given the magnitude and pervasiveness of industrial, economic, and educational changes that are consequences of an information revolution, the use of national policy and planning instruments can be expected to be important. Industrial policy and public investments, including education, are being redefined in order to support and promote high-quality manpower, a requisite for the new technological focus. The national government may be expected to encourage directly through explicit policies and plans and indirectly through exhortation such educational priorities as:

- further development of science education at all levels;
- the widespread use of computers;

- renewed attention to the constraints of traditional teaching methods and examination system on creative thinking in schools;

- expansion of research and library facilities in higher education;

- exploration of university-industry linkages.

Such reforms are not, however, expected to only be the product of centralized educational control. The need for an increased role for the private sector in policy and planning is recognized. And, at all educational levels, local or institutional autonomy is expected to increase and direct government control is expected to be reduced. Increased autonomy is expected to lead to innovation and, particularly in higher education, competition and higher quality. The 1990s apparently will be a period when the status, necessity, and function of national-level planning and policy making will be subjected to intense debate.

Bibliography

Articles and Books

ACEID. *Inventory of Educational Innovations in Asia and the Pacific*, 46-54. Bangkok: Asian Centre of Educational Innovation for Development, 1981.

Reports from six of the participating countries of the Asian Programme of Educational Innovation for Development. An overview includes Korea's radio broadcasting curriculum for elementary schools, the Air and Correspondence High School, and the Air and Correspondence Junior College.

Adams, Don. "Education Change and Korean Development." In *Dynamic Transformation: Korea, NICs and Beyond*, 371-382, edited by Lim, Gill-Chin, and Chong, Wook. Seoul: Myung-Bo Publishing Company, 1990.

Adelman, Irma, ed. *Practical Approaches to Development Planning: Korea's Second Five-Year Plan*. Baltimore: Johns Hopkins University Press, 1969.

Bartz, Carl F. "Higher Learning in the Third Republic." In *Studies in the Development Aspects of Korea*, edited by Nahm, A.C. Kalamazoo, MI: Institute of International and Area Studies, Western Michigan University, 1969.

"Basic Education for the Real World: International Perspectives on Human Resource Development." Proceedings of the International Council on Education for Teaching, 28th World Assembly, 131-134. August 10-14, 1981, Cairo, Egypt. (ED 212 597)

The report from Korea addresses problems of primary and secondary education, such as overcrowded classes, impersonalized relationships between teachers and students, and a lack of emphasis on speech skills and mathematical concepts. A new system for evaluating students' achievement was a major concern at that time.

Blaise, Hans and Davidson, Philip. "Programming Future Changes in the Role of Universities in National Development Planning." In *Role of Universities in National Development Planning in Southeast Asia*, edited by Yip Yat Hoong. Singapore: Regional Institute of Higher Education and Development, 1971.

Byong-Sun, Kwak. "The Impact of the Korean Education Development Institute (KEDI) in Curriculum Development." *Studies in Educational Evaluation*, 13 No. 3 (1987):307-18.

Byun, Hong Kyoo and Others. "Interface Between Education and State Policy: Redesigning Teacher Education Policies in the Context of a Preferable Future." *Education and Polity*, No. 3, Bangkok: UNESCO, Regional Office for Education in Asia and the Pacific, 1988.

Focuses on a number of conceptual issues in teacher education. Recommendations include policy tasks and strategies for a more "humanistic" preservice and inservice training of teachers.

Caiden, Gerald E. and Jung, Yong Duck. "The Political Economy of Korean Development Under the Park Government." In *Administrative Dynamics and Development: The Korean Experience*, edited by B. W. Kim, D. S. Bell, Jr. and C. B. Lee. Seoul: Kyobo Publishing, Inc., 1985.

Chong, T'ae Si. "Korean Education: Yesterday and Tomorrow." *Koreana Quarterly*, 12 No. 3 (Autumn, 1970):66-70.

A review of 25 years of educational growth and identification of the growth targets expressed in the Long-Range Educational Development Plan of Korea (1972-1986).

Chung, Bom mo. "The Role of Government in Higher Education Country Report: Korea." In *The Role of Government in Asian Higher Education Systems: Issues and Prospects*, 51-58, Reports from the 4th Hiroshima International Seminar on Higher Education in Asia, November 25-28, 1987. Hiroshima, Japan: Hiroshima University, Research Institute for Higher Education, 1988. (ED 296 635)

After brief summary of higher education policy change since 1950s, the author describes government control and autonomy of higher education focusing on the introduction of university autonomization policy in 1987.

Chung, Tae Soo. *From Educational Innovation to Classroom Innovation.* Seoul: Bo Jin Jae, 1983.

Cole, David C., and Young, Woo Nam. "The Pattern and Significance of Economic Planning in Korea." In *Practical Approaches to Development Planning: Korea's Second Five-Year Plan*, edited by Irma Adelman. Baltimore: Johns Hopkins University Press, 1969.

Curriculum Committee of Korea Educational Society. *Curriculum Study.* Seoul, 1984.

Dilmy, Anwari. "Nature and Functions of the Regional University." In *Roles of Universities in Local and Regional Development in Southeast Asia*, edited by Yip Yat Hoing. Singapore: Regional Institute of Higher Education and Development, 1973.

Economic Planning Board (EPB). "First Five-Year Plan For Technical Development." Supplement to *First Five-Year Economic Development Plan 1962-1967.* Seoul: EPB, 1962.

Fisher, Joseph. *Universities in Southeast Asia: An Essay on Comparison and Development.* Columbus, OH: Ohio State University Press, 1964.

Han, Sunjoo, ed. *Korea in the Year 2000: Prospects for Development and Change.* Seoul: Asiatic Research Center, Korea University, 1986.

Hardjasoemantri, Koesnadi. "Problems of Expansion Versus Consolidation of Higher Education in Southeast Asia." In *The Growth of Southeast Asian Universities: Expansion Versus Consolidation*, edited by Amnuay Tapingkae. Singapore: Regional Institute of Higher Education and Development, 1974.

Hasan, Parvez and Rao, D. C. *Korea: Policy Issues For Long-Term Development.* A World Bank Report. Baltimore: Johns Hopkins University Press, 1979.

Heslop, Yvonne. "Strategies and Innovations for Nonformal Education for Women." *Asian South Pacific Adult Education Courier* 46 (July, 1989):96.

Hilowitz, Janet. "Education and Training Policies and Programmes To Support Industrial Restructuring in the Republic of Korea, Japan, Singapore and the United States." Training Discussion Paper. Geneva: International Labour Office, 1987.

Offers an intercountry comparison of structural and technological change. Of particular interest is the examination of the range of formal and informal linkages of schooling and training with industry.

Hong, Yi-Sup. *Korea's Self-Identity.* Seoul: Yonsei University Press, 1973.

Hong, Woong-sun; Lee, Yung-dug, Shin, Se-ho, Han, Jong-ha and Park, Kyung-sook. *Final Report of the Elementary-Middle School Development Project.* Occasional Paper 83-4. Seoul: KEDI Press, 1983.

Reports on the objectives, management, instruction and curriculum development associated with the major 1973 reform of elementary and middle school education. The separate evaluation of the implementation by KEDI and USAID are reported, with the statistical analysis and major results. The appendix includes examples of Teacher's Guide and Student's Workbook, as well as an article by Paul H. Masoner.

Hwang, Byung-Tai. "The Status and Issues of Higher Education Finance in Korea." In *Comparative Study of University Finance in Asia. An International Seminar on University Finance.* Seoul: Korean Council for University Education, 1986.

Hwang, Chul-Su. "Primary Education in Revolution?" *Korea Journal,* 9 No. 7 (July, 1969):18-20.

The abrogation of the middle school entrance examination in 1969 and the assignment of all applicants by lottery is a significant change since Hwang claims that the entrance examination had been one of the main factors delaying the reform of elementary education.

Jayasuriya, J.E. *Education in Korea: A Third World Success Story*. Colombo, Sri Lanka: Associated Educational Publishers, 1980.

Jo, Sun Hwan and Seong, Yawang Park, eds. *Second Five-Year Economic Development Plan 1972-1976*, Basic Documents and Selected Papers. Seoul: Sogang University, 1972.

Jung, Song-Hyon. "Political Reform's Impact on Foreign Business." *Korea Business World*, 3 (July 25, 1987):44-45.

KanKuk, Dahah, Gyo Yuk Hyup and Ui Hoe. *Direction of Higher Education Development in Korea*. Seoul: UNESCO, Korean National Commission, 1983.

Kim, Hogwon. "Experimentation in Education, Mastery Learning in Korea." *Studies in Educational Evaluation*, 1 (1975):13-22.

Kim, Jongchol. "Long-Range Educational Planning in Korea." *Korea Journal*, 11 No. 10 (1971):5-11.

Kim, Jongchol. "Educational Planning: Status and Issues in the Republic of Korea." *Journal of the International Society of the Educational Planners*, 2 No. 4 (March, 1976):29-36.

Kim, Jongchol. "Issues of Higher Education in 1980s: The Case of Korea." In *Higher Education for the 1980s: Challenges and Responses*, 129-139. Report of the Hiroshima International Seminar on Higher Education in Asia. January 29-31, 1980. Hiroshima, Japan. (ED 207399)

Contends that higher education in Korea is undergoing transition and transformation that challenges its present and future directions and policies. Issues discussed include: government control vs. institutional autonomy, support of private higher education, and the design of a new model of financing higher education that addresses efficiency and equity.

Kim, Jongchul. "Higher Education Policies in Korea, 1945-1983." *Korea Journal*. (October 1983).

Kim, Nan Su. *Korean Education in Research Perspectives*. Seoul: Jong Gak Publishing Co., 1985. (LA 1331 K517 1985)

This book contains seven papers which report empirical research. Papers focus on citizenship education, planned change in higher education, academic performance in higher education, the issue of quality in higher education, universalization of primary education, and the restructuring of educational administration.

Kim, Shin Bok. *Development Planning Theory*. Seoul: Park Yung Sa, 1983.

Kim, Syng-han H. ed. "A Perspective on the Future Development of Distance Higher Education in Korea." Proceedings of the 4th Symposium, Seoul, Korea, December 12, 1986. (ED 286 489)

This symposium explored the future development of the Korea Air and Correspondence University by addressing the topics of curriculum and faculty development, distance higher education and service for students, and the introduction of new technology for distance education.

Kim, Yoontai and Yun, Chungil. *Manpower Projection and Strategies 1979-91*. Seoul: Korean Educational Development Institute, 1984.

Kim, Young Soo. "Legitimacy: Freedom Fighters and the Succession to Independent Spirit." In *The Identity of the Korean People*. Seoul: Research Center for Peace and Unification, 1983.

Koh, Harold H. "The Early History of U.S. Economic Assistance to the Republic of Korea, 1945-1955." Mimeographed. Cambridge: Harvard Institute for International Development, September 1975.

A useful summary of U.S. involvement in educational planning, and a full evaluation of the American effort to restructure the educational system and to democratize administration.

KCUE (Korean Council for University Education). Current Issues in University Education of Korea and Japan. Proceedings of the 6th International Seminar. Seoul, South Korea, July 7-8, 1987. (ED 291266)

This volume contains seven articles on higher education by different authors. The subjects cover such problems as university administration, social function of universities, student guidance, teaching and curriculum, and the research functions at a university.

KCUE. *Korean Higher Education: Its Development, Aspects and Prospect.* Seoul: KCUE, 1988.

Particularly valuable as a general overview of the development of Korean higher education from early times. This work identifies contemporary problems and discusses directions of possible reform.

KCUE. *Statistical Indicators of Korean Higher Education.* Seoul: KCUE, 1989.

KDI (Korea Development Institute). *The Fifth Five-Year Economic and Social Development Plan 1982-1986.* Seoul: KDI, 1982.

KDI. *Korea Year 2000.* Seoul: Education Planning Board, 1985.

KDI. *Long-Term Prospect for Economic and Social Development 1977-91.* Seoul: KDI, 1978. (HC467 H253 1978)

The long-term prospect on economic and manpower development is suggested along with prospects for overall development for the period of 1977-91. Contents include attention to population growth and structural change, improvement of education, and employment and labor management relations which includes manpower development.

KEDI (Korea Education Development Institute). "Qualitative Improvement of Elementary and Secondary Education." Seminar paper. Seoul: KEDI Press, 1983.

KEDI. *The Long-Term Prospect for Educational Development, 1978-1991.* Seoul: KEDI Press, 1979.

KEDI. *Educational Indicators in Korea*. Seoul: KEDI Press, 1989.

Kraft, Richard H. P. "Implementing Cost-Benefit Research in Education." Paper presented at the annual meeting, American Educational Research Association, April 3-7, 1972, Chicago, IL.

Kwak, Byong-sun. "The Impact of the Korean Education Development Institute (KEDI) in Curriculum Development." *Studies in Educational Evaluation,* 13 (1987):307-318.

Kwak, Byong-sun; Ham, Se-jyung and Kim, Hong-won. *The Preliminary Study for Improving Korean Primary Education.* Seoul: KEDI Press, 1986.

Lee, Chong Hwan. "The Sixth Economic and Social Development Plan of Korea." *Monthly Review,* 20 (December 1986).

Lee, Hahn Been. *Korea: Time, Change and Administration.* Honolulu: East-West Center Press, 1968.

Lee, Jeoung-Neun, et al. "Current Status of Vocational Education and Training in the Republic of Korea." Surveys and Studies in Adult Education. Seoul: KEDI Press, 1979.

Lee, Ki Baik. *A New History of Korea.* Cambridge, MA: Harvard University Press, 1984.

Lee, Kye Woo. *Human Resources Planning in the Republic of Korea. Improving Technical Education and Vocational Training.* Washington, DC: World Bank, 1983.

Lee, Yung Dug. *KEDI's Instructional Strategies.* Paris: UNESCO, International Institute for Educational Planning, 1977.

Lee, Yung Dug. "Tasks for the Qualitative Improvement of Primary and Secondary Education." Paper presented for a seminar on the quality of primary and secondary education. Seoul: KEDI Press, 1983.

Masoner, Paul H. and Klassen, Frank H. "Analytical Case Study of the Korean Educational Development Institute." Final Report. Washington, DC: American Association of Colleges for Teacher Education, 1979.

McCune, Shannon. *Korea: Land of Broken Calm*. Princeton, NJ: D. Van Nostrand Company, 1966.

Min, Kwan Shik. *Innovation and Path of Korean Education*. Seoul: Kwang Myung Chul Pan Sa, 1975.

Ministry of Education (MOE). *Development Direction of School System*. Seoul: MOE Press, 1981.

MOE. "Korean Educational Innovations in the 1980s." White Paper of Educational Administration. Seoul, 1983.

Moon, Yong-Lin. "Facts About Education Present No Shangri-La: Korea's Examination Hall Mars Schooling." *Korean*, 5 No. 2 (1991):30-45.

An overview of the educational system, including administration and finance as of 1987. A comparison of public and private education in Korea, as well as comparing Korea's achievements such as school enrollment ratio, with other major developed countries, concludes the section on schools and students. The section on curriculum analyzes and reproduces MOE's national revised curriculum of 1987.

"Moral Education in Asia." Report of a Joint Study on Moral Education in Asian Countries. Tokyo, Japan: National Institute for Educational Research (1981). (ED 199126)

The report from the Republic of Korea provides an overview of the country's five stages of development of moral education. The objective of moral education (circa 1980) is to produce Koreans who will contribute to the reconstruction and creation of national culture by perfecting self-realization. Curriculum and instructional materials, teacher preparation, and problems in moral education are also discussed.

Office of Planning and Management. *The Education Sector Plan, 1987-1991*. Seoul: MOE, 1987.

Park, Chong-Yul, Kim, Myung-Won, Lee, Jae-Kee and Ahn, Byung-Kyu. *A Study on Higher Education in Korea.* Seoul: Korean Council for University Education, 1986.

Park, Chung-Hee. *Our Nation's Path: Ideology of Social Reconstruction.* Seoul: Dong-A Publishing Company, 1962.

PCER (Presidential Commission on Educational Reform). *Korean Education Reform Toward the 21st Century.* Seoul: Ministry of Education, 1987.

The Asia Society. *Handbook on Korean-U.S. Relations.* New York: The Asia Society.

UNESCO. "Higher Education in Asia and the Pacific." Bulletin No. 24, Bangkok: UNESCO Regional Office for Education in Asia and the Pacific, 1983.

UNESCO. "Implementing Curriculum." A Symposium of Experiences for the Asian Region. Bangkok: UNESCO Regional Office for Education in Asia and the Pacific, 1977.

UNESCO. "Research to Improve Teaching-Learning Practices." Report of a UNESCO Regional Meeting (Inchon, Republic of Korea, October 10-18, 1983). Bangkok: Asian Centre of Educational Innovation for Development, 1984.

UNESCO. "In Search of New Models of Secondary Education." Report of a Task Force Meeting. Jakarta, Indonesia, July 26-31, 1984. Bangkok: UNESCO Regional Office for Education in Asia and the Pacific, 1985.

Wilson, Donald C. et al. *Asia and the Pacific: Issues of Educational Policy, Curriculum, and Practice.* Vancouver: British Columbia University, 1990.

Wilson, Joan B. "School Program Assessment in the Republic of Korea: Changing Strategies in an Era of Reform." Paper presented at the annual meeting of the American Educational Research Association, April, 1990, Boston, MA.

Examines the recommendations of the Presidential Commission on Educational Reform on the evaluation and testing of students. Progress in redesigning curriculum and preparation of new university entrance examination are reviewed.

You, In Jong. "Guidelines for the Redesign of Teacher Education." Paper Presented at the World Assembly of the International Council on Education for Teaching, Washington, DC, 1983.

Yoon-Tai, Kim and Chung-il, Yun. *Manpower Projection and Strategies 1979-1991*. Seoul: KEDI Press, 1984.

This report examines human resource development in Korea from 1961-78 and projects demand and supply of manpower through 1991. The projected gap is identified and strategies are suggested to bring supply into line with demand.

Dissertations

Cho, Young Il. "A Study of Administrative Decision-Making Process for Educational Policies in the Korean Central Government." Ph.D. dissertation, University of Nebraska-Lincoln, 1982.

An analysis of decision making process in the Korean educational system by using Sharkansky's system model suggests that the decision making process can be characterized as a rational and closed system due to limited public participation, professional involvement and insufficient compromises among decision makers and interest groups.

Hentges, Harriet Ann. "The Repatriation and Utilization of High-Level Manpower: A Case Study of the Korea Institute of Science and Technology." Ph.D. dissertation, Johns Hopkins University, 1975.

Kang, Moo Sub. "Design of a Cooperative Educational System for Developing Higher Technical Manpower in Korea." Ph.D. dissertation, Ohio State University, 1982.

Kim, Jae Bum. "The Effects of Selected Independent Variables in Determining Nationwide New Enrollment Quotas of Secondary School Teacher Training Institutions in the Republic of Korea." Ph.D. dissertation, Florida State University, 1973.

Kim, Jin Eun. "An Analysis of the National Planning Process for Educational Development in the Republic of Korea, 1945-1970." Ph.D. dissertation, University of Wisconsin-Madison, 1973.

Kim, Myung Han. "The Educational Policy-Making Process in the Republic of Korea: A Systems Analysis." Ed.D. dissertation, University of North Texas, 1974.

Kim, Shin Bok. "A Systemic Sub-Optimization Model For Educational Planning: With Application to Korea." Ph.D. dissertation, University of Pittsburgh, 1973.

Kim, Yoo Bae. "Forecasting of Economic Structure and the Manpower Requirements in the Rapidly Developing Economy: A Case Study of Korea." Ph.D. dissertation, University of Illinois at Champaign-Urbana, 1977.

Kim, Young Chul. "An Analysis of Selected Variables Affecting the Student Demand for Higher Education in the Republic of Korea." Ph.D. dissertation, Florida State University, 1978.

Kim, Yong Hyun. "Nonformal Education and University Participation: Planning Considerations for Universities of Korea." Ed.D. dissertation, University of Massachusetts, 1984.

Kwak, Soo Il. "Applying the Systems Approach to an Educational System of the Republic of Korea." Ph.D. dissertation, University of Washington, 1974.

La, Ki San. "A Study of Frames of Reference and Preferences Toward Enrollment Policy in Higher Education in Korea." Ph.D. dissertation, University of Pittsburgh, 1986.

This study argues that bureaucratic decision makers and experts significantly differ in their frames of reference and preference toward enrollment policies in higher education. While bureaucrats address enrollment issues in terms of the total society, provosts express the capacity of educational institutions and experts are concerned with equality in education.

Lee, Chongjae. "A Goal Programming Model for Analyzing Educational Input Policy With Application for Korea." Ph.D. dissertation, Florida State University, 1974.

Lee, Hae Young. "The Decline in Employment Opportunities for New College Graduates in Korea: Policy Perspectives." Ph.D. dissertation, University of Maryland-Baltimore County, 1990.

Min, Leo Yoon-Gee. "A Mathematical Programming Model of Educational Planning with Quantitative and Qualitative Sub-Objectives: A Case Study of Korea." Ph.D. dissertation, Stanford University, 1971.

Song, Byung Soon. "Comparative Study of Ideological Influences on Educational Theory and Practice in North and South Korea." Ph.D. dissertation, Wayne State University, 1974.

Song, Yong-Sup. "Development of a Governance Model For Higher Education with a Special Reference to Korea University." Ed.D. dissertation, Texas Tech University, 1975.

Sung, Chung Wha. "Decision Analysis for the Educational Systems in Korea." Ph.D. dissertation, Florida State University, 1977.

Tchoi, Chong Il. "Dynamic Analysis of Korea's College-Educated Manpower Policy and Design of the Stable Manpower Production System." Ph.D. dissertation, University of Minnesota, 1984.

This study is an application of the cobweb manpower model to Korean college educated manpower policy. This model is designed to eliminate the shortcomings of a manpower requirements approach or a rate of return model.

Wilson, Elizabeth Cecil. "The Problem of Value in Technical Assistance in Education: The Case of Korea, 1945-1955." Ed.D. dissertation, University of Maryland, College Park, 1959.

CHAPTER V

Education, Economic and Social Change

In spite of being economically impoverished at the time of achieving national status, cut off from commerce and interchange with North Korea, and devastated by the Korean War, South Korea nevertheless underwent rapid economic development in the 1960s. Its aggressive approach to industrialization and its qualitative improvement of human resources are recognized worldwide as remarkable achievements. Because of its economic advancement, Korea by the 1970s had distinguished itself from the main population of developing countries and had joined such countries as Taiwan, Singapore, Brazil, etc., in being classified as a newly industrialized country (NIC).

Educational Growth

The Korean government in 1948 through its constitution (Article 16) specifically guaranteed equal opportunity for education and free, compulsory education. The Education Law enacted in 1949 also stipulated compulsory education, giving all citizens the right to six years of primary education. Full implementation of these provisions was not realized until well after the armistice of the Korean War; however, by 1953 the enrollment ratio of the 6-11 year old age group had reached 76 percent. The Compulsory Education Accomplishment Plan (1954-59) resulted in a primary enrollment ratio of 96 percent by 1959. This rapid increase was realized even under the severe limitations in the fiscal capability of the government. Within this limited capability, however, most public financial resources were put into primary education. Primary education expenditures comprised approximately 70 percent of the central government's budget in the 1950s.

At the secondary level, increase in enrollments was significant, if less dramatic. In 1950 the secondary school enrollment ratio was 16 percent. Growth through successive decades resulted in an universalization of secondary education by 1990. Higher education, restructured and reorganized after independence from Japanese colonial occupation in 1945, evolved rapidly with both public and private support. By 1990 over one-third of the 18-22 age cohort were enrolled in colleges and universities. Higher education enrollments had grown nearly 20 fold since 1945 and by 1990 Korea ranked third in the world in enrolled students per 100,000 population. Table V.1 shows the rapid growth of all levels of education and indicates the high level of education that had been achieved prior to industrial take-off in the 1960s. Universal primary education preceded the period of sustained economic expansion and the educational foundation for national development was further strengthened by a secondary education system which enrolled approximately one-third of the corresponding age cohort and a higher education system which, although highly restricted, had begun what was to be a long period of growth. Figures V.1 and V.2 show the decrease in illiteracy and growth in enrollment ratios since the 1960s.

The expansion of the educational system was made possible only through the involvement of the private sector. With its limited resources and its commitment to primary education the government had to rely on private institutions to accommodate much of the demand at the secondary and higher levels. In 1945 private secondary schools made up only 17 percent of the total. By 1957 the percentage had increased to 40 percent. The private sector has been important throughout the growth of higher education. Since the mid-1960s private colleges and universities have accounted for over 70 percent of the enrollments. Education was an investment which often brought the investors profit and nearly always brought them status and honor.

Figure V.1 Illiterates as Percentage of Total Population (Age 15 and over)

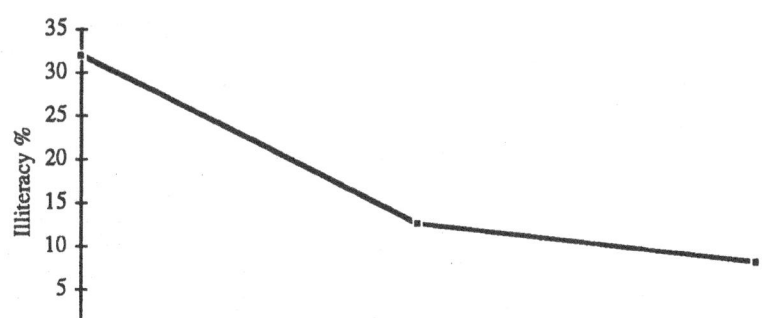

Source: 1966 and 1970 data from *1977 Compendium of Social Statistics* (1980). U.N., Department of International Economics and Social Affairs Statistics Office, New York.
1987 data from *World Quality of Life Indicators* (1989). ABL-CLIO, Inc., Santa Barbara, California.

Figure V.2 Total Enrollment Ratios by Level

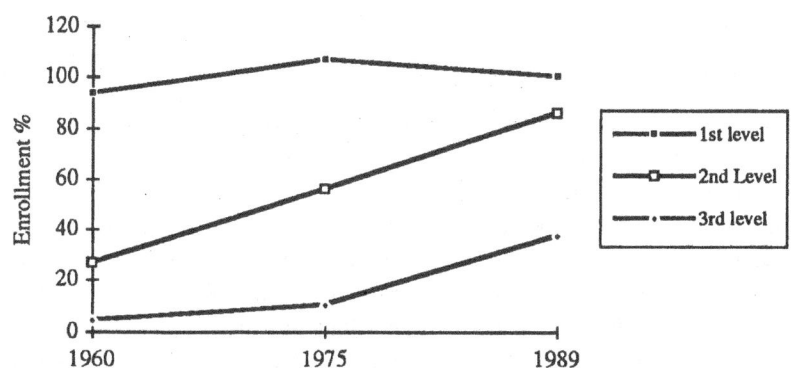

Source: 1960 data from UNESCO (1976). *Unesco Statistical Yearbook*, Paris.
1975 data from UNESCO (1989). *Unesco Statistical Yearbook*, Paris.
1989 data from UNESCO (1990). *Unesco Statistical Yearbook*, Paris.

Table V.1

Enrollment Ratios and Percentages of GNP Spent on Education

Year	Enrollment Ratio (percent)				Percentage Educational Expend. to GNP
	1st Level	2nd Level	1st + 2nd Level	3rd Level	
1950	83	16	52	---	---
1955	89	29	61	---	---
1960	94	27	65	4.6	4.0
1965	100	35	74	6.2	1.8
1970	100	42	75	7.2	3.5
1975	100	56	81	9.6	2.2
1980	100	76	92	14.8	3.4
1985	99	94	95	31.6	4.8
1987	94	95	94	33.9	4.5

Source: UNESCO, *UNESCO Statistical Yearbook (1963-1988)*.

In the 1950s and 1960s, education expanded more rapidly than the economy. In this condition Korea was little different from several other developing countries. Korea, however, unlike many countries, was able to achieve a well-developed system of primary education prior to large-scale efforts at economic modernization. Indeed, growth in all levels of education in Korea preceded the period of rapid economic growth. During most of the post World War II period, Korea's education level has been similar to that of countries with a much higher economic level. McGinn et al. (1980) note that: ". . . a graph plotting a human resources development index (based on proportion of age group enrolled in secondary and tertiary level institutions in the early 1960s) against GNP showed Korea furthest from the regression line of all the 73 nations compared, in the direction of more education than would be expected given GNP" (p. 27). Much of this growth was accomplished despite a low per capita income and relatively low government support for education.

A comparison of Korea's educational growth during its period of industrial development with the educational growth patterns of other newly industrialized countries is provided in Figure V.3. It can be seen that all NICs have highly developed primary levels of education prior to the time of industrial take-off. However, enrollment ratios at the second

Figure V.3 Total Enrollment Ratios by Levels and Stages of Development

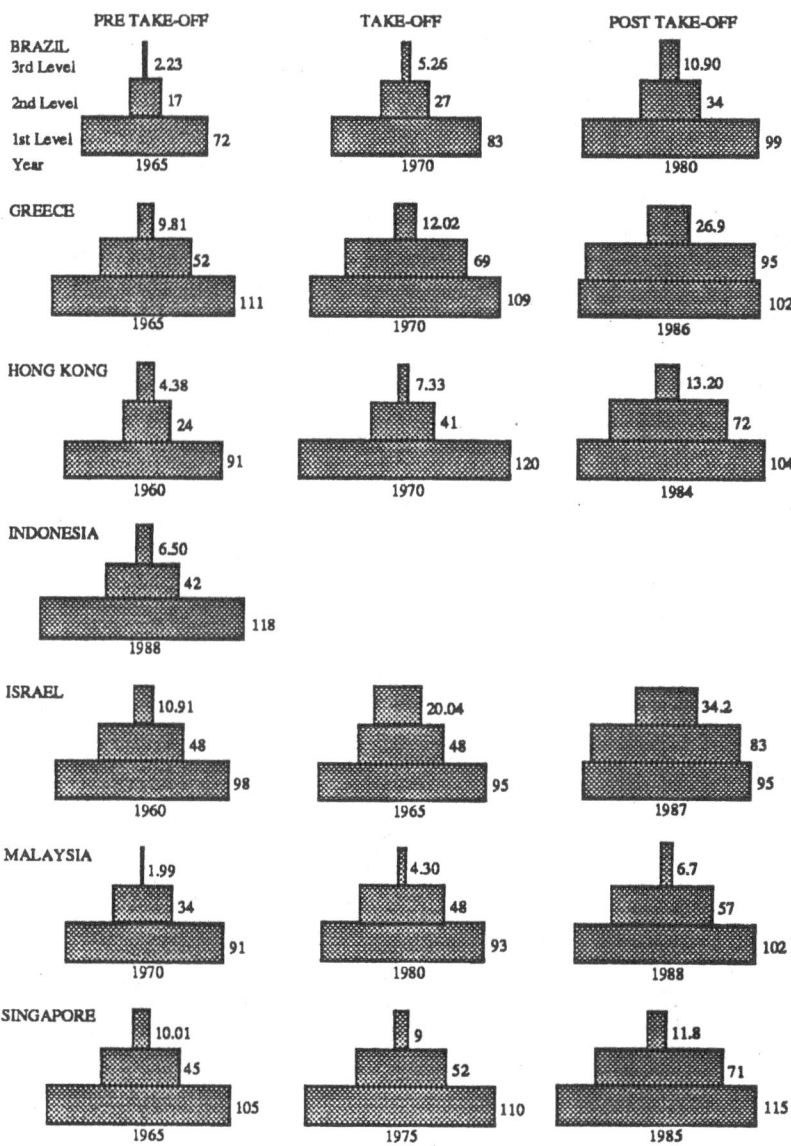

Figure V.3 Total Enrollment Ratios by Levels and Stages of Development (cont'd)

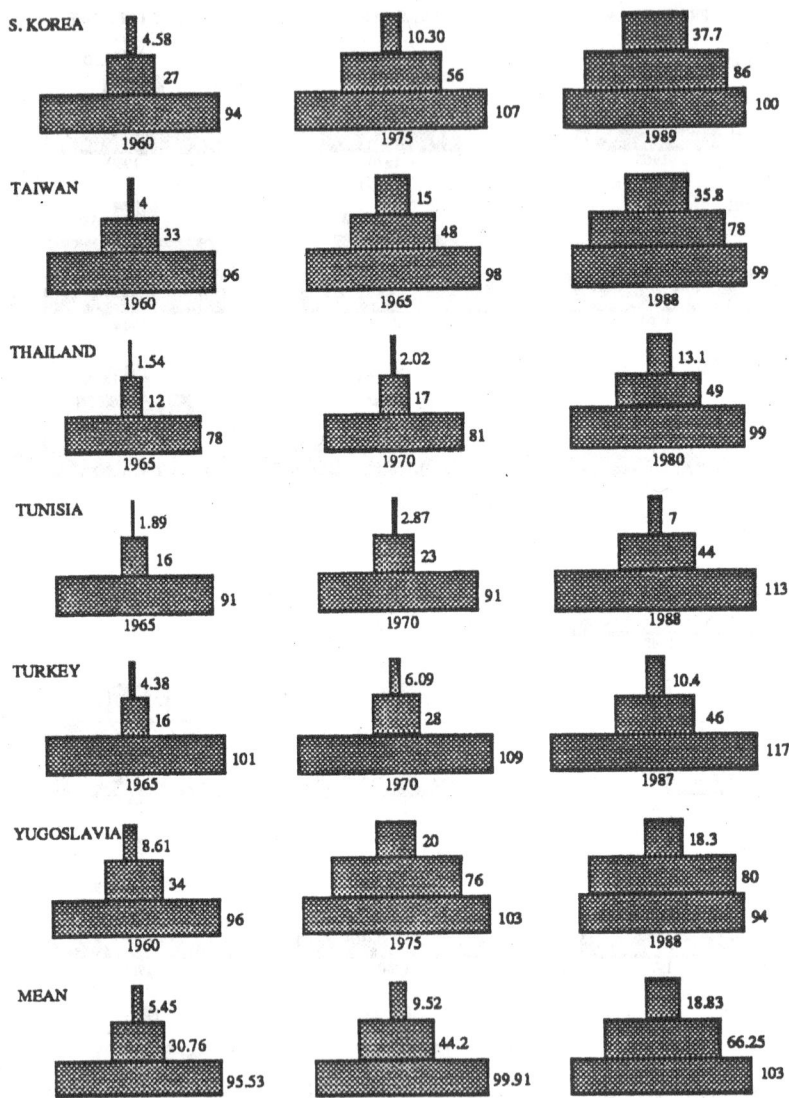

and third levels of education vary widely during early periods of industrialization with Korea and its neighbor Taiwan exhibiting comparatively high enrollment ratios at these levels.

Contextual Explanation of Educational Growth

The international literature of the 1960s generally offered two popular explanations of education's role in development. One held that education is an integral part of the modernization process. In its simplest form modernization theory posits that educated people are more modern and modern people are necessary to build and run complex, contemporary economic, political, and social institutions. Modernization refers to a particular conceptualization of social change which describes development as a transition from a traditional society whose roles are ascribed, functionally diffuse and focussed on particularistic goals to a modern society characterized by clearly identifiable specific roles which are acquired through the application of achievement criteria and are oriented toward universalistic norms. Modernization in both its social and individual meaning is, the theory claims, strongly influenced by education. Education teaches the appropriate value orientations, e.g., personal efficacy, socialization to a rational society, and normative preparation for political elites, thus preparing people for the norms, commitments, and obligations of modern society.

Modernization theory is compatible with the second, or human capital, theory of development--a theory popular in the 1960s which retains its salience today. The core of the human capital argument rests on the idea that education, health, and training are investments with anticipated future individual and social returns. Education is viewed primarily as a system to: 1) endow the labor force with knowledge and skills to make it more productive; 2) create a class of educated leaders; and 3) provide literacy and basic skills for masses.

McGinn et al. (1980) argue that neither human capital theory nor modernization theory offers a fully satisfactory explanation of the early stages of Korean development. In all nations there tends to be, in the aggregate, a positive association between levels of education and income. Although education's "value-added" is to some extent recognized in the Korean marketplace, since Koreans are on the whole paid according to their educational background, the differential impact of education on income is not as great in Korea as in many developing and newly industrialized countries. Yet, high educational demand in Korea has persisted in spite of fluctuating levels of returns and in spite of the fact that families contribute significantly and directly to educational costs.

An understanding of the extent and pattern of educational growth in Korea must include a variety of considerations which go beyond the modernization and human capital explanations and recognize a number of contextual conditions and influences. The acceptance by Korean governments of external pressure to create a strong capitalistic state with constitutional rights for all citizens led to the correlative assumption of the necessity for extensive literacy and basic education as basic human rights. The universalization of primary education was high on the agenda of each successive Korean government from 1948 through the 1950s. Secondly, the internal dynamics of the educational system with its upward pressure for growth created increasing demand for secondary and higher education. This self-generating demand was further legitimated by policies anticipating future labor needs. The special needs for high-level manpower were apparent as Korean industry increasingly engaged in high-technology development and application. However, explanations of educational trends would be incomplete without looking further into Korea's history. To understand Korea's educational growth the time frame of analysis must be stretched to many decades, perhaps even to centuries. The current demand for education is at least partly a consequence of actions, ideas, cultural predispositions found deep in Korea's past. Both scholars and casual observers from the 1950s to the present have commented on the high value placed on education by most Koreans. No financial or other incentives were needed, as are in several LDCs today, to encourage parents to send their children to school. Neither distance nor inclement weather seemed to stem the desire for schooling. Stories were widely told of parents who sold their only ox to pay for school fees.

Although difficult to interpret in terms of precise impact the Confucian heritage may have contributed to the context of change. The sober, practical ethics of Confucianism, originally elitist in its appeal, over the centuries impacted on the general population. As a sort of historical pragmatism it gave impetus to a form of government and bureaucracy which incorporated disciplined and consistent administration. As reflected in the phrase *Gun-Sa Bu Il Che* (King, teacher and father are one body) teachers and teaching were highly revered. The Confucian legacy also left a zeal for learning, an image of a cultured, accomplished person and a drive for education at all costs. Education became a widely accepted, unquestioned goal.

The general respect and pervasive drive for education with its deep historical roots provided a context that allowed rapid expansion of educational facilities and opportunities when only modest additional fiscal resources were available. The historical presence of the valued tradition of education may well have been a more significant determinant of the rapid educational development of Korea in the early stages of the industrialization than the explicit development policies initiated in the 1950s or the series of 5-year national educational plans begun in the 1960s.

Finally, the possibility of global influences on Korean educational expansion should not be ignored. There are competing explanations of factors exogenous to an educational system which may influence educational growth. Modernization theory, as has been noted, reflects a common view by considering only the internal development characteristics of the nation-state. Recently world systems approaches have been put forward to explain educational expansion as a process independent of variations in national social or economic structures but influenced primarily by world economic or cultural relationships. Choi (1988) compared effects of national and global factors on the expansion of Korean secondary school enrollments during the period 1955-1986. Two of Choi's findings in particular are worthy of note: 1) neither national development factors nor world cultural integration factors had significant effects; and 2) several foreign dependency factors did have significant effect. While the Choi study does not provide overwhelming support for the world systems position it does strongly suggest that secondary educational expansion in Korea was not simply a result of internal or national forces. A caveat must be inserted, however. Without rejecting the existence of global influences there is the possibility that national factors other than those examined by Choi, and not as easily quantified as those discussed above, have affected educational change and growth in Korea.

Financing Educational Growth

In 1957 Korea spent only 0.9 percent of its GNP on education. Since 1970 the amount of the GNP spent on education has varied but rarely exceeded 3 percent (see Figure V.4). Moreover, between 1965 and 1975 the increase in public expenditures for education grew at a rate slightly less than the rate of growth of the GNP. During the 1950s the ratio of the Ministry of Education (MOE) budget to total government budget ranged between 1 percent and 11 percent. Since the mid-1960s the public expenditures on education ranged between 15 percent and 22 percent of total government expenditures (see Figure V.5 and Table V.2).

These data reflect a central government effort in education which was well below that extended by governments in many countries. However, the pattern of paying for education in Korea has been quite unlike the typical pattern of third world countries where little cost is incurred by students or their families for education. In Korea parents traditionally have been expected to make a financial contribution to education above their contribution through taxes. Parents thus pay fees toward support of public schools and support a large system of private schooling. In the 1950s the central government was financing only about 10 percent of the total costs of education. At the local level during the early stages of sustained development parents contributed over 50 percent of the costs of local schools. Current sources of school expenditures are shown in Table V.2.

Figure V.4 Total Educational Expenditures as Percent of GNP and Percent of Total Government Expenditures

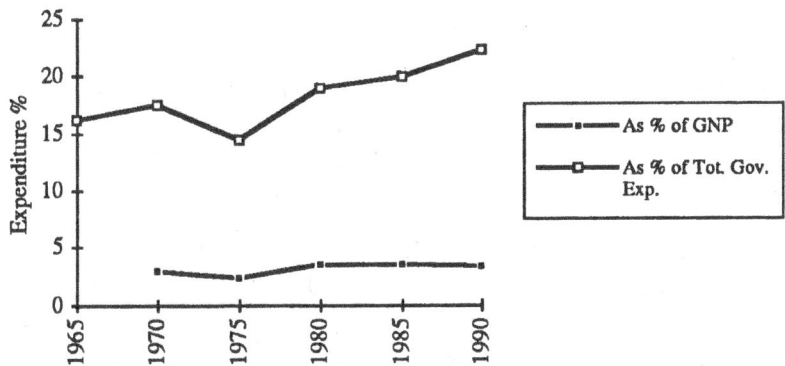

Source: "Educational expenditures as percent of government expenditures" data from *Statistical Yearbook of Education* (1990). MOE, Republic of Korea.
"Educational expenditure as percent of GNP" data from Dong-Kun, Kim and J.R., Kim, "Education in Korea: Efficiency vs. Equity," *The Korean Journal of Policy Studies*, v.5, pp.53-58.
Note: 1990 data for educational expenditure as percent of GNP is estimated value.

Figure V.5 Percent of National Educational Expenditure by Level

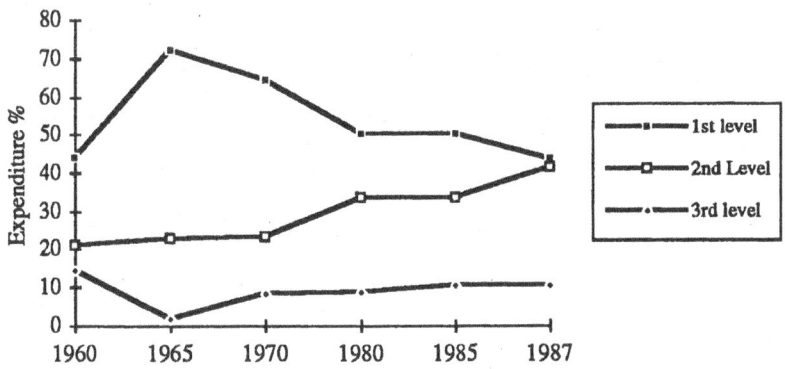

Source: 1960-1985 data from UNESCO (1989). *Unesco Statistical Yearbook*, Paris.
1987 data from UNESCO (1990). *Unesco Statistical Yearbook*, Paris.

The present system of financing education was reorganized in 1970 with the purpose of integrating the many kinds of different fees. However, problems and inequities persist. For example, at present, every student pays the same amount of Parent Teacher Association (PTA) fee (by school level) regardless of his or her economic capabilities. As seen in Table V.2, this source accounts for over 13 percent of the total educational expenditures. The private costs of education have persisted at a high rate and currently take the share of about 50 percent among the total educational costs (see Table V.3). Korean educators argue that the extent of private costs represent a potential danger which may contribute to educational and social inequities.

There are, in addition, somewhat hidden costs borne by parents and students which add to the financial burden of educational attainment. The severe competition for entrance into colleges and universities, for example, has led to family, supported extra-school preparation for entrance examinations such as private tutoring and the purchase of expensive instructional materials and equipment.

Table V.2

Composition of Revenue Sources of School Expenditures By Levels

Unit: percent

Source	Average	Primary School	Middle School	High School	Junior College	College/Univ.
Total	100.00	100.00	100.00	100.00	100.00	100.00
Public Source	56.04	97.84	59.32	26.87	17.43	27.60
Central Government	46.99	97.59	45.55	18.57	7.54	9.54
Local Government or others	9.05	0.25	13.77	8.30	9.89	18.07
Private Source	43.85	2.16	40.68	72.62	82.57	72.40
Tuition/Fees	30.73	0.98	30.51	58.81	55.85	43.08
PTA Fees	13.12	1.18	10.17	13.81	26.72	29.32

Source: Ministry of Education, *Statistical Yearbook of Education*, 1989.

Table V.3

Share of Private Costs in School Education by Levels

				Unit:	percent
Levels	1968	1970	1977	1982	1985
Average	37.48	36.87	33.51	37.09	50.19
Primary School	51.15	37.30	36.51	37.29	50.50
Middle School	55.76	44.57	33.03	44.06	53.29
High School	47.40	45.93	30.72	40.34	58.60
College/University	38.54	27.65	26.60	34.10	41.71

Source: Kong, Eun-Bae and Chun, Se-Yeoung, *Diagnostic Study on Educational Investment Policies in Korea*, Seoul: KEDI, 1989.

Distribution of Educational Opportunity

In many countries rapid aggregate educational growth is associated with wide disparities in the distribution of education. In Korea disparities have been discernable between rural and urban educational opportunities and between male and female educational opportunities. University education, for example, remains disproportionately male and is disproportionately available in larger cities and the more industrialized provinces.

Intermittently throughout the period of rapid growth in enrollments issues of equity were raised particularly by educators, but at least at the secondary and higher levels these concerns were not in the forefront until the system was well developed. In response to regional disparities the Government has, however, played a role in creating policies designed to equalize opportunity of access--particularly between Seoul and the provinces. Efforts in this regard included both restraints on enrollments on institutions located in Seoul and subsidies allowing improvements in provincial institutions.

Data are available to examine in detail interregional differences in middle school educational opportunities. Table V.4 identifies the percentage of elementary school graduates by sex advancing to middle schools in the mid-1970s, a decade after Korea began rapid, sustained economic growth. The advantages in educational opportunity of males over females and in the two major cities over more rural provinces is apparent.

Clearly economic takeoff was accompanied by discernible unequal distribution of educational opportunities. Kim, S.C. (1979) plotted Lorenz curves for the interregional advance ratios from elementary to middle schools and obtained a Gini Index of 0.056. In comparison with disparities in educational opportunities found within many developing and newly industrialized countries this index should be considered low. Rapid educational growth has not created geographic or gender parity in education but neither has it resulted in great regional differences in access to primary and middle schools in Korea.

Table V.4

Advance Ratio in 1976

Region	Total	By Sex	
		Female	Male
Seoul	89.9	86.9	92.4
Busan (Pusan)	87.7	83.4	91.4
Je Ju	86.3	80.8	91.8
Kyung Buk	80.3	73.4	86.4
Kyung Gi	80.2	75.4	84.7
Kyung Nam	80.0	73.8	85.8
Choong Nam	75.4	67.7	82.6
Choong Buk	74.4	65.7	82.5
Jeon Buk	70.2	61.6	78.2
Jeon Nam	67.9	58.5	76.7
Kang Won	66.5	57.0	75.2
National Average	78.3	71.4	84.5

Sources: NIEE *Statistical Yearbook of Education, 1976*, MOE, 1976:70-71. See Appendix 1-5. Seoul and Pusan because of their size have a region-like status.

Clearly, inequities in educational opportunities for high quality schooling are present in contemporary Korea. A major innovation in the 1970s designed to reduce between school differences in educational quality appeared to have some potential for equalizing educational opportunity. The persistence of sex differences in educational opportunities in particular warrants recognition. The number of female students although growing steadily since 1960 their proportionate representation, in higher education has decreased. Figures V.6 and V.7

describe enrollment ratios by gender at each educational level. In terms of access equality of opportunity between males and females in primary education was achieved by 1975 and by 1989 was nearly achieved in secondary education.

In higher education although the numbers of female students have been growing steadily their proportionate representation has decreased.

In 1973, the Ministry of Education set forth the High School Equalization Policy (HSEP) which reformed the high school entrance examination system in an attempt to remove inequities among academic high schools in terms of school facilities, finances, and teacher quality. Um explains:

> In the implementation of the policy, middle school graduates who passed the United Examination for High School Entrance were mandatorily assigned to academic high schools on the basis of their resident areas, . . . public or private. By revising the law of the standard of school facilities and equipment, the Ministry of Education financially supported the schools whose conditions were below the standard levels. To improve and to decrease the gaps of teacher quality, they offered various inservice teacher training programs and implemented a circulating system of teacher assignment among public schools and private schools (1990:120).

The HSEP enforced in Seoul and Pusan in 1974 was expanded to 18 other major cities by 1981. Through implementation of HSEP, the differences in students' ability among high schools appear to have been reduced (see Table V.5.)

Figure V.6 Enrollment Ratios by Gender - 1st Level

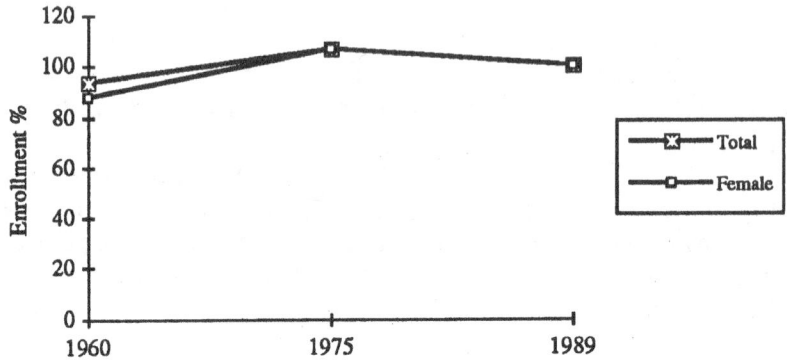

Source: 1960 data from UNESCO (1976). *Unesco Statistical Yearbook*, Paris.
1975 data from UNESCO (1989). *Unesco Statistical Yearbook*, Paris.
1989 data from UNESCO (1990). *Unesco Statistical Yearbook*, Paris.

Figure V.7 Enrollment Ratios by Gender - 2nd Level

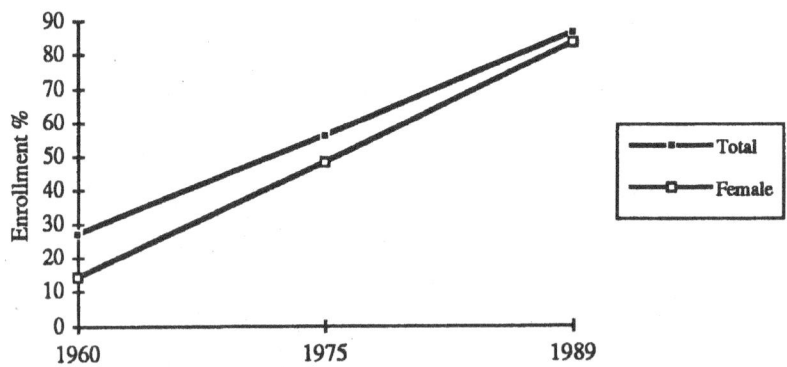

Source: 1960 data from UNESCO (1976). *Unesco Statistical Yearbook*, Paris.
1975 data from UNESCO (1989). *Unesco Statistical Yearbook*, Paris.
1989 data from UNESCO (1990). *Unesco Statistical Yearbook*, Paris.

Figure V.8 Enrollment Ratios by Gender - 3rd Level

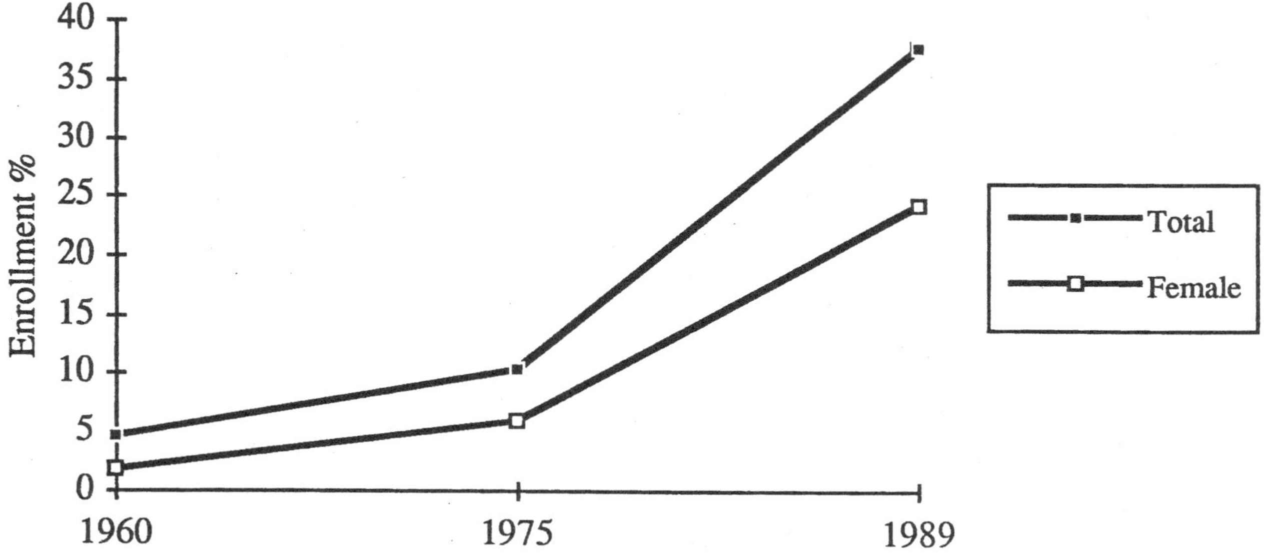

Source: 1960 data from UNESCO (1976). *Unesco Statistical Yearbook*, Paris.
1975 data from UNESCO (1989). *Unesco Statistical Yearbook*, Paris.
1989 data from UNESCO (1990). *Unesco Statistical Yearbook*, Paris.

Table V.5

Students Entering IQ Distribution Before and After the Implementation of the HSEP (in Percentage)

Time	School Type	IQ Scores		
		>120	100-119	100<
Before	Prestigious Schools	58.3	39.0	2.7 (100 percent)
(1973)	Less Prestigious Schools	8.5	54.6	36.9
After	Prestigious Schools	18.3	55.5	26.2
(1976)	Less Prestigious Schools	16.2	58.3	25.2

Source: KEDI, *Evaluation Study of the HSEP*, Seoul (1978):23.

Fiscal limitations and possibly other constraints, however, led the government to suspend the implementation of the HSEP to other areas after 1980. Even in the high schools in the urban areas which continued implementation of the policy, quality gaps in school facilities and teachers have remained among the high schools (Ministry of Education, 1980). Moreover, new, prestigious academic high schools have emerged.

Education and Economic Growth

Korea is a country with a limited endowment of natural resources. It has, for example, few mineral resources and no petroleum. Being extremely mountainous, only approximately one-fourth of its land area was cultivated in 1960. Korea's remarkable growth was largely initiated and sustained by intensive development of export-oriented industries fueled by a high rate of investment in both physical and human capital. From the mid-1960s through the 1980s the ratio of total investment per income averaged roughly 30 percent annually while the ratio of total expenditures per income was rising approximately 4 percent. During this period Korea exhibited a high rate of real export growth, averaging over 15 percent. High investment and high growth rates were accompanied by slow population growth, further stimulating economic development. Until the 1970s the agricultural sector was relatively ignored.

Although there is little argument concerning the magnitude of Korea's economic growth there is some debate over the pattern of distribution of income. KEDI's *The Long Term Prospect of Education Development 1978-91* noted:

> Although rapid economic growth has been sustained since the 1960s, the distribution of income in Korea has been relatively equitable by international standards until recently. This is largely attributed to the sustained development of labor-intensive industries and the Saemaul (New Community) Movement which is aimed at reducing income disparities. *However, the current conglomeration tendency of business firms and the resulting disparities in wages are increasingly impairing the equitable status of income* (KEDI, 1979:202).

Data available on income inequality and poverty allow some comparisons between Korea and other countries. In Korea the Gini coefficient of income among households decreased, suggesting a reduction in inequality of income distribution between 1965-1970 and between 1976-1982. However, the Gini coefficient registered an increase (suggesting an increase in inequality of income distribution) between 1965-1982. Other data show a steady decrease in the proportion of Korean households with incomes below a constant real poverty line between 1965-1980 (ibid, 24). Thus on the whole the Korean population seems to be achieving higher incomes but the gap between the income levels of rich and poor appears to be wider in the 1980s than in the 1970s.

Both the high productivity ratio of industry and manufacturing and the decreasing population growth rate may be attributed in part to high educational levels. Education has facilitated the structured adjustment of the shifts of labor force from agriculture and underemployment to higher productivity activities in manufacturing and export-oriented industries. Comparatively high female enrollments in primary and secondary levels of education, with enrollment ratios reaching over 90 percent by the mid-1980s, undoubtedly contributed to the decline in fertility rates. From an international perspective Korea was "over developed" educationally compared to countries with a similar level of economic development.

The productivity of the Korean workforce has also often been seen as making an important direct contribution to economic productivity. Cole comments:

> In addition to the underlying strength deriving from the educational system, the Korean labor force has other attributes that have enhanced its contribution to economic growth. Korean workers have been described by one manpower specialist as "adaptable, trainable, manually dexterous, and accustomed to arduous work for long hours" (Cole, 1975:138).

The early years of the industrial take-off period saw a rapid shift in employment structure and worker productivity. Employment in agriculture, forestry and fisheries remained relatively constant while employment in mining and manufacturing, and to lesser extent social overhead and service increased. These employment shifts are related to changes in the output of the sectors. However, the dramatic increase in the value added per worker is the major contributing factor to productivity growth. Cole concludes: ". . . of the roughly 60 percent increase in value added, one-third can be attributed to increased employment and about two-thirds to rising production per worker" (1975:139).

The contribution of education to Korea's economic growth directly through improvement of skills and productive capacities and indirectly through reductions in fertility is widely accepted by Korean scholars. The economic effects of educational or human-capital investment are further demonstrated by rates of return studies (Psacharopoulas [1990:17] has suggested that the percentage contribution of education to Korea's annual economic growth rate was 15.9).

The industrial path taken by Korea required a highly skilled, adaptive labor force. In spite of the rapid educational expansion there was fierce recruiting competition for college graduates by corporations in the 1970s. However, the history of demand for entrance to higher education does not appear to have been closely related, nor immediately responsive, to occupational variables or labor force participation rates. In the case of women, fewer than half of whom are employed after completion of university education, the general uncertainty of economic benefits does not appear to be a deterrent to educational attainment.

Education and Social Change

Paralleling the remarkable educational growth during the industrial take-off period were equally remarkable changes in Korean society. A few examples will suggest the direction of the social transformation taking place. Table V.6 shows the significant improvements taking place in selected indicators of mortality during the early stages of industrialization. A decline in birth rates during the 1970s can be attributed to the national attention given to family planning during the 1960s and 1970s. During this period in the use of contraceptive devices by females took place among all age groups. Moreover, rapid growth was reflected in both rural and urban areas and at various educational levels.

Table V.6

Korea Health Index (1955-1970)

	Percentages			
	1955	1960	1965	1970
Average life length				
Male	51	54	54	63
Female	54	58	60	67
Infant death rate (on 1,000 born infants)	78	69	52	49
Death Rate (on 1,000 persons)	14.3	13.0	11.9	8.5

Source: Hakchung Choo and James Jeffers, "Health and Economic and Social Development." Unpublished paper studied for the research on Korea Modernization. KDI, Seoul, 1976:13.

In pre-colonial Korea social status was associated with family background and ownership of land. Increasingly social status has become less associated with family background. The three emerging indicators of status tend to be wealth, and income, education and occupation. Under

Japanese colonialism the hierarchy of social structure placed Japanese bureaucrats at the top, followed in descending order of status and power by landlords, merchants and peasants. Industrialization brought a new occupational structure and new sources of wealth and income and new demands on education which itself was associated directly with both income and status (see Table V.7).

Differences between regions in the determinants of status appear not to be great. Wealth and educational level dominate the explanatory factors for social class across urban, suburban and rural populations. Some variation among occupations is visible in perception of factors determining social class. The respect for income is highest among laborers and small entrepreneurs but is strong among all occupational groups. Education is also seen as a formidable factor by all occupational groups with technicians (technically trained professionals) being the only group making education the most influential factor.

Table V.8 identifies factors determining social class as perceived by social class members. Again, wealth and education are chosen as the main determinants of social class. Upper class respondents, that is, those who perceive themselves belonging to the upper class, evaluate occupation as being a much less influential factor in determining status than do respondents from other social classes. However, all groups studied, whether divided by region, occupations or classes, chose wealth and education as dominant factors in determining social class. Somewhat surprising is the consistently low evaluation given to income as a factor.

Table V.7

Social Class Evaluation Factor By Occupation

Factor Occupation	Percentages						
	Income	Education	Occupation	Family Background	House	Personality	Total
Employer	47.7	33.0	11.9	3.7	1.8	--	99.9
Small Entrp.	51.0	27.8	13.1	2.5	3.2	0.2	100.0
Farmer	45.7	36.6	8.7	3.6	3.3	0.7	100.0
Technicians	35.6	50.8	8.5	1.7	1.7	--	100.0
Office People	40.7	33.4	16.5	5.7	2.7	--	99.9
Laborer	58.7	18.8	15.5	2.3	2.3	0.5	100.0
Women	39.3	33.3	16.9	3.4	2.8	0.8	99.9
Others	64.3	14.3	14.3	--	--	--	100.0
Unemployed	43.2	31.8	12.1	8.3	4.5	--	99.9
TOTAL	45.7	31.4	13.9	3.9	2.9	0.3	99.9

Source: C.J. Lee (1988). *A Study of Korean Social Class*. Unpublished monograph. Also see B.S. Kim et al., 1982 *Schooling and Social Achievement*. Seoul, KEDI.

Table V.8

Social Class Evaluation Factor by Perception of Self's Class

Factor Perception	Percentages						
	Wealth	Educ. Level	Occupat.	Income	Family Background	House	Personality	Total
Upper	48.3	37.9	3.4	—	3.4	—	6.9	99.9
Upper-middle	40.7	37.4	13.8	3.4	2.7	0.3	1.7	100.0
Lower-middle	42.6	31.4	16.1	4.6	2.9	0.5	1.8	99.9
Upper-low	47.5	30.7	11.9	3.6	3.6	0.3	2.4	100.0
Lowest	51.4	27.5	14.3	3.9	2.0	0.2	0.7	100.0
TOTAL	45.7	31.4	13.9	3.9	2.9	0.3	1.8	99.9

Source: Ibid., p. 338.

Comparisons over time of criteria for determining social status are difficult to locate; however, there is some evidence that the importance of the criterion of wealth has declined over the last two decades. Increasing in significance are education and occupation. New determinants of status have meant changes in the age structure of the social classes resulting in the domination of the middle classes by the younger age groups. This characteristic may be assumed to be the product of industrialization and the rapid growth of education. Higher educational levels in Korea are associated with younger age groupings; higher educational levels are also associated with higher status and higher paid occupations. Korea's economic development has differentially advantaged the younger generation.

Growth in educational and employment opportunities in higher-status occupations have contributed to a significant level of intergenerational social mobility. There is evidence of both upward and downward mobility from all social classes. Many persons currently with middle- or upper- class status, represent upward mobility from the status of their parents. However, Korean social research suggests that it is in the lowest class where there is the highest continuance of social class status. The lowest percentage of continuance of social class apparently is found in the upper class.

The role of education in social-status attainment and intergenerational social mobility has been examined in some detail by Kim (1984). In a study in major urban areas of employed males (ages 25-65) Kim studied the interaction of family background, school, and personal attributes. Schooling was found to be more directly influential than personal traits or family background factors in determination of social status. Also demonstrated was the significant influence of father's educational background on the number of years of schooling of the sons. In this study all sub-variables of social achievement, i.e., occupational status, ascribed class, life satisfaction, and self-evaluation, were influenced more by the extent and quality of schooling than by personal traits and family background. Upward mobility influenced by educational attainment was particularly recognizable in the many sons of skilled workers who have entered white-collar and managerial positions.

In the process of industrialization and the restructuring of social distinctions, social values represent both influential inputs and consequences. One Korean source summarizes the changes in social values between 1945 and the mid-1980s:

- In the 1950s, wealth, power, status, and expedient commitments became important values; moral values were perceived as declining.

- In the 1960s the traditional family system and social cohesiveness were weakened with the emergence of individualism and materialism. There was a heightening of values emphasizing national development, patriotism, confidence in Korean culture, worth of self, quality of life, equity between men and women, and small families. Furthermore, values of participation and cooperation were integrated into Korean value systems during this period.

- In the 1970s, urbanization and industrialization resulted in the emergence of some differences between regions and social classes. The values of diligence and wealth declined somewhat and non-materialistic values gained in importance. Part of the population embraced the values of social justice, equity, human rights and social welfare and thus there was a "consciousness raising of people."

- In the 1980s, the values of wealth, health, and hedonistic orientations were continued and heightened. Nationalism as a value is in retreat. The value of fellowship as part of friendship has gained in priority (Kang, 1985:10424-10425).

Education, Politics and Government

The political evolvement of contemporary Korea has not been marked with as much success as the development of the economy. Rapid economic growth did not lead easily or quickly to political democracy. Indeed, the basic transformation of the economic structure occurred in a period when the degree of authoritarianism was increasing in the political system and process. Particularly after the 1961 military coup Korea developed effective central authority and efficient bureaucracy in support of economic modernization.

Education like other major institutions was expected to respond to mandates and laws set forth by the central government. Immediately after the establishment of the Republic several anti-government rebellions broke out involving dissident soldiers, some civilians (reputedly communist cells), and many students. Government security regulations tightened and many of the individual rights guaranteed by the constitution were restricted. There were mass student strikes and boycotts of classes in high schools and colleges. The student activists basically were seeking opportunities to participate in political activities without school or governmental interference.

One of the major responses of the government directed toward curbing student political activisim was the creation of the Student Defense Corps under a Ministry of Education Ordinance in 1949. This ordinance identified the objectives of the Corps as the promotion among students of patriotism and ideological unity, qualities needed in building the nation's defense strength. Choe describes the evolvement of the corps:

> . . . its organization clearly resembled that of military units whose structure was highly centralized. The Corps' supreme commandant was the President of the Republic. The Minister of Education held a position as Central Commandant of the corps, who had an authority to control over all matters of its administration. The provincial governor was entitled as the commandant of the local unit whose position was solely responsible to carry out its central policy, while a school principal assumed the position as the head of its school unit. Each unit of the Corps had an advisory committee which consisted of 10 members who were appointed by the President at the Central and provincial levels to advise on its major policies. At each school level, the guidance committee was organized to give proper guidance to students in each extracurricular activity area. The principal and all faculty members automatically became the chairman or full members of the committee. A remarkable thing to note was that all extracurricular activities programs were carried out in the structure of the corps except such few groups as YMCA, YWCA, and in Catholic and Buddhist student organizations which were independently governed by the students themselves (1971).

The interaction of successive political regimes and politically active students was at best distrustful and often involved violence. A broad-based student movement succeeded in overthrowing the existing autocratic government in 1960. The Park- and Chun-led governments (1961-1986) monitored student activism and sought to control any student anti-government movements. From the mid-1960s a number of national laws and policies were enacted to extend the central government's control over both private and public colleges and universities. These actions involved the setting of student quotas, influence of entrance and exit policies, appointment of senior administrators, development of rules pertaining to fiscal and personnel management of private institutions, and establishment of tenure and appointment policies for faculty members. Most recently, activist students have made a major issue of the lack of student involvement in university governance which they view as an indicator of the need for democratization of higher education. The government, apparently seeking to avoid the strengthening of student power, has prohibited student participation in important university decisions.

However, the link between politics and education is a two-way street. Most scholars and experienced educational administrators agree that educational policymaking and reform are profoundly political processes. On the other hand, education is widely believed to contribute to citizens' understanding of political processes and to the quality of government. A satisfactory quantification of these relationships, however, is difficult. Yet there is some empirical evidence that in Korea level of education is associated with political participation and political beliefs and, since the 1960s, increasingly advanced education appears to be associated with attainment of high-level political and administrative positions.

As early as the 1970s the level of education attained was influencing various forms of individual political participation (Table V.9). The minimal political involvement of citizens with no formal education is striking. With the exception of "listening to radio" no form of participation draws over 6 percent of the respondents. It would appear that education contributes to the confidence or feeling of effectiveness of citizens in their relationships with politics.

The findings on the relation of education and political participation support the research on broader social values in Korea which shows that the higher the level of education the higher the concern for the future of the country and the stronger the commitment to a society ruled by law. The educational level of both appointed and elected officials has continued to increase over the last few decades. New senior appointees in the Ministry of Education in the 1970s and 1980s had a higher educational level than their predecessors and the educational level of Congressmen over time shows the same trend (Table V.10).

Table V.9

Degree of Political Participation by Educational Level

Form of Participation	Percentages		
Educational Level	Non-Educated	Elementary School	More than Secondary School
Contribution for Political Purpose	0.2	0.8	1.0
Effort to Influence Public Policies of Central Government	0.2	2.5	7.2
Providing Time for Political Activity	1.4	5.1	7.9
Affiliating With a Political Party	1.4	6.9	7.2
Effort to Influence Public Policies of Local Government	3.6	13.7	20.7
Watching Election Campaign With Attention	5.7	19.1	36.1
Talking With Others About Political Affairs	3.0	16.5	48.2
Reading Magazines	2.5	24.1	63.9
Reading Newspapers	2.8	31.0	71.5
Listening to Radio	30.8	59.6	78.0

Source: Lee, Young Ho. "Education and Political Development." In Lee, Young Dug et al., *Education's Contribution to National Development*. Seoul: MOE, 1976:202.

Table V.10

Educational Level of Congress

Term Education Level	1	2	3	4	5	6	7	8	9	10	Total
Non-Education & Chinese Classics	4.5	1.9	1.5	1.7	2.4	—	0.6	—	—	1.5	1.4
Elem. Sch. Grad.	12.5	4.8	10.8	5.2	5.8	1.7	1.1	0.5	0.7	—	4.5
Middle Sch. Grad.	23.5	25.2	32.1	26.6	19.3	1.7	1.1	—	—	—	10.9
High Sch. Grad.	—	—	—	—	13.7	10.9	5.7	5.9	6.1	2.2	4.7
2-Yr. College Grad.	19.0	20.0	10.9	18.0	17.9	9.7	9.7	4.9	2.7	—	12.3
College Grad.	39.0	48.1	44.7	48.5	49.0	63.5	63.2	65.2	60.0	38.6	51.2
Graduate School	—	—	—	—	2.1	8.6	14.9	23.0	29.5	58.4	14.4
Others	1.5	—	—	—	—	2.2	1.1	0.5	—	0.3	0.5
TOTAL (n)	200	210	203	233	291	172	170	204	145	274	2,056

Source: Ibid.

Summary

The Korean economy and society have undergone dramatic transformations over the past few decades. A poor agricultural country has evolved into a strong industrial state. Agricultural workers and their children have been turned into manufacturing and service workers. Urbanization has created cities which are both the producers and consumers in the world marketplace of goods, technology and ideas. Rural areas have also participated in this transformation, developing higher levels of productivity and consumption.

Education has been an integral part of industrial transformation, contributing new skills, creating new values, and conveying new status (see Table V.11). Education persists in high demand and the majority of Koreans are willing to make great sacrifices to assist their sons and daughters in attaining entrance to institutions of higher education.

Educational certification, particularly at the secondary and higher education levels, offers both economic and noneconomic benefits. Rapid educational expansion may have inflated educational requirements for many occupations. Employers with a choice use educational certification as a screening device for ability, and for high-status occupations the prestige of the university awarding the degree also becomes crucial in employee selection.

Table V.11

Educational and Social Changes in the Development of Korea

Educational Development	Pre-Industrial Society 1950s	Transition Period 1960-1970	Industrial Society 1970-Present
Basic Education	Well developed primary education; extensive literacy	Universalization of Primary Education	Concentration on qualitative improvements
Secondary Education	Elite secondary system; emphasis on college preparatory	Rapid expansion of lower secondary education; attempt to vocationalize curricula	Universalization of lower secondary schools; upper secondary schools becoming comprehensive; major qualitative improvements
Higher Education	Elite traditional autonomous professional colleges; growth of private institutions	Rapid expansion; modernization of professional curricula; wide range in quality of institutions	"Massification" of higher education; increased institutional autonomy; strong efforts at quality control
Financing Education	Emphasis on public resources; bulk of education budget for primary education; some reliance on contributions at all educational levels	Continuing priority for primary education; increased privatization of costs of secondary and higher education; significant family expenses at all levels	Growing balance within education budget of funding for different educational levels; extensive burdens of costs of education borne by families
Planning Strategies	Centralized, top-down control; short and medium terms; use of rationalist models within acceptable political context	Top-down approach modified by local innovations and growth of private education; short and medium term emphasis; growing involvement of educational professionals	Mixed top-down with local, regional based institutional options; medium and long range perspective planning; professional debate over effectiveness of planning

Table V.11 continued
Educational and Social Changes in the Development of Korea

Educational Development	Pre-Industrial Society 1950s	Transition Period 1960-1970	Industrial Society 1970-Present
Role of State	Emerging strong central leadership; provision of resources for capacity building; educational agenda setting	Commitment to and suspicion of education; use of mandates and inducements to foster educational growth as a contribution to a strong nation-state; encouragement of state controlled, private education; educational growth legitimation to state	Continued commitment to and suspicion of education; caution with respect to educational autonomy; fear of student power, coordination between public and private education efforts; sharing educational agenda setting with educational professionals; significant but slowly decreasing influence in shaping educational issues and debates
Individual and Social Values	Some breakdown of traditional value, roles and relationships	Strengthening of materialism and individualism; growing pride in nation's accomplishments	Emerging criticism of "western" values (particularly youth with advanced education); attempts at redefining quality of life; concern for cultural identity
Status	Status associated with family, land ownership, wealth, and education	Status primarily associated with wealth and education; emerging technical/professional middle class	Education an increasingly important requisite for status; education the major determinant of social mobility; middle classes younger in age
Equity	Advanced educational opportunity strongly influenced by class, wealth, geography and gender	Inequalities in educational opportunities due to wealth and gender remain significant	Inequalities in educational opportunities stabilized or slightly reduced; inequalities less than many developing and industrialized countries

Bibliography

Articles and Books

Adams, Don K. "Education Change and Korean Development." In *Dynamic Transformation: Korea, NICs and Beyond*. 371-382, edited by Lim, Gill-Chin, and Chong, Wook. Seoul: Myung-Bo Publishing Company, 1990.

Ahn, Hae Kyun. "Administrative Changes and Elite Dynamics: The Patterns of Elite Mobilization and Integration in Korea." *Journal of Asiatic Studies* (November 1972): 110-132.

An, Nack Young. "Student Activism and Dissent in Korea: The World's Oldest Tradition of Its Kind." *Chronicle of Higher Education*, 34 No. 4 (September 23, 1987): B1.

ARTEP, eds. *Manpower Planning in Asian Countries*. Singapore: RIHED, 1985.

Bae, Cheon-Ung, Choi, Sang-Keun and Park, In-Jong. *Analysis of Korean Views of Education*. Seoul: KEDI Press, 1986. (in Korean)

Bae, Jong Keun. "Study on Optimalization and Economic Effectiveness of Educational Investment." Academic Research Report. Seoul: Ministry of Education, 1977.

Bahl, Roy, Kim, Chuk-kyo, and Park, Chong-kee. *Public Finances During the Korean Modernization Process*. Studies in the Modernization of the Republic of Korea: 1945-1975. Harvard East Asian monographs 107. Cambridge: Harvard University Press, 1986. (HJ1400.5 B34)

Ban, Sung-hwan, Moon, Pal-yong, and Perkins, Dwight H. *Rural Development*. Studies in the Modernization of the Republic of Korea: 1945-1975. Harvard East Asian monographs 89. Cambridge: Harvard University Press, 1980. (HD2095.5 B37)

Blaise, Hans C. "The University and National Development." In *The Role of Asian Universities in a Changing World*, edited by K. S. Nijhar. Kuala Lumpur: Academic Staff Association, University of Malaya, 1972.

Brandt, Vincent S. R. "Rural Development in South Korea." *Asian Affairs: An American Review*, 6 (January/February 1979):48-63.

Reviews development in rural areas of Korea since the late 19th century, with particular emphasis on rural to urban migration, governmental investment in agriculture, transportation and mass communications, and cooperative village improvement projects.

Caldwell, J. Alexander. "The Economic and Financial Outlook for the Developing Countries: Trends and Issues." In *Political Change and Economic Future of East Asia*, edited by R. Robert. Honolulu, Hawaii: Pacific Forum, 1981.

Cha, Kyung Soo. "Model for Measuring Equality of Educational Opportunity in Korea." *Educational Research* (1973).

Chen, Edward K. Y. *Hyper Growth in Asia Economies: A Comparative Study of Hong Kong, Japan, Korea, Singapore, and Taiwan.* New York: Holmes & Meier, 1979.

Choi, Hyung-sup. "Approaches to Technological Manpower Development-The Korean Experience." In *UNESCO in Asia and the Pacific: 40 Years On*, 177-188, edited by Cahill, Bruce. UNESCO: Asia and the Pacific, 1986. (ED 282 677)

The author describes the role of education in supplying high caliber scientists and engineers in Korea. Korea's technical qualification system as related to education is outlined.

Chung, Jin-Young. "South Korea Strategies for Dynamic Transformation 1961-88." In *Dynamic Transformation: Korea, NICs and Beyond*, edited by Lim, Gill-Chin, and Chong, Wook. Seoul: Myung-Bo Publishing Company, 1990.

Cole, David C. and Park, Yung-chul. *Financial Development in Korea, 1945-1978*. Studies in the Modernization of the Republic of Korea: 1945-1975. Harvard East Asian monographs 106. Cambridge: Harvard University Press, 1983. (HC467 C65)

Dutta, Ratna. "The Process of Modernization: Some Structural Constraints." In *Studies in Asian Social Development*, No. 2, edited by Suren Navlakha. New Delhi, India: Vikas Publishing House, 1974.

Edberg, Hakan. "The South Korean Challenges." *Institutional Investor*, New York, April 1978.

Faraj, Abdulatif-Hussein. "Higher Education and Economic Development in South Asian Countries." *Higher Education Review*, 21 No. 1 (Fall 1988):9-26.

Golladay, Frederick and King, Timothy. "Social Development." In *Korea: Policy Issues for Long-Term Development*. 135-172, edited by Hassan, Parvez and Rao, D. C. Baltimore: Johns Hopkins University Press, 1979. (HC467 153 1979)

Examines the process of national development, in relation to the growth of the educational system and skill formation after 1950. Major issues of educational policy and their emphasis on social development issues in Korea are described.

Hasan, Parvez. *Korea: Problems and Issues in a Rapidly Growing Economy*. Baltimore: Johns Hopkins University Press, 1976.

A World Bank country economic report. Contends that the phenomenal economic progress of the Republic of Korea during 1963-74 has been the result of the interaction of economic, political, and social factors. Export expansion and long-range strategic planning are cited as central elements of economic development with manufactured exports as the nucleus of growth.

Ha, Tae Hung. *Guide To Korean Culture*. Seoul: Yonsei University Press, 1968.

Hollander, Edward D. *The Role of Manpower in Korean Economic Development*. Korea: United States Operations Mission to Korea, 1966.

Hong, Sung Chick. "Values of Korean College Students." *The Journal of Asiatic Studies* (May 1963).

Hong, Sung Chick. *The Intellectual and Modernization: A Study of Korean Attitudes*. Korea: Social Research Institute, Korea University, 1967.

Hughes, Phillip. "Social and Technological Interaction with Education: Redesigning Structures, Preparing Personnel." Asian Programme of Educational Innovation for Development. Occasional Paper No. 13. Bangkok: UNESCO, Regional Office for Education in Asia and the Pacific, 1984.

Huq, Muhammad Shamsul. *Education and Development Strategy In Southeast Asia*. Honolulu: East-West Center Press, 1965.

Hyde, Georgie D. M. *South Korea: Education, Culture, and Economy*. New York: St. Martin's Press, 1988. (DS922.2 H93)

The author briefly introduces the Korean educational administration system, supervision and management, and discusses economic development in the areas of science and technology, industry, business and finance, trade, and commerce in 1970s.

Ihm, Chon Sun. "South Korea's Economic Development." *Social Studies* 79, No. 4 (July-August 1988):165-69.

Jayasuriya, J. E. *Education in Korea: A Third World Success Story*. Colombo, Sri Lanka: Associated Educational Publishers, 1980. (LA1331 J39).

An attempt to explain education as the base of Korean development by reviews of the historical background, religion and culture, educational development from 37 B.C. to 1905, education during Japanese occupation and education since independence. The content of second part of the book includes examination of the legal basis, goals of education, organizational structure and educational planning of the whole system. The conclusion projects national trends and the future of Korean education.

Jones, Leroy P. and SaKong, Il. *Government Business and Entrepreneurship in Economic Development: The Korean Case.* Studies in the Modernization of the Republic of Korea: 1945-1975. Harvard East Asian monographs 91. Cambridge: Harvard University, 1980. (HC467 J65)

Kaltsounis, Theodore and Shin, Se-Ho. "South Korea: A Country on the Move." *Social Studies*, 79 No. 4 (July-August 1988):137-39.

Kang, Eun-Bae and Chun, Se-Yeoung. *Diagnostic Study on Educational Investment Policies in Korea.* Seoul: KEDI Press, 1989.

Kang, Sin Pyo. "The Changes and Problems of Korean Society." *Beop Moon*, 30 (1985):10424-10425. (in Korean)

Kang, Sung-Chul. "Development of Human Resources: Korea's Most Utmost Task." *Korea News Review* 12 (January 1984).

Kantasewi, Niphon. "Higher Education and Economic Growth in Thailand." In *Higher Education and Economic Growth in Southeast Asia*, edited by Amnuay Tapingkae. Singapore: Regional Institute of Higher Education.

KCUE (Korean Council for University Education). *Equity, Quality and Cost in Higher Education: Research Study on the Republic of Korea.* Seoul: KCUE, 1988.

An attempt to assess the achievements and problems of Korean higher education with respect to access discrimination, academic quality and cost. Interuniversity comparisons are provided.

KDI (Korea Development Institute). *Long-Term Prospect for Economic and Social Development 1977-91*. Seoul: KDI Press, 1978. (HC467 H253 1978)

KDI. *Korea's Economy: Past and Present*. Seoul: KDI Press, 1982.

KEDI. *Evaluation Study of the HSEP*. Seoul: KEDI Press, 1978.

KEDI. "Social Development and Education in the 2000s." Report Commemorating the 10th Anniversary of KEDI. Seoul: KEDI Press, 1983.

KEDI. *Korean Education 2000*. Seoul: KEDI Press, 1985.

Korea Chamber of Commerce and Industry. "Economic Development and Educational Investment." Seoul: The Korea Chamber of Commerce and Industry, 1973.

Kim, Bun-Woong, Bell, D. S., Jr. and Lee, C. B., eds. *Administrative Dynamics and Development: The Korean Experience*. Seoul: Kyobo Publishing Inc., 1985.

A collection of articles on political and social development. Included is a discussion of the ways the administration developed under the Park government relied on bureaucratic and political elite culture which slowed down democratic movements.

Kim, Byong-sung. *Schooling and Social Achievement*. Seoul: KEDI Press, 1984.

According to this report, schooling is the most important variable and accounts for about 17 percent of the variance in social achievement. About 4 percent of variance in the social achievement was explained by the combination of family and individual variables.

Kim, Jong Chul. *Popularization of Higher Education and Excellence Education*. Seoul: KCUE, and UNESCO Korean National Commission, 1983.

Kim, Kwang-suk and Roemer, Michael. *Growth and Structural Transformation*. Studies in the Modernization of the Republic of Korea: 1945-1975. Harvard East Asian monographs 86. Cambridge: Harvard University, 1979. (HC467 K512)

Kim, Kyung-dong. "Social Change and Societal Development in Korea Since 1945: Modernization with Uneven Development." *Korean and World Affairs: A Quarterly Review*, 9 (Winter 1985): 56-788.

An overview of social and economic development over a thirty-year period, explaining educational growth as indirectly related to the evolvement of other social institutions.

Kim, Okgill. "The Place of Women's Colleges, The Korean Experience: Ewha University. *New Frontiers in Education* 8, No. 1 (July 1978):47-56.

Kim, Soung-Yee and Stinner, William F. "Social Origins, Educational Attainment and the Timing of Marriage and First Birth Among Korean Women." *Journal of Marriage and the Family*, 42 No. 3 (August 1980):671-78.

Kim, Young-Bong and McGinn, M.F. *Education and Economic Development in Korea*. Seoul: Korea Development Institute, 1980.

Kim, Young-chul, Kong, Eun-bae and Lee, Yun-sik. *Educational Investment and Optimum Unit Cost*. Seoul: KEDI Press, 1980

Kim, Young-chul and Kong, Eun-bae. *Educational Contribution to the Economic Development in Korea*. Seoul: KEDI Press, 1986.

Koh, Hesung and Chun, Comp. *Studies of Korean and Japanese Women: An Analytical Guide*. New Haven, CT: Human Relations Area Files, Inc., 1981.

Koo, Hagen. "Transformation of the Korean Class Structure: The Impact of Dependent Development." *Research in Social Stratification and Mobility*, 4 (1975):129-148.

"Korea Forms Graduate Institute in Science." *Chemical and Engineering News,* 50 No. 31 (December 1972):9.

Korea University. International Conference on the Problems of Modernization in Asia. June 28-July 7, 1965. Asiatic Research Center, Korea.

Krueger, Anne O. *The Developmental Role of the Foreign Sector and Aid.* Studies in the Modernization of the Republic of Korea: 1945-1975. Harvard East Asian monographs 87. Cambridge: Harvard University, 1979. (HF3830.5.Z5 K78)

Kuznets, Paul W. *Economic Growth and Structure in the Republic of Korea.* New Haven, CT: Yale University Press, 1985.

Lee, Chong Jae. "Social Class and Distribution of Educational Opportunity." *Social Science Journal,* 9 (1982):7-36. (HN 730.5 A65)

The relationship between education, educational opportunity and social mobility were investigated. Conceptions of equality of educational opportunity and research questions for further study of equality of educational opportunity in Korea are suggested.

Lee, Chong Jae. "Social Constructions of Schooling." Research Report No. 142. Seoul: KEDI Press, 1984.

Draws on Peter Berger's social construction model to conceptualize Korean schooling and to report the results of a survey which indicates that parents tend to hold a "Humanistic" view of the purpose of schooling.

Lee, Jong Jae, Chung, Younae, Lee, Inhyo and Lee, Yongro. "Social Construction of Schooling: Dominant Patterns and Conflicts." Seoul, Korea: KEDI Press, 1981. (in Korean)

Lee, Kye Woo. "Equity and an Alternative Educational Method: A Korean Case Study." *Comparative Education Review,* 25 No. 1 (February 1981):45-63.

Lee, Kyu Hoo. "Ideological Direction of National Development for the Fifth Republic." Policy Research, Summer 1984, Democratic Justice Party Policy Research Institute.

Lee, Man Gap. *Sociology and Social Change in Korea*. Seoul: Seoul National University Press, 1984.

Lee, Sungho. "Science and Higher Education in Korea." Paper presented at the annual meeting of the American Educational Research Association, April 1988, New Orleans, LA.

Lee, Young Dug, Lee, Sang Joo and Kim, Shin Bok. *Educational Contribution to National Development (1945-1975)*. Seoul: KEDI Press 1976.

Lew, Seok Choon. "Life in South Korea Today." *Social Studies*, 79 No. 4 (July-August 1988): 161-164.

Limbird, Martin, et al. "The Korea Papers: Profiles in Educational Exchange." NAFSA Field Service Working Paper 10. Washington, DC: National Association for Foreign Student Affairs, Field Service Program. n.d.

Consists of four papers which discuss a variety of topics related to education of Koreans in the U.S. the employment of the U.S.-educated Koreans and an analysis of the linguistic and cultural differences in the U.S. and Korean social relationships. A separate paper focuses on political activism on the campus of Seoul National University.

Mason, Andrew, et al. "Population Growth and Economic Development: Lessons from Selected Asian Countries." Policy Development Studies, No. 10. New York: United Nations Fund for Population Activities, 1986.

Mason, Edward S., et al. *The Economic and Social Modernization of the Republic of Korea*. Studies in the Modernization of the Republic of Korea: 1945-1975. Harvard East Asian monographs 92. Cambridge: Harvard University, 1980. (HC467 E26)

Mayer, Victor J. and Fortner, Rosanne W. "Internationalizing Science Education: The Korean Example." *School Science and Mathematics*, 91 No. 3 (1991):111-15.

McVoy, Edgar C. *Manpower Development and Utilization in Korea.* Washington DC: United States Department of Labor, 1965.

Mills, Edwin S. and Song, Byung Nak. *Urbanization and Urban Problems.* Studies in the Modernization of the Republic of Korea: 1945-1975. Harvard East Asian monographs 88. Cambridge: Harvard University, 1979. (HT147K6 M54)

Moos, Felix. *Some Observations on Korean Cultural Change 1966-1967.* Washington DC: US AID, United States Operations Mission to Korea, 1967.

Moskowitz, Karl. "Korean Development and Korean Studies-Review Article." *Journal of Asian Studies*, 42 No. 1 (November 1982):63-90.

A review of the "Studies on the Modernization of the Republic of Korea: 1945-1975," the monograph series published by The Council on East Asian Studies, at Harvard University, including "Education and Development in Korea" written by McGinn et al. 1980.

Mukerjee, Dilip. *Lessons from Korea's Industrial Experience.* Kuala Lumpur: Institute of Strategic and International Studies, Malaysia, 1986.

Nam, Woo Hyun and Jung, Chang Young. *Economic Value Analysis of Educational Investment in Korea.* Seoul: KDI, 1973.

National Bureau of Statistics. *Korea Statistical Year-Book, 1988.* Seoul: Economic Planning Board, 1988.

Newland, Kathleen. "Women and Population Growth: Choice Beyond Child-bearing." *Worldwatch* Paper 16 (1977).

NIERT (MOE). *Education in Korea 1979-1980.* Seoul: MOE, 1980.

Office of Planning and Coordination. "Evaluation Report of the Third Five-Year Economic Development Plan." Seoul: Office of the Prime Minister, 1975.

Oh, Byung-Hun. "University Students and Politics in Korea." Paper presented at the Conference on Students and Politics, March 27-April 1, 1967. Center for International Affairs, Harvard University, and the University of Puerto Rico.

Park, Chong-kee. *Human Resources and Social Development in Korea.* Seoul: KDI, 1980. (HC467 E77 v.4)

    Chapters on population and the quality of labor, trend of economic growth, and human resource development are used to evaluate the contribution of education to economic growth.

Park, Chung Hee. *Korea Reborn: A Model for Development.* Englewood Cliffs, New Jersey: Prentice-Hall, 1979.

Park, Seil. "Social and Private Rate of Return to Education in Korea." *The Korea Development Review*, 4 (September 1982):94-124.

Psacharopoulas, George and Tilak, J.B.G. "Schooling and Equity." In *Essays on Poverty, Equity and Growth*, 53-78, edited by Psacharopoulas, G. Oxford: Pergamon Press, 1991.

Repetto, Robert, et al. *Economic Development, Population Policy, and Demographic Transition in the Republic of Korea.* Studies in the Modernization of the Republic of Korea: 1945-1975. Harvard East Asian monographs 93. Cambridge: Harvard University, 1981. (HB3652.5 A3 E28)

Sarkar, N. K. "Development Models in Practice: The South Korean Case." *Social Structure Development Strategy.* New Delhi, India: People's Publishing House, Ltd., 1978.

Schubert, Jane G. "Education and Modernization: A Method for Establishing The Relationship." Washington, DC: American Institute for Research, 1987. (ED 142 566)

Describes a method of impact assessment designed to examine the outcomes in developing countries of participant training program sponsored by the U.S. Agency for International Development (USAID). Korea was one of three field assessment sites. Data indicate that USAID participants were making contributions to the development of the host countries and that these contributions can be attributed to their participant training experience.

Scitovsky, Tibor. "Economic Development in Taiwan and South Korea, 1965-81." In *Models of Development: A Comparative Study of Economic Growth in South Korea and Taiwan*, edited by Lau, Lawrence J. San Francisco: The Institute for Contemporary Studies, 1986.

Shemick, John M. "Korea Lets Vocational-Industrial Education Pave the Way for 1980." *School-Shop*, 35 No. 6 (June 1976):50-1.

Steinberg, David I. "Development Lessons from the Korean Experience-A Review Article." *Journal of Asian Studies*, 42 No. 1 (November 1982):91-104.

A review article in which the role of education in economic development and wealth distribution in Korea as explained in the "Studies of the Modernization of the Republic of Korea, 1945-1975" (Harvard East Asian monographs), is compared with McGinn et al.'s "Education and Development in Korea."

Sunoo, Harold Hakwon. *America's Dilemma in Asia: The Case of South Korea*. Chicago: Nelson-Hall, 1979. (DS 917 35 S66)

The overview of modernization and traditional value systems of Korea show that the role of the educational system during President Park Chung Hee's rule was designed mainly to prevent social change.

UNESCO. *Self-Propelled Development of Korean Society*. Seoul: Korean National Commission for UNESCO, 1984.

UNESCO. "A Study of the Contribution of Population Education to Educational Renewal and Innovation in the Republic of Korea." In *Study of the Contribution of Population Education to Educational Renewal and Innovation in El Salvador, the Republic of Korea, Philippines and Tunisia*, 53-94, Coordinate Action Programme for the Advancement of Population Education (CAPAPE), Paris: UNESCO 1980. (ED 199 075)

Contents include demographic, economic and educational characteristics, population education programs, population education curriculum, teacher training for population education, research and evaluation of population education, and an assessment of the contribution of population education to Korea's development.

Westphal, Larry E., Rhee, Yung W. and Pursell, Carry. "Korean Industrial Competence: Where It Came From." Washington DC: The World Bank, 1981. (qHC467 W45)

A historical perspective on direct foreign investment in Korea, sources of technology and organization of the export activities in Korea.

Whittaker, David. *Higher Education and Societal Change: The Vanguard Personality Syndrome of University Students.* Vancouver, British Columbia: The University of British Columbia, 1988.

Yat, Hoong Yip, ed. *Role of Universities in National Development Planning in Southeast Asia.* Singapore: Regional Institute of Higher Education and Development, 1971.

Yun, Chung il and Park, Jong yul. *Status on and Problems of Educational Finance.* Seoul: KEDI Press, 1977.

Yun, Chung il and Jim, Dong-seob. *The Priorities of Investment for the Development of Korean Education.* Seoul: KEDI Press, 1983.

Dissertations

Barnes, Elaine Milam. "The Schools of Taegu, Kyongsang Pukto Province, Korea, in 1954-1955: An Investigation Into the Interaction Between Culture and Education." Ed.D. dissertation, University of Maryland-College Park, 1960.

Cha, Jongchun. "Social Stratification and Group Formation in Contemporary Korea." Ph.D. dissertation, The University of Wisconsin, 1987.

An investigation of the significance of various group formation processes for social stratification of Korean society. Attention is given to the school clique, the preference for big firms, regionalism and status-conscious mate selection.

Chang, Yong Sun. "Philosophy of Morality, Development, and Moral Education Among Late Adolescents and Young Adults--Emphasis on Korea (Youth, College Student, Character Formation)." Ph.D. dissertation, University of Michigan, 1985.

Choe, Byung Sook. "The Impact of the Government Policy on the Development of Education in the First Republic of Korea." Ph.D. dissertation, University of Pittsburgh, 1971.

A historical, descriptive study of how socio-political factors affected the educational system and how education was used to achieve the political goal of economic growth in the First Republic of Korea from 1948 to 1960.

Choi, Ju won. "Program Design for Women in Development: Implications for Korea." Ed.D. dissertation, Columbia University Teachers College, 1986.

The factors which contribute to unemployment and limited self-development of middle-class Korean women are attributed to the lack of information about appropriate learning models. This is addressed by designing a program for the development of women.

Chung, Sae Gu. "The Political Socialization of Selected Elementary and Middle School Students in the Republic of Korea: Political Knowledge, Political Trust and Political Efficacy." Ph.D. dissertation, Florida State University, 1973.

Cole, Ross Harold. "The Koreanization of Elementary Citizenship Education in South Korea." Ph.D. dissertation, Arizona State University, 1975.

Coleman, Craig S. "Career Expectations and Aspirations of Male High School Seniors in the Republic of Korea." Ph.D. dissertation, University of Southern California, 1985.

This study attempts to explore the influence of Korean culture and economic and social development policies and goals on career expectations and aspirations of Korean male high school seniors.

Duressa, Berhanu. "A Systems Model of Human Resource Utilization: An Analysis of Five Major Components in Deliberate National Development (Hong Kong, Japan, Korea, Singapore, Taiwan)." Ph.D. dissertation, Florida State University, 1985.

The development of a qualitative, conceptual systems model which examines the interaction and interdependencies of five components of development--capital, education, political, entrepreneurship, and technology. The researcher concluded that the economic growth of the countries was mainly achieved as a consequence of those components.

Hahn, Meerha. "An Investigation of Factors in School Productivity: The Input-Output Analysis of School Performance in High Schools of Seoul, Korea." Ph.D. dissertation, State University of New York at Buffalo, 1982.

Develops a school management system model and examines the relationship between school inputs and outputs in Seoul's high schools. This study concludes that the schools are indeed important in influencing pupil achievement, however, school characteristics are not dependent upon the student socio-economic status.

Hess, Peter Neal. "Demographic Factors in South Korean Economic Development." Ph.D. dissertation, The University of North Carolina at Chapel Hill, 1982.

This empirical study assesses the demographic factors, particularly human capital in Korean economic development. The conclusion is that human capital formation has been a significant and pervasive factor in recent South Korean economic development.

Hong, Doo Seung. "Social Stratification and Social Values in Contemporary Korea." Ph.D. dissertation, University of Chicago, 1980.

Ihm, Chon Sun. "Cohort Shifts, Occupation and Economic Benefits of Education in Korea: The Impact of Educational Expansion in a Dynamic Economy." Ed.D. dissertation, Harvard University, 1990.

Jin, Misug. "A Comparison of the Subsequent Career Activities of Vocational and Academic High School Graduates in Korea: Implications For the Role of Vocational Education in Enhancing Social Equity." Ed.D. dissertation, Harvard University, 1988.

Joung, Chin Whan. "A Conceptual Model for Enhancing the Relevance of Vocational-Technical High School Education in Meeting the Socio-Economic Needs of Korea." Ph.D. dissertation, Ohio State University, 1982.

An attempt to provide an operational definition of educational relevance and to develop a conceptual model evaluating the extent to which Korean vocational-technical high school education is relevant.

Jung, Pilsoo. "Economic Development and the Distribution of Welfare in Korea." Ph.D. dissertation, University of Texas at Austin, 1988.

Jung, Yongduck. "Development, Distributive Justice, and Public Policy: The Case of Korea." Ph.D. dissertation, The University of Southern California, 1981.

This historical and empirical study indicates that the traditional Korean society was strongly committed to egalitarianism till the mid-19th century when the modernization movement had changed this commitment. Survey results indicate that the Koreans do not consider income distribution as a criterion for equality, and that they support strongly a meritocratic principle of justice distribution.

Kang, Jong Geun. "Cultural Indicators: The Korean Cultural Outlook Profile." Ph.D. dissertation, University of Massachusetts, 1989.

Kim, Chung Han. "Changing Functions of Women's Higher Education in the Republic of Korea: A Study of Educational Equality Between Men and Women." Ph.D. dissertation, George Peabody College for Teachers of Vanderbilt University, 1975.

Kim, Kyung Keun. "Schooling and Married Women's Work In A Developing Country: The Case of the Republic of Korea." Ph.D. dissertation, University of Chicago, 1990.

Kim, Nang Nang. "The Educational and Occupational Backgrounds of the South Korean Political Elite: 1948-1976." Ed.D. dissertation, Columbia University Teachers College, 1981.

A descriptive study attempting to explain the education and occupational background of political elite. Although role of education in the formation of political elite groups is not clear, bureaucrats, intellectuals, and business executives are represented in higher numbers among the political elites in Korea.

Kim, Ohn Juh. "Child and Parent Attributions for School Achievement as a Function of Cultural Background and Parent-Child Relations." Ed.D. dissertation, University of Toronto, 1986.

Kim, Oksoon. "The Effect of Family Background on Educational and Occupational Attainment of Korean Adults." Ph.D. dissertation, University of Southern California, 1988.

Kim, Ukhwan. "An Examination of the Interplay of Culture and Education in Korea: A Comparative Study." Ph.D. dissertation, Claremont Graduate School, 1972.

Examines the effect of culture on the educational system, and suggests intervention in the educational program of Korean schools within a cultural context. Advances the argument that if Korea is to utilize the dynamic characteristics of democratic thinking, the presence of undemocratic cultural forces must be recognized, teachers must be cognizant of cultural influences that are working against them.

Kim, Young Hwa. "Education and Gender Inequality in Earnings in the Structured Labor Market: A Case Study of Korea." Ph.D. dissertation, Stanford University, 1987.

Examines the sources of gender inequality in earnings in the labor market of Korea. This study concluded that the earnings of workers are substantially associated with the level of schooling, the major field of study, and firm tenure for both sexes and a most important source of gender inequality in earnings is that men are rewarded for being married whereas women are not.

Kuark, John Yoon Tai. "A Comparative Study of Economic Development in North and South Korea During the Post-War Period." Ph.D. dissertation, University of Minnesota, 1966.

Lee, Aie Rie. "Value Cleavages and Political Attitudes: The Case of Korea." Ph.D. dissertation, Florida State University, 1989.

Lee, Jong Hun. "A Proposed Model of Social Change in Korea Through the Ministry of Korea Christian Academy." Ph.D. dissertation, School of Theology at Claremont, 1984.

This study developed a new curriculum of social education with focus on Christian spirituality, and proposes to disseminate such a program through the Ministry of Korea Christian Academy.

Lee, Joung Woo. "Economic Development and Wage Inequality in South Korea." Ph.D. dissertation, Harvard University, 1983.

Examines wage inequality, wage distribution, rates of return to higher education and discrimination by gender over the period of Korea's rapid economic development.

Lee, Kang Ro. "Democratization and the Social Movements in South Korea: The Dynamics of the Bureaucratic Mobilizational Regime." Ph.D. dissertation, University of Wisconsin-Madison, 1990.

Lee, Kyung Jo. "Social Origins and Backgrounds of Representatives of National Assembly in South Korea, 1948-1961. Ph.D. dissertation, Claremont Graduate School, 1975.

Lee, Nam Young. "The Democratic Belief System: A Study of the Political Culture in South Korea." Ph.D. dissertation, University of Iowa, 1984.

Lee, Young-Ho. "The Political Culture of Modernizing Society: Political Attitudes and Democracy in Korea." Ph.D. dissertation, Yale University, 1969.

Lim, Hyun-chin. "Dependent Development in the World-System: The Case of South Korea, 1963-1979." Ph.D. dissertation, Harvard University, 1982.

This study explores the underlying nature of late, dependent, and capitalist development in South Korea. The major findings of this study are that the model of dependent development in a modified form is more useful in analyzing South Korea's development experience than the orthodox dependency perspective. In addition the dependent development of Korea displays its own unique character.

Oh, Jisoo. "Korea and Democracy: An Examination of Attitude Adaptability." Ph.D. dissertation, Claremont Graduate School, 1989.

Paik, Sung Joon. "Male-Female Earnings Differentials in Korea: The Role of Education (Earnings Differentials)." Ed.D. dissertation, Harvard University, 1990.

Park, Bu Kwon. "The State, Class and Educational Policy: A Case Study of South Korea's High School Equalization Policy." Ph.D. dissertation, University of Wisconsin-Madison, 1988.

Park, Kyung-Nan Choo. "Labor Force Participation of Professional Women in Korea." Ed.D. dissertation, Boston University School of Education, 1979.

Park, Seong-Hee. "Rates of Return to College Education in Korea From 1977 To 1986." Ph.D. dissertation, University of Southern California, 1989.

Park, Young Jin. "Women's Labor Force Participation in Korea: Trends in Levels, Patterns and Differentials During 1960-1980 (Labor Patterns)." Ph.D. dissertation, University of Pennsylvania, 1990.

Ryoo, Jai Kyung. "Changes in Rates of Return to Education Over Time: The Case Study of Korea." Ph.D. dissertation, Stanford University, 1988.

Shin, Doh Chull. "Socio-Economic Development and Democratization in South Korea: A Time-Series Analysis." Ph.D. dissertation, University of Illinois at Urbana-Champaign, 1972.

Shin, Kunza. "A Study of the Determinants of Higher Educational Aspirations of Korean Women." Ph.D. dissertation, University of Pittsburgh, 1981.

The question-whether the parents' position in a stratification system influence the level of aspirations of adolescents is investigated by using Sewell's model. This study concludes that 6 of the hypothesized factors significant others' influence; academic performance; socio-economic status; mental ability; sex; and living in urban centers-yield high correlations, the only exception, compared to the model was the "academic self-concept" variable.

Song, Byung Soon. "Comparative Study of Ideological Influence on Educational Theory and Practice in North and South Korea." Ph.D. dissertation, Wayne State University, 1974.

An examination of the major religious and political influences on education as Korean society evolved from an ancient homogeneous culture to a relatively high level of industrialization.

Song, Dae Sung. "National Development of South Korea and Taiwan: A Different Case of Dependency Theory." Ph.D. dissertation, University of Michigan, 1984.

Swisher, Ralph Blakeslee. "Passing the Threshold to Modernity in Rural South Korea: The Convergence of Elite Communication, Popular Frame of Reference, and Institutional Capacity." Ph.D. dissertation, University of Pittsburgh, 1972.

Um, Sangheon. "Factors That Relate To Student Achievement in Korean Academic High Schools." Ph.D. dissertation, University of Pittsburgh, 1990.

Yamazaki, Makoto. "The 'Japanese Model' in Korean Economic Development After 1953." Ph.D. dissertation, Duke University, 1984.

CHAPTER VI

Epilogue

It has been said that an art collector is naturally drawn to Florence, Italy, and a mountain climber is naturally drawn to the Himalayas. In somewhat the same way contemporary students and scholars of development and modernization are attracted to East Asia. It is in Japan, Korea, Taiwan, and the "city states" of Hong Kong and Singapore where the most rapid, dramatic changes in industrialization and related social changes within the last century have taken place. Historically the West, which has provided the most significant examples of industrialization--particularly capitalist industrialization--is now being joined with a second, perhaps different, model. Moreover, there is a significant possibility that this "miracle" will be extended during the coming decades to other Pacific Rim Asian countries. East, and increasingly southeast, Asia have become or are becoming viewed as giant laboratories for the scrutiny of many of the countries of the developing world.

Explaining Educational and Economic Growth

The commitment to growth describes many of the changes in contemporary Korea: economic growth, industrial growth, urban growth, physical and human capital growth. Educational growth and its contribution to national development are subjects of praise in most

English-language sources on Korea. Typically, Korea has been seen as offering a good argument for the importance of human resources in economic growth and modernization. A significant level of literacy and extensive educational development preceded industrialization and continued educational expansion at all levels, and increased attention to qualitative improvement has paralleled economic development and social change.

The Korean educational system has had a symbiotic relationship with the state. The state played an important role in the growth and development of the educational system. The state was a consistent advocate for change, distributor of resources, supporter of demands for access and equity, and mobilizer of the private sector. Educational development in turn contributed legitimacy to the state as an effective provider of one of the strongest demands of the people.

The pragmatic quality of national policies encouraging freer markets and private sector activities has been interpreted as a contributing factor to industrialization. Private education is frequently described as making a crucial contribution to the extension of educational opportunities --a claim particularly true in secondary and higher education where many sectarian and nonsectarian colleges and universities have prospered.

The cultural context for educational, social and economic change has also been noted. Cultural supports include the traditional honor and respect shown for accomplishments of educated persons, the enormous continuing prestige of formal education as a process, and the high achievement motivation of youth and adults. These values were translated into educational outlays. The direct financial contributions of parents in the form of school materials, equipment, and direct and indirect contributions to the teachers' welfare are difficult to quantify precisely. Yet these efforts may well have been an indispensable key to the continued growth of the system and to maintenance of minimum standards of quality during the pre economic take-off stage.

The interpretations identified above are all supported by considerable evidence. More tenuous, however, than the conclusions themselves are their underlying causes or stimuli. What are the roots of the cultural and institutional conditions which explain the acceptance of change, dedication to education and commitment to competition? There may be no fully satisfactory answers to this broad question. There are, however, a number of hypotheses which have been woven into two main arguments: cultural and institutional.

The cultural argument emphasizes that the people of Korea have been conditioned by centuries of history. For example, in spite of a deep reverence for the past, several cultural traditions have served to anchor contemporary Korean society firmly in the ongoing conditions and problems of this world and not a world of the hereafter. Contemporary Confucianism emphasizes a disciplined life style and a positive attitude toward active participation in civic and political affairs. Buddhism as transformed in East Asia became a world affirming religion; "the true body of Buddha is the world as we know it empirically." The cultural and religious traditions (including the various folk religions), rather than denying the importance of life in this world, encourage a pragmatic approach to coping with life's conditions and problems. A variant of the culturalist argument focuses on the historical deprivations and the repeated struggles for survival which led to intense frustrations and, over time, resulted in innovative and risk-taking behavior to achieve need gratification.

The second, or institutionalist, argument downplays the importance of cultural factors in the economic success of Korea and emphasizes specific policies, plans, and organizations. This argument points to such factors as: a stable political system; a resilient private sector; successively hierarchical but relatively lean governments; and a centrist policy and planning mechanism which, although powerful, was flexible in adjusting to economic uncertainties and opportunities. Institutionalists point out that the various cultural elements had existed long before economic take-off with little noticeable impact.

Thus the cultural argument emphasizes the historical traditions and unique value systems which have evolved long before the creation of the contemporary nation-state. The institutional argument, in contrast, focuses on individual and organizational responses to the technical and administrative problems of economic growth. The institutional model, as technique and technology, may be directly exportable to developing countries seeking to emulate Korea. The cultural model is less amenable to transferability.

Educational and Social Problems

Economic and educational successes have been accompanied by serious persisting political, social, and educational problems. Some scholars have argued that successful international economic competitiveness has come as the result of labor exploitation reflected in low worker pay and long working hours. Korea has also been described as a repressive state with limited regard for citizen or worker rights.

Social inequities persist and social institutions and systems for protecting the health and welfare of the poor are still underdeveloped.

Korean education has also directly been subjected to extensive criticism by Korean educators and citizens. The education system exhibits rigidity and uniformity and frequently does not respond well to the heterogeneity of abilities and interests among students. Regardless of locality or future plans of students the curriculum remains essentially the same. The elite character of the system is demonstrated by the widely recognized gradation of status of educational programs at all levels from the kindergarten to the prestigious departments in elite universities. Teachers are often described as having low morale, a condition resulting from a combination of low salaries, parental pressure, and low autonomy. Progress in schooling is dominated by examinations which in turn dominate curriculum and instruction. The influence of the crucial and unavoidable examinations extends into the home, affecting allocation of family resources and family time. Examination success demands extra school, private tutoring, the purchase of books and various instructional aids, and the organization of an educationally conducive environment in the home.

Koreans as individuals and as parents invest heavily in education. There is, nevertheless, a severe problem related to the fiscal support of the educational system. Korean educators tend to interpret the amount of public expenditure (4.5 percent of GNP in 1987, 21.2 percent in 1989 at national budget) to be inadequate. Much of the real cost of schooling at all levels continues to be borne by parents, thus putting a disproportionate burden on those with lower incomes.

But some of the criticism of Korean educators is more general and goes to the core of the meaning and purpose of education. As an instrument of the state, education, critics argue, has been used to perpetuate cold war attitudes, transmit anticommunism as an interpretation of democracy, rationalize a series of totalitarian governments, act as handmaiden to economic production, and assist in a process of social control by linking occupational position and status to educational credentials. The foundations of direct instrumental use of education sometimes have been traced to the colonial policy of Japan. However, the attempts in the 1960s to foster education for national unity and modernization, and more explicitly in the 1960s and 1970s to design education for economic growth, were interpreted by some educators as a continued perversion of the more fundamental goal of achieving self-realization through education.

The period of the 1970s has been labelled the "period of developmental education" (Kim, p. 13). At this time the Korean government placed economic growth squarely on center stage. When a major policy conflict arose between the Ministry of Education and the National Economic Planning Board over the quota of new entrants to higher education the recommendation of the latter body became policy. In the actions to ensure that all institutions fully supported economic growth the terms "first economy" and "second economy" identified an important distinction. The "first economy" referred to the traditional meaning of economy as the sector of society committed to the production of goods and services. The "second economy" referred to the values, attitudes and life-styles assumed to be supportive of successful economic growth. Education was expected to be the foundation for both economies.

Thus, some Korean educators argue that the core, intrinsic value of education has been lost. Its scope and content have been determined by particular political and economic agendas, sometimes to the detriment of the larger society. The long-range educational goals of contributing to the individual moral and intellectual growth and to the development of national culture, it is argued, were often ignored or painfully subverted. Figure VI.1 provides an overall critique of Korean education as interpreted by the PCER. It could perhaps be viewed as a summary of educational problems frequently articulated by Korean educators.

Basically, these criticisms reflect the peculiar pattern of Korean history--its colonial past, its centrality in the East-West ideological conflict, and the internal exercises of political power. However, some of the criticisms echo the concerns voiced by educators and citizens from many countries in all historical periods when groups or individuals in power have sought to utilize educational programs and processes for their particular interests. Yet, there is still another message in these critical interpretations, one being heard increasingly among the rapidly industrializing countries caught in a global economic, cultural, and communication environment. Economic growth in Korea and elsewhere is frequently accompanied by social, political, and cultural costs. If taking place under a repressive state, growth and change are often associated with lack of human rights, labor exploitation, and the underdevelopment of certain social institutions. The complex interplay of a political stability, international markets, and internal investment priorities which support economic productivity may particularly neglect, for example, the rural and less privileged elements of society and may sharpen social divisions based on income.

216   *Education and Social Change in Korea*

Figure VI.1   PCER Analysis of Educational problems

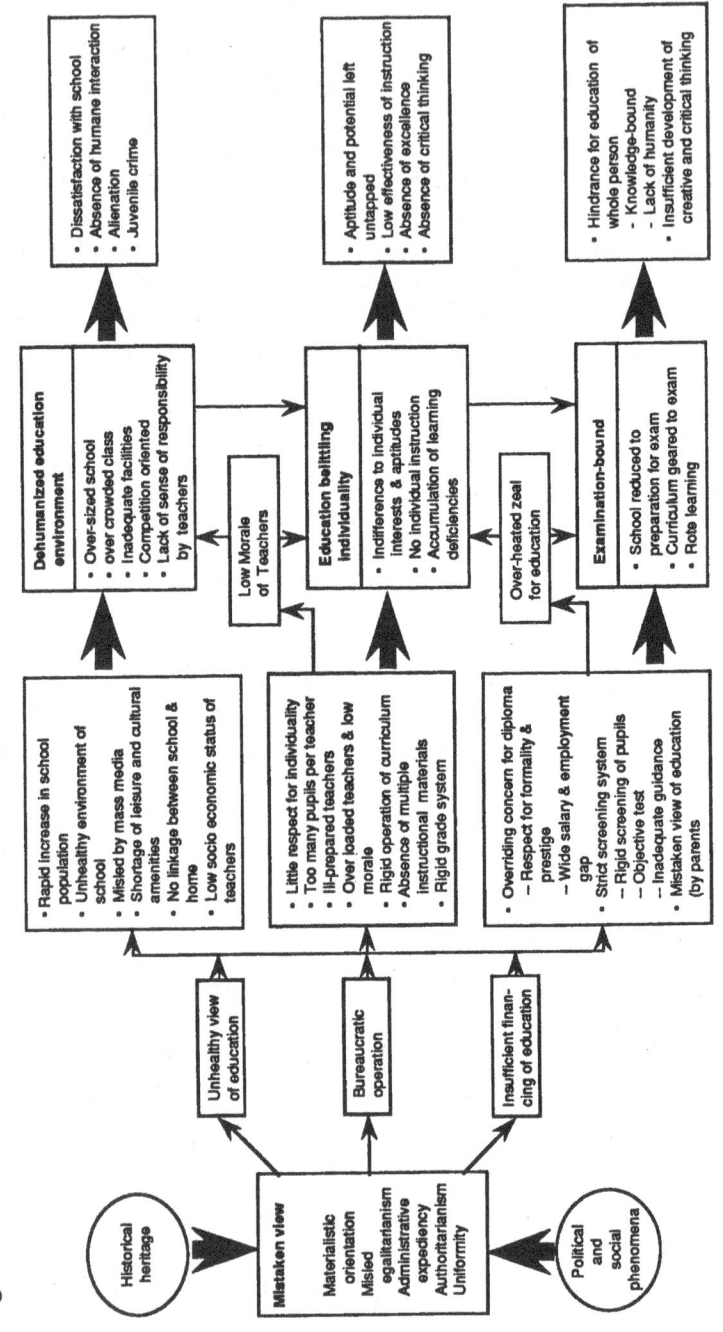

Source: PCER. Korean education Reform Toward the 21st Century. Seoul: MOE, 1987: 27.

Trends and Strategies

Korean educators and social scientists tend to see their country entering a new era in the 1990s. Expectations are that industrialization with an emphasis on further development of high technology and service industries will continue to result in the evolvement of an "information society." Korea will become an increasingly urbanized, consumer-oriented society with a slowly aging population. Further, political democratization is predicted and is expected to be accompanied by heightened political consciousness and high expectations for government competence in the delivery of social services and in maintenance of a rising standard of living. Closer ties with North Korea are anticipated to bring problems in the rationalization of two different ideologies and contrasting production and educational systems, but also to allow greater economic potential, and eventually a more powerful nation state. A larger middle class will be vigorous in placing additional demands on public and private services, including cultural and recreational opportunities.

The Korean accomplishments in education since the establishment of the first Republic in 1948 have been many. As has been documented, the amazing growth of formal and nonformal educational opportunity has resulted in one of the world's most quantitatively developed educational systems. One consequence of this growth is a population whose average length of schooling exceeds nine years. The social, political, and economic effects of educational growth and development in Korea, although to some extent problematic, include recognized contributions to social mobility, attainment of social status, acquisition of social and cultural values, political socialization, political participation and leadership, national unity and nationalism, and development of human capital which has contributed to higher economic productivity. Yet the anticipated future social, economic, and political changes identified above are interpreted by current scholars and policymakers as requiring a more effective educational system.

Contemporary Korean education appears to be undergoing a wide-ranging critique which may lay the foundation for large-scale reform and structural change. Nearly every major aspect of the educational system and its linkages with society is being reexamined. Although Korean educators, citizens, and political leaders are proud of Korea's educational accomplishments criticism is extensive, problems are seen as serious, and fundamental changes are sought.

Koreans speak of the "mistaken view of education" which has characterized Korean educational development. Basically, this criticism is a reaction against the perceived narrowness of the past interpretation of the purpose of schooling. In practice each level of schooling has tended to be treated as a vehicle for advancing to the next higher level--the ultimate criterion of educational achievement being a university diploma. Indeed, not only has the university degree become a requisite for an increasing number of occupations but there is the danger that it has become a measure of the worth and character of the individual.

The report of the Presidential Commission for Educational Reform (1987) in considering educational changes necessary to cope with the challenges of the 21st century identified no fewer than 42 tasks (Table VI.1). The document, *Korean Education 2000* (1985), although not presenting a summary list of proposed reforms appears to be in general agreement with the PCER document on needed educational changes. Although space does not permit a detailed review and analysis of each of the many proposed reforms, an attempt is made here to examine the major directions and recommendations identified in these two reports. These may be grouped under three categories: goals and ideology; equity; effectiveness and quality, and equalizing educational opportunity.

Table VI.1.

Major Reform Proposals by PCER

A. Establishment of Korean Education Ideology

B. Goals and Directions of Education Reform

- General Goals and Aims of Education
- Directions and Strategies for the Reform of Primary, Secondary, and Higher Education
- Nonformal Education

C. Selected Policies for Education Reform

- Modification of the Basic School System
- Reform of the Entrance Examination System
- Increasing Autonomy of Education Administration
- Improvement of Education Policy for Private Schools

- Development of Gifted and Talented Students
- Innovation of Science and Technology Education
- Strengthening Computer Education in Schools
- Feasibility of an Education Broadcasting System
- Development of Career Education
- Development of Education Programs for the Information Society
- Establishment of a Life-long Education System

D. Upgrading the Quality of Basic Education

- Promotion of Kindergarten Education
- Extension of Compulsory Education to Middle School
- Updating of the School Curriculum and Textbooks
- Improvement of Foreign Language Education
- Innovation of Vocational Education
- Promotion of Guidance Programs for Youth
- Improvement of Teacher Preparation Programs
- Promotion of Education in Seoul for Korean Residents Abroad

E. Pursuit of Excellence in Higher Education

- Upgrading the Quality of University Education
- Upgrading the Quality of Graduate Education
- Promotion of Junior College Education
- Improvement of the Quota System
- Reform of the Entrance Examination
- Promotion of Colleges and Universities in Non-metropolitan Areas
- Upgrading Criteria for Physical Facilities and Equipment
- Establishment of School-industry Cooperative System
- Development of Education Programs for Global Understanding

F. Foundation for Education Development

- Innovation of Teaching Methods
- Promotion of Special Education

- Improvement of Education Environment
- Promotion of Life-long Education
- Maximizing the Efficiency of Education Administration
- Diversification of Financial Resources for Education
- Indices for Education Development
- Increasing the Effectiveness of Education Financing
- Modernization of Educational Facilities and Equipment
- Promotion of Non-formal Education

Out of the defined tasks, the Presidential Commission for Education Reform advanced 10 major tasks which deserve higher priority. They are called 'Highlights of the Education Reform.'

1) Modification of the Basic School System
2) Reform of the Entrance Examination System
3) Improvement of Education Facilities and Environment
4) Enhancement of Teacher Quality
5) Revision of the Curriculum and Teaching Method
6) Strengthening of Science and Technology Education
7) Pursuit of Excellence in Higher Education
8) Institutionalization of Life-long Education
9) Increasing Autonomy of Education Administration
10) Expanding Education Investment

Goals and Ideology

Hongik in gan is expected to continue to serve as the basic ideal for education. The PCER document suggests that Hongik in gan implies four attributes to be developed through education: 1) *Humanity* (respect for individuals, harmony, equality); 2) *National Identity* (consciousness of distinctive features of country, self realization in context of relationship to others, pride in nation); 3) *Morality* (faithfulness, honesty, altruism, cooperation and trust); and 4) *Pioneering Spirit* (openness to change, future oriented). Acquisition of these attributes leads to the development of the three basic characteristics of the educated person: *self-reliance, creativity, and moral consciousness.*

Korean Education 2000, in essential agreement with the PCER interpretation, describes the ideal profile of an educated person as "a person capable of self-realization" (1987:83). This summary view is elaborated with eight characteristics: "subjective consciousness," creative, moral, intelligent, democratic, cosmopolitan, healthy, and motivated to learn. Subjective consciousness suggests a person adaptable, committed to self-growth, and inner-directed in terms of motivation. Creativity implies a capability to seek and be empathic with change. A person with moral consciousness is "cooperative, disposed for the common good of the society and altruistic works," is "conscious of individual responsibilities vis-a-vis the society," and "continuously seeks the ways of ensuring harmonious coexistence with others" (KEDI, 1985:86). A democratic person values and respects participation and accepts the accompanying responsibilities. Intelligence appears to be primarily associated with "scientific thinking" and rationality tempered by a sense of justice. Being cosmopolitan means demonstrating recognition of the idea that the world is a global village and one community. A healthy person understands the stresses and social fragmentation which may come with modern society and recognizes his or her changing physical emotional and spiritual needs.

Because of their high level of abstraction these goals pertaining to the individual may look little different from what might be forthcoming from many countries. Yet each goal carries the implication of adaptation and interpretation within the evolving context of Korea. As aggressive as Korea has been in interacting with, and borrowing from, other economic, political and cultural systems, Korean leaders increasingly seek to develop a future which respects the past but doesn't resurrect it. The goal for the decade ahead at the individual and societal levels is not just further "modernization" but Korean "modernization."

Effectiveness and Quality

Strategies being considered for qualitative reform at the primary and secondary levels give attention to nearly every aspect of content, teaching, administration, organization and facilities. The focus on curriculum and instruction emphasizes the need for individualization of materials and further diversification of content. The move toward less standardization recognizes the range of ability and backgrounds now found among the student body in primary and secondary schools. Diversification of instructional methods implies a reaction against the labor intensive, teacher-focussed approach to the teaching-learning process and an introduction of a more active learning model which includes use of a variety of media and technology. Moreover, reforms in instruction and curriculum must respond more fully to the extension of compulsory education through nine years, the near universalization of senior secondary school, and a possible changing structure of primary and secondary education (PCER, 1987:75). More effective teaching requires more effective teacher preparation and perhaps higher teacher incentives and rewards. Reforms under consideration in pre-service and in-service teacher preparation emphasize the need for more depth of training in the disciplines and a higher level of professional knowledge. Such preparation will place new demands on departments and schools of education in colleges and universities.

If equality is defined as maximization of each student's chance to achieve his/her potential uniformity of educational programs can be viewed as obstructive. In most Korean schools little adjustment or adaptation is made for personal attributes in curriculum or classroom management. The causes of learning deficiencies are rarely diagnosed, resulting in the failure of schools to assist many children in realizing their educational potential.

The ever present influence of the university entrance requirements affects and, indeed, to a considerable extent defines educational quality. What are and what are not criteria for admission and what is and what is not covered in the examination defines the focus of schooling. Moreover, the downward influence of examinations and the structure of the exams themselves have shaped a learning process which focuses on examining the kinds of knowledge tested in examinations. The selection process at best evaluates a narrow band of academic qualities assumed to be necessary for study in the next higher rung of the educational ladder. For example, three-fourths of all high school students participate in the preparatory program for universities. Yet, only one-third of those who try succeed in the university entrance examination.

Like teaching, administration and management are viewed as needing further professionalization. Currently, the central government is the major actor in educational policy making and administration. The Ministry of Education has direct control over important decisions in higher education and shares control of elementary and secondary education with provincial administrative "Boards of Education." The changing school population, new educational expectations, reforms in instruction and curriculum, higher quality teachers and increased local educational autonomy require new, more demanding forms of administrative leadership and support.

Proposed increases in administrative decentralization and institutional autonomy suggest more responsibility, more decision authority, and potentially more creative initiatives at each educational level from elementary schools through universities. Leadership from the Ministry of Education is increasingly viewed as focussing on planning, policy, and coordination activities. Reformed provincial and local boards of education are expected to have authority to formulate as well as implement innovations, including those concerned with new sources of fiscal support. In terms of primary and secondary education the changes being sought recognize that a commitment to effective schooling and to professionalization of educational personnel means, among other things, institutionalization of school-based management with expectations that local administrators will provide programmatic leadership. Autonomy with its various organizational, curricular and fiscal implications, while defended on essentially the same grounds as autonomy at lower educational levels, has become even more of a professional and ideological *cause celebre* for teaching and administrative personnel.

Equalizing Educational Opportunity

Korea, through its constitution, various educational laws and policies, has removed many barriers to educational opportunity. As discussed in Chapter V, however, the universalization of elementary and secondary education, and the massification of higher education have not eliminated disparities in education based on financial ability, locality, gender, and student characteristics.

The selection processes have implications for equity at each educational level. The educational system purports to screen on the basis of academic ability, reserving the upper rungs of the educational ladder for the most academically talented. However, differential advantage is realized from the earliest grades because of qualitative differences in school facilities, equipment, and teaching. Secondly, the ability of parents to create the extra-school environment of tutors, books, computers and various instructional supplements depends on family income.

Korean educational development in general has reached a stage where equity concerns go beyond formal provisions of access to the core system of formal education. Korean educators appear to be taking a multifaceted approach to reduction of inequalities in educational opportunities by largely focusing on qualitative changes at each level of the system and by examining potential innovations designed to distribute education to new segments of the population. The air and correspondence high schools and university have reached thousands of adults and youth not served by mainstream educational institutions. Industry has responded favorably to government urging in building special high schools to serve employees. The expansion of public and private preschool education is being encouraged with a long-range target of 100 percent enrollment of this age cohort during the first decade of the 21st century. At the elementary and secondary levels qualitative differences in instruction and facilities may be reduced by incentives for teachers to teach in less popular areas, through standardization of teacher workload, and by enforcing minimum requirements for equipment and specialized facilities.

Rapid economic modernization in Korea has been associated with loss of some traditional values and institutions, transformation of such basic institutions as the family and school, and the widening cultural and behavioral gaps between older and younger generations. "Korean values and behavior patterns-for better or worse-are moving in the direction of the world's industrialized societies" (Macdonald, 1990:12). Most of the complex individual and social problems associated with societal changes were not foreseen and proactive planning was not undertaken in earlier stages of educational development. The deep concerns with the breakdown in traditional institutions, the confusion by displays of "alien" culture, and the realization of the costs of material advances are leading in Korea, as in many newly industrialized nations, to a profound search for cultural identity and moral integration. Fundamental questions persist: Which new patterns of social roles and human relationships are acceptable? What criteria other than historical traditions may help in this choice? What policies and programs can best educate children and adults for the future and at the same time strengthen rather than weaken cultural identity and perserve the valued cultural heritage?

Bibliography

Articles and Books

Covell, Jon Carter. *Korea's Cultural Roots.* Fifth edition. Seoul: Hooym International Publishing Co., 1983.

Cumings Bruce. *The Two Koreas.* New York: Foreign Policy Association, 1984.

deBary, William T. and Haboush, JaHyun Kim, eds. *The Rise of Neo-Confucianism in Korea.* New York: Columbia University Press, 1985.

Han, Sungjoo. *The Failure of Democracy in South Korea.* Berkeley: University of California Press, 1975.

Han, Sunjoo and Myers, Robert J. eds. *Korea: The Year 2000.* New York: Carnegie Council on Ethics and International Affairs, 1987.

Kim, Ilpyong J. and Kihl, Young Whan, eds. *Political Change in South Korea.* New York: Korean PWPA, Inc.; distributed by Paragon House Publishers, 1988.

Morse, Ronald A., ed. *Wild Asters: Exploration in Korean Thought.* Lanham, Md.: University Press of America, 1987.

Oh, Joun Kie-Change. *Korea: Democracy on Trial.* New York: Cornell University Press, 1968.

Yi, Man Gap. *Sociology and Social Change in Korea.* Seoul: Seoul National University Press, 1982.

Yim, Yong Sun. "The Significance of the January 22 Unification Proposal." *Korea and World Affaiirs,* 6 No. 1 (1982):19-38.

Dissertations

Cha, Poong Ro. "A Feminist Perspective on Education for Human Liberation in a Korean Context." Ph.D. dissertation, School of Theology at Claremont, 1985.

Chung, Kyung Ae. "A Comparative Study of Principals' Work Behavior (Korea)." Ph.D. dissertation, University of Utah, 1987.

The study concludes that Korean principals tend to be more "desk bound" (26% of their time) compared to their American counterparts, and spend a relatively small portion of their time on classroom observation, processing, and monitoring. They spent no time teaching and more than one-third of the principals' time was spent in verbal contacts.

Graw, Leroy H. "The Correlations Between Management/Leadership Style Perceptions of Korean Academic High School Principals and Student Scores on Standardized Achievement Tests." Ed.D. dissertation, University of Southern California, 1980.

Using a translated "Profile of a School" instrument and student achievement scores on the college entrance examination served to determine if the management/leadership styles of principals were related to student achievement. Students' achievement scores were not significantly correlated with any measures of principal management/leadership style.

Huh, Kyung Chul. "The Role of Teacher Logic and Clarity in Student Achievement." Ph.D. dissertation, Stanford University, 1986.

A study using correlations to research teachers' use of logic and clarity in instruction and student achievement

Jang, Me Seok. "Principals' Leadership and Communication, and Teacher Job Satisfaction in Korea." Ph.D. dissertation, University of Missouri-Columbia, 1987.

Data from 555 public elementary school teachers were collected by using 3 instruments translated from English. The canonical correlation for seven leadership variables and two job satisfaction variables revealed that the more the principal's leadership behavior is viewed as being supportive of teachers, facilitative of the work of the school, possessing goal emphasis, and receptive to teacher's ideas, the more likely it is that teachers' intrinsic and extrinsic job satisfaction will be higher.

Jun, Sung Yun. "Principal Leadership, Teacher Job Satisfaction and Student Achievement in Selected Korean Elementary Schools." Ph.D. dissertation, Florida State University, 1981.

Stepwise multiple regression analysis was utilized to determine the relative contribution of staff variables in explaining the outcomes of the new instructional program. Questionnaires were collected from 280 principals, 903 fourth grade teachers, and their students. Teachers' professional experience was found to exert a significant influence on student achievement, teacher job satisfaction, and preference for new instructional programs.

Kim, Haeja. "Sex Role Stereotyping in Elementary Reading Textbooks in Korea." Ph.D. dissertation, University of Pittsburgh, 1987.

Kim, Jung Han. "Development of an Instrument for the Evaluation of Administrative Staff in the Republic of Korea." Ph.D. dissertation, University of North Texas, 1984.

Kim, Nam Il. "The Relationship Between School Principal Leadership Behavior and Teacher Stress, Satisfaction, and Performance in the Schools of Inchon, Korea." Ed.D. dissertation, University of Georgia, 1986.

Lee, Kyunghui. "An Assessment of Attitudes of Faculty Men and Faculty Women in Higher Education in the Republic of Korea (Sexual Discrimination)." Ed.D. dissertation, Western Michigan University, 1985.

An assessment of the differences in the attitudes between faculty men and women toward faculty women in Korean higher education. The study showed consistent differences between men and women regarding: employment opportunities, advancement opportunities, teaching effectiveness, research and scholarly writing, personality characteristics, acceptance by associates, and use of full potential.

Park, Kyung Jae. "Instructional Methods and Media: Issues Surrounding the Open Colleges of Korea." Ed.D. dissertation, University of Massachusetts, 1986.

The study identified the problems and constraints working people perceive in continuing their education at an open college, and examines the need for the open college staff to develop appropriate instructional methods and media. The study consists of two cases, a students' survey, and a needs assessment.

Ro, Jong Hee. "An Investigation of Organizational Climate in Elementary Schools in the Province of Chollabukdo, Korea." Ph.D. dissertation, University of Southern Mississippi, 1981.

The organizational climate of elementary schools in the province of Chollabukdo was investigated by replicating the Halpin and Croft questionnaire. Factor analysis and a varimmax rotational solution were applied. The five factors identified in the Korean version are principal support, teacher disengagement, teacher esprit, hindrance, and principal task emphasis.

Song, Wha Sop. "The Secondary School Principalship in Korea." Ph.D. dissertation, Columbia University Teachers College, 1981.

This study investigates the perceptions of teachers and administrators regarding the actual and ideal role of secondary school principals in Korea and offers guidelines for principal training programs.

Wong, Sang Bong. "An Investigation of Emphasis Given to Teaching Basic Skills for Entry-Level Employment in Korean Vocational High Schools." Ph.D. dissertation, University of Illinois at Urbana-Champaign, 1987.

INDEX

Academic High School 56, 137, 205, 226
Administration of Education 70, 72, 91
Adult Education 39, 71, 84, 88, 91, 94, 145, 149
    Air and Correspondence College 29, 31
    Air and Correspondence High School 29, 142
Annual Report of the [Colonial] Government 13
Autonomy 28, 31, 35, 74, 83, 87, 90, 111, 125-127, 137, 140, 141, 144, 146, 188, 214, 218, 220, 222, 223

Blue House 123
Boards of Education 69, 72, 74, 78, 79, 125, 135, 222, 223
Buddhism 4, 5, 8, 38, 213

Charter of National Education 130, 133
Chinese influence 3
Christian Missionaries 10
    Choson 8, 9, 11, 13, 16, 34
    Choson Christian College 11, 16
Colleges and Universities 24, 25, 31, 56, 60, 61, 65, 66, 68, 72, 74, 78, 130, 133, 158, 168, 184, 212, 219, 222
Compulsory Education Accomplishment Plan 157
Confucianism 4, 5, 7, 8, 10, 38, 164, 213, 225
Confucius 4
Council for Long-Range Educational Planning (CLEP) 122
Curriculum xi, xvi, 5, 9, 10, 16, 19, 27, 38, 39, 45-52, 56, 58, 62, 64, 65, 72, 74, 84, 89, 94, 100-103, 113, 114, 115, 116, 118, 129-131, 133, 134, 142, 143, 144, 145, 147-152, 202, 207, 214, 219, 220, 221, 222
    Textbooks 19, 114

Decentralization 83, 105, 121, 135, 140, 222
Dong To (oriental learning) 99

Economic Growth xv, 3, 27, 97, 116, 131, 160, 169, 174-176, 182, 194, 197, 200, 201, 203, 204, 211, 212-215
Economic Planning Board (EPB) 121-123, 144

Education and political participation 20, 43, 184
Education Law of 1949 20, 43
Education tax 79, 125, 134
Education Yearbook of Korea 24
Educational costs 164, 168
Educational Expenditures xiii, xiv, 78, 79, 86, 168
Educational Goals 19, 92, 129, 215
Educational Growth 3, 143, 157, 160, 163-165, 169, 170, 177,
         188, 196, 211, 217
Educational Opportunity 11, 71, 169, 170, 189, 197, 217, 218,
         223
Educational planning xvi, 20, 32, 35, 36, 39, 83, 87, 105, 121,
         122, 123, 124, 127, 131, 132, 138, 140, 146,
         147, 149, 154, 194
Educational Policy 3, 14, 35, 40, 85, 116, 118, 121-123, 125,
         128, 134, 153, 184, 192, 208, 222
Educational Reconstruction Plan, 1962-1966 128
Elementary and Primary Education
         Elementary School (Kuckmin Hakyo) 46
         Primary School 15, 30, 39, 48
Enrollment ratios xi, xiii, xiv, 158, 160, 163, 171, 175
Entrance examination to middle school 49, 131
Equalizing Educational Opportunity 170, 218, 223
Ewha Haktang 11
Ewha University 11, 196

Filial piety 4, 5, 7, 8
Finance 31, 36, 78-81, 92, 122, 125, 145, 150, 193, 202
Financing education 168, 188
First Five-Year Educational Development Plan (1972-1976) 130
Five-Year Economic Development Plans 128
Five-Year Educational Development Plan, 1977-1981 132

Gender xiv, xv, 170, 171, 189, 207, 223
Goals 18-20, 22, 26, 54, 60, 70, 91, 92, 129, 138, 139, 163,
         194, 204, 215, 218, 220, 221
Graduate School 66-68, 94, 186, 206, 208
Gun Ja 8
Gun-Sa Bu Il Che (King, teacher and father are one body) 164

Heavy and chemical industrialization (HCI) 28

High School (Kodung Hakyo) 52
High School Equalization Policy (HSEP) 171
Higher Education xi, xv, 5, 13, 14, 24, 25, 27-29, 31, 35, 40,
41, 53, 56, 60-63, 65-67, 74, 79, 80, 82-88,
90, 95, 99, 100, 108, 109, 111, 114, 117, 126,
128, 129, 130, 132, 134, 136, 140, 141, 143,
144, 145-148, 151, 153, 154, 158, 164, 170,
171, 176, 184, 187, 188, 190, 192, 194, 195,
198, 202, 206, 207, 212, 215, 218-220, 222,
223, 227, 228
Hongik in gan 20, 21, 220
Human capital theory 163
Human resources xv, 87, 149, 157, 160, 194, 200, 212
Hwarangdo 5
Hyanggyo 5, 9

Illiteracy 70, 85, 126, 158
Independence Movement 13, 39
Indigenous Knowledge System 107
Inequities in educational opportunities 170
Information society xv, 58, 140, 217, 219

Japanese Annexation 9, 11
Japanese Colonial Government 15, 18, 34
Japanese Imperial Rescript of Education 12
Jeonmum Hakyo 15
Junior College 63, 68, 132, 142, 219

Kindergarten (Yuchiwon) 45
Koguryo 4
Korea Education 2000 54
Korean Advanced Institute of Science 109
Korean alphabet (Han'gul) 70
Korean Council for University Education (KCUE) 74, 92
Korean culture 3, 4, 14, 17, 40, 47, 118, 182, 192, 204
Korean Development Institute (KDI) 121, 123, 138
Korean education xi, xv, xvi, 4, 18, 19, 27, 33-36, 38, 39, 43,
60, 82-84, 86, 87, 90, 97, 99, 100, 105, 111,
113, 115, 117-119, 124, 133, 134, 137-139,
143, 147, 149, 150, 194, 195, 202, 214, 215,
217, 218, 220

Korean Education Reform Toward the 21st Century 124, 138, 139
Korean Educational Development Institute (KEDI) 29, 122, 131
Korean Federation of Education Associations (KFEA) 70
Korean Institute of Science and Technology 109
Koryo xi, xiii, 5, 7, 8
Kuk Ja Gam xi, 5, 7
Kukhak 5
Kwago 5
Kyungsung Imperial University 15

Literacy 70, 71, 91, 163, 164, 188, 212
Local administrative bodies 74
Long-Term Educational Planning 138
Lottery system 56

Middle School (Chung Hakyo) 49
Military coup in 1961 26
Ministry of Education (MOE) 72, 125, 165
Ministry of Home Affairs 128
Modernization 17, 37, 41, 88, 160, 163-165, 177, 182, 188, 190, 192-194, 196-201, 206, 211, 212, 214, 220, 221, 224

National Commission of Education (NCE) 125
National Confucian Academy (Taehak) 5
National Confucian College (Kukhak) 5
National Educators' Labor Union (NELU) 70
New Educational System 19, 118, 131-133
Newly industrialized countries (NICs) 108
Non-Formal Education xi, 36, 70-72, 86, 94, 218, 220

Pacific Rim xv, 211
Paekche 4, 5
Park Chung Hee 26, 201
Park Military Government 128
Policy Making xvi, 30, 116, 121, 125, 127, 140, 141, 222
Pre-Education Promotion Law 45
Preliminary Examination for College Entrance 130, 132
Presidential Commission 54, 79, 87, 90, 124, 125, 134, 135, 138, 139, 151, 152, 218, 220

Presidential Commission for Education Reform (PCER) 124
Private education 52, 123, 150, 188, 212
Private School Law 126
Private schools 15, 19, 56, 78, 80, 86, 126, 171, 218
Public semi-official social educational system 5

Republic of Korea xvi, 17, 20, 23, 37-40, 82, 83, 87, 88, 91, 93, 94, 95, 115, 116, 118, 145, 147, 149-151, 153, 190, 192, 194, 196-204, 206, 227
Revenues for education 79, 80
Royal examination system 8

Saemaul Undong (New Community Movement) 29
Second Economic Development Plan 129
Secondary Education 16, 26, 28, 32, 35, 49, 54, 63, 67, 68, 78, 79, 80, 92, 129, 130, 136, 140, 142, 148, 149, 151, 158, 171, 188, 222, 223
Seoul National University 35, 66, 198
Shamanisn 4, 5
Silhak 10
Silla 4, 5
Sirhak 10
Six-Year Plan for Completion of Compulsory Education 127
Sixth Five-Year Plan 135
Social Change iii, xv, 91, 157, 163, 177, 196, 198, 201, 207, 212, 225
Social mobility 181, 189, 197, 217
Songgyun-gwan 9
South Korea xv, xvi, 3, 4, 17, 28, 32, 33, 40, 41, 70, 88, 92, 94, 118, 119, 148, 154, 157, 191, 193, 194, 198, 201, 204, 205, 207-210, 225
Special Education (T'uksu Hakyo) 60
Statistical Yearbook of Education 45, 47, 50, 53, 61, 62, 72, 88, 168, 170
Student Defense Corps 56, 183
Study abroad 106
Sukmyong University 16
Supreme Council for National Reconstruction 126

Taiwan xv, 108, 157, 163, 191, 201, 204, 210, 211
Taoism 5

Teachers and Teacher Education 67
Teachers' Organizations 70, 89
Temporary Exception in Education 126
The state 4, 8, 26, 27, 29, 30, 33, 78, 208, 212, 214
Three Kingdoms Period 4
Transnational Knowledge System 97, 98, 109

U.S. Military Government 17, 20, 82
Unit of Social Studies Education (USSE, a special unit of KEDI) 102
United States Influences 99

Vocational High School 54, 58, 138

War-Time Union Colleges 25
War-Time Education 23, 24

Yonsei University 11, 33, 34, 66, 87, 145, 192